ROCK AND ROSES
SECOND EDITION

MOUNTAINEERING ESSAYS BY SOME OF THE
WORLD'S BEST WOMEN CLIMBERS
OF THE 20TH CENTURY

Mikel Vause, editor

Mountain N' Air Books
La Crescenta, CA
91224 - USA

Rock and Roses ©
Mountaineering Essays, including some by the best women climbers in the World
in the 20th Century
Compiled and edited by Mikel Vause, Ph D, 1952–
Copyright in 1999 by Mountain N' Air Books

Second edition (revised and expanded), 1999, 2001
First edition, 1990

Published in the United States of America by
Mountain N' Air Books - P.O. Box 12540, La Crescenta, CA 91224 USA
Phones: (800)446-9696, (818) 248-9345
Faxes: (800)303-5578, (818) 248-6516
e-mail: publisher@mountain-n-air.com

Cover photos:
Alison Osius climbing , by Brian Bailey
Background, Mountains and Rivers Corel Photo-CD collection.
Cover and book design by Gilberto d'Urso
Printed on demand
#001-0301

LIBRARY OF CONGRESS CARD NUMBER: 99-067293

Vause, Mikel editor
Contributors: Rosie Andrews, Beth Bennet, Arlene Blum, Julie Brugger, Rosemary Cohen, Susan Edwards, Catherine Freer, Sue Giller, Linda Givler, Sibylle C. Hechtel, Lynn Hill, Cherie Bremer-Kamp, Magda Nos King, Lilace A. Mellin, Ruth Dyar Mendenhall, Dorcas S. Miller, Sally Moser, Alison Osius, Wendy Roberts, Moira Viggers, Laura Waterman, Annie Whitehouse, Elizabeth D. Woolsey. Sally Zigmond, Gabriela Zim—Second edition, 1999

LCCN: 99-067293

ISBN 1-879415-28-3

Climbing, Women Adventures, Literature, essays, mountaineering
I.Title

ISBN: 1-879415-28-3

TABLE OF CONTENTS

ACKNOWLEDGMENTS

I would like to acknowledge all the women who have contributed to this collection for their abilities as mountaineers, historians (and history makers), and writers. Climbing is hard, writing about it is harder. All have excelled in both.

I also wish to thank my wife, Janis, for her continual support and encouragement and for her love of mountains and willingness to share (and climb) them with me. I am lucky to have three wonderful daughters, Kelly, Emily, and Sarah, who are complete individuals—some are mothers, all are athletes and intellectuals, and bring they bring me a great deal of joy. And for my son, Jared, my regular climbing partner who loves and respects his mother and sisters.

Thanks also to Gilberto d'Urso, editor and publisher of *Mountain N' Air Books*, for all his efforts in bringing this project to a successful conclusion (again).

PREFACE

In the introduction to the first edition of *Rock and Roses,* back in *1990,* I stated women were finally coming into their own as climbers and that it was reflected in their writing. Over the almost ten years since *Rock and Roses* was first published, not only have women arrived on the mountaineering scene, they have established themselves and are pushing the limits of climbing difficulty and standards, as well as strong expedition and organizational leadership. Many of the contributors to the first edition are still actively involved in the world of mountaineering and their essays, though nine years old, are still very relevant, possibly reaching the status of classics. These, coupled with a number of new essays by both new climbers and well as those who have been associated with the climbing world for many years, helps expand the scope and vision of a collection of writings by "some of the best climbers in the world."

New in this expanded edition of *Rock and Roses* are works by experienced expedition and big wall climbers like Magda King and Lynn Hill; editors, scholars, and activists like Sally Moser, Alison Osius; rock climbers like Susan Edwards, Lilace Mellin, Moria Viggers, and Sally Zigmond. The varied backgrounds and writing styles of the women in this collection come together to celebrate the well established strength and creativity of women's climbing.

Mikel Vause
Ogden, Utah
1999

Words from the Editor back in 1990

People need to participate in adventure, to pioneer new frontiers, sometimes even at the risk of life, and to do it under their own power using few or possibly none of technology's products to add an even greater feeling of accomplishment and contribute to their ascent—physically and spiritually.

When one thinks of mountaineering, generally it is in the masculine sense, and in the past men was mostly responsible for the advances made in the sport. But today things have changed. Women have taken an active role in the development of new and difficult routes in all of the major mountain ranges of the world.

The essays contained in this collection are those of women. Women bold enough to break the old ideological mode set for them by society and to go seeking adventure. The writings herein approach climbing with the same poetic enthusiasm as the scholar climbers of the "Golden Age."

Rather than mere journalistic reports of climbs that are filled with unimaginative route and equipment descriptions, the reader finds stimulating philosophical treatments of universal issues with climbing as the central focus. Each the essay, in this compilation, draw the reader into an active participation with its author. Whether it be responding to the death of a friend or family member as in the works of Linda Givler, and Julie Brugger or the pressures of being a lone woman on an all male climb, as with the essays by Arlene Blum and Alison Osius. In some of the essays, the reader is confronted with logistical problems that are inherent with climbing, particularly those of an expedition leader, as in Post Card, by Sue Giller. Other essays deal with the history of women's climbing and with the history comes an appreciation for the obstacles women had to face and overcome in an endeavor that has, with few exceptions, been dominated by men, as is clear when reading Ruth Dyar Mendenhall, Laura Waterman and Betty Woolsey.

From a literary standpoint, about the best compliment an author can receive from a reader is to find that the reader actively participated with the author while reading. Each of the essays mentioned here and all those others in this collection represent the kind of literature that pulls the reader in, forcing involvement in much the same way climbing does.

The contributors come from vast and varied backgrounds, everything from climbing guides to journalists and scientists. But what is most exciting about this collection is that it represents the innermost thoughts and feelings of women from vastly different backgrounds that are strung together by a common element: climbing mountains.

Mikel Vause, 1990

"You Don't See *That* Everyday"

Gabriela Zim

Climbing legend has it that just after leading the stove-legs pitch on El Capitan Beverly Johnson looked up and saw what she believed to be a haul bag plummeting directly towards her. As the flailing mass flew by and hit the earth with the unmistakable sound of crushing human flesh Bev is said to have turned to her partner and remarked cooly, "Well, you don't see that every day," and continued climbing.

Legends, however, are often a combination of fact and fiction and this one is no exception. In actuality, Bev's partner Dan Asay uttered the quotable phrase and Bev herself was quite shaken up by the event. But this legend, although it isn't what happened, portrays an image of Beverly firmly rooted in reality. Beverly Johnson a.k.a. "Big Wall Bev" was a climber of legendary proportions, and was once named "the best woman climber in the world." In addition to her climbing she was also a remarkable skier, pilot and film maker. She has been called, "The Amelia Earheart of Outdoor Adventure." What separates Bev from an impressive but two-dimensional tick list of world exploration and adventure though, is the acknowledgment by nearly all her partners of her unique spirit. She found intense joy in the journey, not just the discovery, and the journey of her life is a story that needs no exaggeration.

Johnny Carson: " . . .Why do you do it?"

Bev: "I have no idea."

Beverly Ann Johnson was born the daughter of Edward and Doreen Johnson on April 22, 1947, in Annapolis, Maryland, where her father, a lieutenant commander at the time, was an engineering post graduate student at the naval academy. She started ballet at twelve and gymnastics at fifteen. Seemingly more at home in the air than on the ground, after successfully finishing a challenging routine on the uneven parallel bars, Beverly tripped on the floor walking back to her seat and broke her wrist. Later in the season she was crushed when she received second place in a meet in which she had competed despite having her cast removed only five days earlier. She had been marked down for favoring her healthy arm.

Beverly was a reluctant debutante, but made her debut at the Holly Ball in Arlington, Virginia, where her family settled in 1964. Later as a climbing bum in Yosemite Valley she would be chided for her debutante past. She went to Kent State where she raced sailboats on the Great Lakes in "frost-bite regattas," The warmth of California beckoned though, and enticed by their excellent gymnastics program, she decided to transfer to UCLA. After she had filled out the paperwork, sent it in, and been accepted, however, she realized she had gotten herself admitted to USC. With a characteristic non-chalance she went anyway, and through her geology major she discovered the mountains—though at the time women were not allowed on the field trips.

Her acquisition of a new rope made her a popular climbing partner, and soon enough she had found Yosemite. Bev quit school within one semester of graduation and after a brief stint living at home, climbing uninspired lo-cal rocks, she moved to the Valley and began what would become an intense and remarkable life of outdoor adventure.

1969 was the end of what climbing writer and historian Steve Roper has called the "Golden Age" of Yosemite climbing. It was a time when men such as Warren Harding, Yvon Chouinard and Royal Robbins were making a name for themselves on every granite monolith in sight. In their wake came the next generation, beginning in 1971. A decade of free-climbing was ush-ered in by a Camp 4 cast led by characters such as Jim Bridwell, Kim Schmitz, and John Long. It was among these rapscallions that Bev looked for her teachers.

Bev found a mentor and sometimes boyfriend in Bridwell, though she was clearly not one of his groupies. He says, "She was the first 'one of the guys' girls. She wasn't a female with an attitude. You could joke or tease her and she'd have something to say. We didn't take girls climbing, but we'd take her. If she could do it, it was 5.9, if she couldn't, it was 5.10." Some-what annoyed by Bridwell's rating system, Bev had her own ways of dealing with "the boys." Malinda Chouinard, who lived with Bev in the Valley in the early 70's, recalls, "Bev slept with her climbing rack as her pillow, and her pillow at the door of our tent, and whenever there were scary noises she would reach down and throw a handful of pitons. She said they were good for man or beast."

Bev's climbing progressed rapidly. From 1971 through 1972 she climbed extensively with Barry Bates. He remembers, "Certainly some of the most memorable routes I did were with her. Lunatic Fringe, we did the first ascent of that together, and Five and Dime, and Vanishing Point, a lot of those routes are rated about 10c, and back then that was the standard of the day. She was able to follow some of those routes, at that point she wasn't up to leading them yet, and a few years later she was leading without too much trouble. Back then I think following those routes was in some respects physically harder than leading them, because we were still climbing with pitons and you had to hang there and actually pound things back and forth to get them out. It was pretty demanding, just physically, to hang there and get the stuff out."

Over the years Bev completed some of the most difficult routes in the Valley including New Dimensions (the first climb to be rated 5.11.) She was particularly known for her finesse in off-widths and chimneys. As one of her partners put it, "She was a master of the off-width, very smooth, very solid, very much in command."

Peter Hackett met Bev in the Valley in the summer of 1974. Bev taught Hackett to climb, encouraging him to pursue his natural talent for face climbing. Bev was "the only woman considered one of the best climbers in the Valley," says Hackett, although, he adds, "She didn't have the sense of being a pioneer. She was very down to earth, if anything a little too self-deprecating. She would never brag about her feats."

Bev stood 5'6", and was known for her amazingly strong legs. Her 17" calves inspired one friend to write, "How I envied Beverly her astounding calves! I could easily believe she could do anything she wanted when I looked at her calves. There for a while I tried especially to develop my calves because with calves like that I knew I could do anything too."

Bev spent close to nine years living seasonally in the Valley during which time she supported herself working as a member of the Yosemite Search and Rescue team, and the helicopter and fire crews.

Hearing about Beverly and her climbing feats was what brought Sibyle Hechtel, who was to become a leading woman climber herself, to Yosemite.

"To give you an idea of the times," explains Hechtel, "in all the years I'd climbed I never saw another woman climbing other than my mother. Climbing through '69, '70, '71 without seeing another woman climbing, not even once.

I heard of Bev and I knew who she was long before I met her. It was in '71. I was in college, and I heard about all this woman in Yosemite who led

5.9, which was pretty spectacular in those days. So I packed up everything and drove to Yosemite, and moved into Camp 4.

Beverly was my big hero, she was my idol, I mean a woman who climbed, and led stuff!"

"I remember once sitting in the Four Seasons cafeteria and Beverly came over to me," says Hechtel. "She'd heard I was climbing harder stuff, and I was all excited and impressed because here was this great god Beverly coming over to talk to me, and I said 'Wow, how many pull-ups can you do?' and she said, 'Oh no, I can't do any, I just do back flips.'"

An avid cross-country skier, Bev spent several winter seasons living in Squaw Valley, near Lake Tahoe, where she learned to alpine ski. Bridwell described Bev's learning style in a June '94 article for Climbing.

"Bev's ski equipment was comprised of hand-me-downs. I gave her some 207 French team skis and cut-down poles. She got boots from the sister of a friend. . . From time to time I would see her long enough to pass her some brief instructional tips, and then she'd be off on her oversized skis. . . One stormy day, I was stationed on the steepest hill. . . Up ahead I spied a lone skier making big, smooth, fast turns. . . After 200 yards of semi-reckless abandon I could make out it was a woman smokin' down the hill. . . It was Beverly. Bev was like that when it came to picking up skills. You'd turn your back and the next thing you knew she had improved twice as much as you thought possible."

Hechtel, who often joined Bev in Tahoe recalls, "She [Bev] took me on some great trips. One night she decided that what we really should do was hitch-hike down to Lee Vining, ski across the Sierra Nevada, ski in and climb Whitney, then ski over to Yosemite, since we couldn't really drive around that way since all the roads were still closed. Now I'd never been on cross-country skis in my life. So we left. To hitchhiked to Reno, down 395 in the middle of this huge blizzard. It was pitch dark. Got to Lee Vining at mid-night, or one in the morning, and decided we really had to find a place to bivy where we wouldn't freeze our asses off, since we hadn't brought a tent, for some inexplicable reason. So we found this junked car, and we're walking towards this car, and Bev says, 'Oh, what if there's snakes in it?' So here's Beverly my hero, leading me across this Trans-Sierra mid-winter trip, getting worried about snakes. I looked at her and said, 'Beverly, it's like zero degrees. . . ' So we decided yes, yes, the snake threat was probably not really serious.

This is the story of my life with Beverly; it was all stuff like that. It never occurred to me that there was anything we couldn't do, or wouldn't do. I always thought that Bev could do everything, and Bev could do anything."

Everything and anything was Bev's mode of operation as she continued to climb at the limit of Valley climbing. She and Hechtel made the first all-female ascent of El Cap, climbing the Triple Direct . Climbing with Dan Asay in 1977 she was the first woman to climb El Cap swinging leads. She made numerous first ascents, among them. . . She was first woman on the Search and Rescue team. The first woman Fire Crew Boss and Helitack Rescue Leader. However, it was her 1978 El Cap solo ascent of Dihedral Wall that catapulted her into national celebrity, and made "Big Wall Bev" a household name.

The publicity generated by Bev's solo climb was amazing, and she received more press coverage in the Bay Area papers than the Pope, who was visiting San Francisco at the time. The Los Angeles Times reported, "Day after day during the ascent, hundreds of persons stood on the Valley floor and watched through binoculars and telescopes as Miss Johnson laboriously worked her way up the granite wall. On Thursday, two helicopters and an airplane, apparently carrying photographers, buzzed the monolith repeatedly. This aroused the ire of the rangers, who said the aircraft were much too close for the well being of the climber. But nothing seemed to bother the tiny figure of Miss Johnson."

Bev was invited on The Johnny Carson Show (they played "Climb Every Mountain" as she walked on stage) and the TV game show To Tell the Truth. As contestant number three she sat on a panel of three women whose job it was to each convince the celebrity judges that she was the real "adventurer and explorer, Beverly Johnson." When asked, "Number three, how do you know when you're ready [for a climb]?" Bev replied, "You try, if you don't make it, you're not ready." Unfortunately for Bev and her teammates, all the judges recognized her as the true Beverly Johnson. They explained that her blase answers to their questions about life on the edge had given her away.

In a film made of all-women's expedition she led to New Guinea she voiced her own thoughts on the importance of getting to the top.

It's curious how enjoyable summits are. It's not conquest, there aren't prizes, you don't expect a brass band, and sure enough, when you get there, there isn't one. . . but you're so glad to be alive.

Though she did receive a brass band after El Cap, Bev's "blase" attitude towards her accomplishments wasn't due to arrogance or self-centeredness. Bev was often one of the few, if not the only, woman participating to the degree she did, in activities that are overwhelmingly male dominated. What she did accomplish during her life is certainly more impressive in light of the social expectations for women, especially prior to the late seventies. Yet Bev never saw her gender as anything more than a part of who she was, just as she was a climber, a skier, a pilot, a film maker. There were too few women climbing in the 70s for her to serve as a role model to the same degree as such visible female climbers today, like Lynn Hill and Robyn Erbesfield. Though she did serve to inspire other women, such as Sibyle Hechtel, being a spokeswoman for women in the outdoors was never part of Bev's agenda. Bev didn't set her compass by society's map, as she showed time and again, one of her most remarkable qualities was her simple obliviousness of conventional expectations.

Outside of the press coverage, Bev's legacy is not tangled in gender lines. In the recollections of her friends it is the not her impact as "the first woman to. . ." her memory evokes, but rather the attention she paid to the details of their relationship. Mike Graber remembers, "I first met Bev when she was a member of the Yosemite rescue camp. My climbing partner, Rick Ridgeway, broke his leg on Mt. Watkins and she ran up Tenaya Canyon, arriving hours before the rest of the rescue. I have this memory of how she wore her headlamp, not around her forehead, but around her neck, so as not to wreck people's night vision by blasting them with a direct beam." Hechtel recalls, "One of Beverly's best friends in the Valley was Donna Pritchard, a part-time ranger who broke her neck in a car accident and was paralyzed from the neck down. Beverly was the one who took care of her. Bev was always wheeling Donna around, would take her everywhere, and that was her thing, to take care of Donna."

Her solo of El Cap can be seen as a crossroads for Bev between the life of a Yosemite climbing bum and the life of a global adventurer and Hollywood film maker. While she began the climb with almost no fanfare, alerting only a few friends to her plans, she emerged on the summit into a swarm of reporters and cameras. And this was not an unconscious transition in her life. Barry Bates recalls hearing that Bev, aware of the interest her climb had fostered, stopped before finishing the final section of the climb to wash her face and comb her hair in preparation for meeting the photographers on the summit. She wasn't naive about the power of the visual image.

This transition was in large part due to her relationship with Mike Hoover which began in 1976. They were married in 1981. Hoover, a climber and cinematographer, is known for his relentless perfectionism and his often obsessive motivation. Many thought that in Bev, Mike had finally found someone who could keep up with him. Hoover asserts however, that the reverse was actually true. He describes his first meeting with Bev. "While climbing in Yosemite, [I] bumped into her on the wall—she was leading up the most difficult route on the pinnacle and I had just finished one of the easiest." However, Hoover came face to face with Bev only after first dropping a rope on her party unannounced. Hoover was impressed with Bev, but was not destined to have a cordial meeting with her until several years and misadventures later. After many encounters in ill-fated locations such as the hospital bedside of Bev's boyfriend (who had taken a near fatal fall while climbing with Hoover,) they did begin dating after Hoover hired Bev to work as a double for a TV pilot he was filming.

Although Bev had been involved with film and television as a stunt woman and rigging advisor it was through Hoover she moved behind the camera, both as a camera woman and later as an expert sound technician who designed and built much of her own equipment. One of Bev's most valuable assets on any shoot was her ability to fix any piece of technical equipment, and often in extremely adverse conditions. Bruce Brown, whom she worked for on the shoot of Endless Summer II in 1992 recalls, "I remember in Hawaii, the plastic lid on [the film canister] was warped so it was touching the reel. And she went and got some sand from the beach, and put it on the stove and heated it up and poured it on the lid and molded it and put the lid back on. And it was fixed."

This ingenuity was especially useful when, in 1979 Mike and Bev went on the first of a series of expeditions to Antarctica. Their work there typified the unique documentary production style they would become known for. Along with veteran climbers Mike Graber and Rick Ridgeway, Mike and Bev composed a team in which each member worked both in front of and behind the camera. There was no separation between climbers and film crew. "Other people take the film crew and then the film crew shoots those people," says Graber. "On a trip like [Antarctica] when it's so expensive to get down there, and the budget's so tight, there can only be four people. [And that meant] those four people had to be the film crew, the sound crew and everything. And they had to repair stuff. It's really pretty amazing to think that four people produced that film and everyone is in it."

John Wade, celebrity panelist on To Tell the Truth: "What's the difference between climbing ice as opposed to rock?

Bev: "Ice is colder."

* * *

Over the years Bev made over seven trips to Antarctica, both filming and exploring. Antarctica resonated something within Bev. Janet Kellam, a friend who joined Bev on a 1990 trip to "the big ice", remarked, "Beverly was very much a part of Antarctica. She knew the moods and whims of this endless continent, she understood its grace and power she thrived there." Kellam described her own first impressions of the frozen continent in her journal. "Wednesday January 31st 1990. Bev came down below and woke me at 4:00am. The Peninsula was ahead and just visible. A soft violet rose color on a vast horizon. I'm really glad she cared enough to wake me. . . Beautiful light, a clear morning. I don't believe that I'll experience anything quite like this again. So beautiful, so free. . . crystalline, magical, endless."

Antarctica also offered Bev the chance in 1990 to be the first person to fly a gyrocopter in on the frozen continent. Her ability to fly the gyrocopter (an adapted lightweight helicopter) was a great boost for the expedition, which used her flight to scout out routes through the ice, saving the group weeks in navigational time.

Stranded in a tent for days during one Antarctica trip Bev spoke about finding serenity and stability in the eye of the storm.

I like 'em [storms]. In fact, I think maybe it makes me feel secure. It makes me feel that everything's normal. It gives a little bit of order, maybe a little bit of pattern to an otherwise pretty order less existence.

Lives in the States presented it own constant maelstrom of preparations, travel, projects, and epics. But regardless of if the storm was literal or figurative, Bev maintained the ability to assess a situation and make decisions, take what she needed and ignore the rest, and to find the silver lining.

Bev loved to fly, and owned her own plane, a single engine Mooney. Her attitude towards this passion was the same as that which drove her climbing, film making and exploration, a potent mixture of inventiveness, courage, and practicality. Robert Duncan tells of one misadventure flying with Bev in her Mooney returning to LA after surveying land in Wyoming for the show Survival of the Fittest. "We stopped in Salt Lake for fuel," recalls Duncan. "Bev checked the plane out and we took off. An hour and a half later Bev asked to tap the Oil Pressure Gauge which I did. But it still showed zero pressure! 'We're going to have to land.' Bev announced. Bev raised a United Airlines pilot on the radio, told him where we were, where we were headed and asked him to call Flight Control in Salt Lake in our behalf. He wished us good luck. By this time the engine had finally quit but fortunately a Mooney will glide for ever, or ten years, which ever comes first. The landing site we were aiming for was a small airport which we later learned had a

5,000 foot paved runway. With the silence of a glider and the temperature climbing in the cabin because of the desert heat we floated along until we could see a tiny speck on the horizon. Suddenly we were right there. Bev set the Mooney down gently and we rolled to a stop. When I finally got back, Barbara [Duncan's wife who knew about the situation] gave me a long look and said, 'ROBERT, don't you ever do that to me again!" When I asked what she meant, Barbara said, 'Don't be so blase about it.' I just laughed and said, 'Hey, I was with Beverly!'"

In addition to other projects, from 1983 to 1987 Bev helped Mike on extensive coverage of the war in Afghanistan. The conditions there were insane, they often worked with limited supplies of food and water, traveling on foot at night, constantly plagued by various forms of dysentery. Again it was Bev's stability and compassion that others recall. Mike Graber, who worked on several trips to Afghanistan said, "She was the best of all of us—stronger, smarter, and balanced emotionally. Shit, she was sane!" This reflection is more powerful in the context of the adventure film business, a world driven by eight cylinder egos and four-wheel drive motivation, where Bev was a greatly appreciated anomaly.

Mike Hoover remembered one close call, "[Mike] Graber, [Ron] Peers, and I had been in for a long time. We were going all over trying to get [film] coverage of Russian tanks. We all were sick, but I was probably the sickest, mainly with dysentery. I was just coming down with a severe form of arthritis related to the dysentery, which made it so I couldn't walk. So when I was overdue and she [Bev] got tired of making long distance calls [from the States] she just decided to come over. She followed the few leads she had, and showed up with a small camel caravan. We waited for two days until it was safe to cross the desert; because crossing the desert you were real vulnerable to MIG attack. She put me on a camel and took me out, and right in the middle of the desert we did get attacked by MIGs. They weren't really weren't interested in us though, they made a couple of passes, and dropped bombs that were far away. . ." Hoover did make it to medical assistance.

The quality of Bev's life is reflected in the memories of her friends and relatives, memories of how she made them feel. Says John Long, "She was always real impressed with what I was doing, but I haven't done a lot of what she's done. I'm not sure she had a clear picture of how impressive and voluminous her life was. She had no ego at all. She was totally gracious and unassuming." Bev had the ability to open people up and walk right into their hearts armed only with her smile. Again and again her stability, good heartedness and concern for those around her is what rises to the surface of the stories of her adventures, and the descriptions others offer. Long continues, "She was always doing real hairball stuff, but her head was screwed on tight, that's for sure." As Hoover put it, "She just knew who she was, she looked in the mirror and saw what was there."

Bev's life contains events and deeds of a phosphorescent magnitude, but the afterglow she left is one of unassuming care for others, and a joy for living. One friend wrote, "Beverly set an example for me. . . I learned that a person can be strong—stronger than anybody—and still be a warm and gentle, caring and understanding person. I also learned that the biggest flames tend to put out the least amount of smoke."

Bev loved the classics. A dream of hers was to work at a small college, teaching ancient history and Greek mythology. A classic is defined as, "of recognized value. . .serving as a standard of excellence, historically memorable, a work of enduring excellence; also: its author." Bev authored many classics; epic adventures from the North to South Poles, the jungles of Venezuela, the skies of the Antarctic and the big walls of Yosemite filled the pages of her life, and the film she shot. I never met Bev, never climbed with her. In high school, newly introduced to the world of climbing and the outdoors, I imagined living a life of nomadic adventure. It was hard to find female role models and my heroes were Indiana Jones and the weathered men, the hardened mountaineers, I would see in National Geographic. I can't say I ever stifled my climbing dreams because my heroes were men, but it sure would have been nice, to have known Beverly.

Bev was a pioneer climber, explorer, and pilot, an accomplished skier, a mechanical wizard, and one of the most capable camera and sound technicians in the film business. Untimely death, though not a daily occurrence, was an accepted occupational hazard. On April 3, 1994 at the age of 47, Bev was killed in a helicopter accident while returning from a backcountry ski trip. Some shook their heads to consider that a woman who had traveled to the North and South Poles, climbed throughout the world, led an expedition across Greenland and parachuted into New Guinea, died during a comparatively mundane adventure. Others were consoled that she died outdoors, doing something she loved. Either way, she is gone. But her life, well, it's like the legend, " . . .you don't see that every day."

Bev sent her condolences to Mike Graber after a mutual friend of theirs died, and shared her thoughts on mortality and a lifestyle always flirting with the boundaries of death. She wrote:

"If she had bee a whiner, she would have lived. If she had been less brave, less determined, she would have bagged the whole thing long ago.

...Time makes the pain less though it never really goes away. In a sense it is good that it doesn't. To forget is to lose the only sort of immortality worth having, which is a place in the heart of those you loved."

Bev's heart beats on.

Gabriela Zim is a sportclimber, a graduate from of UC-Davis and presently attending UC–Berkeley Law School. She is the author of Beverly Johnson biography, "The View from The Edge: Life and Landscapes of Beverly Johnson" (Mountain N' Air Books), and the third generation women in her family to be published. She started her journalist career as an intern for *Climbing Magazine*.

Freeing the Nose

Lynn Hill

In the aftermath of my competitive career, I felt a renewed sense of freedom and spirit toward rock climbing. What I wanted the most of all was the freedom to pursue rock climbing again in the beautiful natural environment. I wanted to invest myself in an effort that had meaning to me. One challenge that had long been lingering in the back of my mind came to surface: to free climb the Nose route on El Capitan. A comment made by John Long played in my mind: "You should try free climbing the Nose." John was not alone in his opinion that this was one of the greatest remaining free climbing challenges in America. Numerous climbers tried to free climb the Nose over the previous decade but none had been successful.

Ever since I first laid eyes on El Capitan at the age of thirteen while on a camping trip with my family, this magnificent wall of rock inspired a sense of excitement and intrigue. Little did I know at the time that it would become the scene of my future adventures, and a major milestone in my life as a climber.

Some twenty years after my first view of this gigantic wall of rock, I found myself suspended 2000 feet off the Valley floor, hanging at the belay under the Great Roof on El Capitan. I was climbing with a British climber named Simon Nadin, whom I had met several years before, while competing on the World Cup competition circuit in Europe. When we first met in 1989, Simon had just entered his first competition and ended up finishing the year as the first World Cup champion in the history of the sport.

I felt an immediate sense of camaraderie with Simon and respected his humble, understated personality and spirit toward climbing. Though Simon had never climbed a big wall, I was confident of his ability since he started to climbing back in the days of "traditional style." In addition to his brilliant free climbing ability, he was quite good at evaluating risk and placing natural protection in cracks. These skills were becoming obsolete already, in the opinion of the majority of rock climbers involved in the competition game at that time.

When Simon and I happened to cross paths at Cave Rock, we discovered our mutual desire to try free climbing the Nose route on El Capitan. Within an hour of our chance meeting, Simon had postponed his return flight back to Britain. Five days later, we found ourselves hanging under the famous Great Roof, one of the key sections of difficulty yet to be free climbed for the first time in the 35 year history of the route. In 1981, Ray Jardine was the first person to attempt free climbing the Nose route, but after several unsuccessful tries to free climb past the Great Roof, Ray abandoned his attempt.

This was our third day on the route, and the power of gravity seemed to increase the higher we climbed. After climbing from 5:30 A.M. until midnight the previous day, I began to feel the accumulation of fatigue after twenty-two free climbing pitches. In addition to the challenge of the free climbing itself we were climbing with the extra weight of two ropes, a heavy rack of gear, and the need to haul our cumbersome haul bag. That fateful morning, when Simon and I woke up on Camp Four feeling tired, with swollen hands and the Great Roof looming just above our heads, we had no idea what was in store for us.

Simon went up to try free climbing this Great Roof pitch first, but quickly determined that it would be too difficult for him to do it on that day. Although having small fingers was an advantage, after having gone up twice to work out the moves and one failed effort on the lead, I wasn't sure if I had enough remaining strength, energy, or concentration to make a successful free ascent that day.

On my next try, while lay backing up the lower section of the crack, I conserved my energy by climbing as fluidly and as relaxed as possible. I felt surprisingly strong through the first series of difficult moves, but as I began to execute one of the last ones, my timing and body position were slightly off. As I thrust my finger tips into the small under cling slot my foot popped off and suddenly, I found myself dangling two thousand feet above the ground.

After lowering back down to the belay and allowing a team of Croatian climbers to pass, I noticed the shadows of the trees sketching long across the meadow on the Valley floor below. I decided to skip the idea of trying to further optimize the crux moves under the roof. I had limited daylight and energy left and I was hoping that pure motivation would be enough to carry me through on my final attempt to lead this pitch. Either I would make it on my next try, or we would be obliged to continue up the route and forfeit the "all-free" effort.

While resting at the belay before my final effort, I had plenty of time to contemplate the situation. I imagined what it must have been like for Warren Harding, who had pioneered the first ascent in 1958. I also reflected on my own experiences on this route when I first climbed it in 1979, and then again the summer before when Hans Florine and I climbed it in a one-day marathon. Here I was in 1993; about to play out my chances of trying to free climb this legendary Great Roof.

As I looked out across the Valley at the face of Middle Cathedral, I noticed a shadow in the form of a heart. This symbolic form reminded me of the values that have inspired my most remarkable efforts in climbing. Cultivating my feelings of passion for what I truly believe and love is what has always enabled me to tap the source of my being and access the tremendous power of the human spirit. As I had done so many times before on difficult climbs and in the realm of competition. I needed to direct all of my attention and energy toward succeeding on this one final effort. Free climbing this historic route had great meaning for me and I was prepared to commit myself entirely to realize this dream. Somehow, I felt this was my destiny and I convinced myself that fate would play in my favor.

Once again, I made my way up the lower crack feeling relaxed and smooth. I continued with a bit less authority on the first series of difficult moves as I felt my strength waning. These observations did not penetrate my will to persevere. I made it past the move where I had fallen on my previous attempt. Just as I was making the last hard move my foot popped off its delicate purchase against the face. Miraculously, my head touched the roof just at the right moment to steady me, and I propelled myself onward. In the next instant I extended my arm to the limit of its range and drove my fingers precisely into a small under cling finger lock. After a few more moves, I found myself standing beside one of the Croatian climbers at the belay. Both of us were quite surprised by what had just taken place.

Although happy to have finally free climbed the Great Roof, I knew there was one more key pitch above Camp Six that had yet to be free climbed. Intimidated by its reputation as being "reachy," I had my doubts about my chances of finding a possible solution. Simon was disappointed that he hadn't been able to free climb the Great Roof but there was a good chance that the situation would be reversed above Camp Six.

In the early days, the goal was simply to climb to the summit using whatever means available. Later it became a question of style and equipment and the speed of ascent. My own quest was to try free climbing the route, to climb every move free by simply adapting my personal dimensions to the natural form of the rock. Perhaps the next challenge would be to do it all free in a day, then to do every pitch on sight next to do every pitch on-sight in a day and so on. The common denominator of all these challenges was the constant search for new ways of evoking a sense of meaning and personal discovery.

As I engaged in the process of exploring unusual techniques and body positions on this holdout pitch, I was increasingly appreciative of its extraordinary nature. Climbing it free would involve problems requiring ingenuity and technical finesse of the kind that I had rarely, if ever, encountered on any other route. After numerous tries over a three-day period I discovered a bizarre sequence of moves involving delicate smears, tenuous stems, back stepping, cross stepping, laybacking, arm bars, pinching and palming up this shallow dihedral. Ironically, what initially appeared to be a pitch that would be desperate for a small person, turned out to be a unique expanse of rock that almost seemed as though it was custom designed for someone of my body dimensions and background in climbing.

Meanwhile, Brooke focused his efforts on his own face variation to the left. Despite the intense heat spell, I was eventually able to climb this pitch with only one fall and felt confident that it would be possible to free climb under cooler conditions. Brooke and I decided to hike back down to the Valley floor to attempt the route from the ground.

We were well prepared with plenty of food this time, water, equipment and we had a much better strategy for budgeting time and energy. We felt sense of harmony in this spectacular environment. Once again, I found myself dangling at the belay, 2000 feet above the ground under the Greet Roof. However, this time I managed to lead it on my first try. At the end of the day I led the Glowering Spot pitch while still warm and loose, thereby eliminating the burden of having to climb it in the morning.

Before getting there however, we overcame one more particularly difficult pitch above Camp Five called the "Glowering Spot." The next morning, we quickly organized our gear and shared our last bit of food; one half of an Energy Bar and a single date each. We made sure to start before our Croatian friends, so we would arrive at Camp Six quickly and with plenty of energy left.

The Glowering Spot pitch turned out to be a horrendous way to warm up for the day. Simon did an excellent job of leading up this thin, tedious, 5.12c pitch using occasional stemming possibilities in the nearby dihedral to stop and place small wired stoppers. I was grateful that Simon had led this pitch since it was all I could do to concentrate on free climbing it, while one of the Croatians was literally climbing at my heels.

We finally arrived at Camp Six, tired but hopeful. I went up first to check out the crux moves, but was quickly discouraged. Indeed, it was a "reachy" boulder problem, with little in the way of intermediate holds to accommodate my small body size. Simon went up next and after a few tries, he too determined the moves to be relatively extreme and improbable under his current tired condition.

I decided, as a last resort, to check on the original aid line up a shallow, flaring dihedral to the right. There did not appear to be many possibilities of free climbing over to this shallow dihedral, nor did appeared to be much in the way of a crack or any other significant holds inside the corner itself. I did manage to traverse over to the dihedral, but getting around the smooth, rounded arete and into the corner itself seemed absurdly difficult. The only possible feature that I could imagine using to pull myself around the arete and into the corner was a small finger tip jam that was currently occupied by an old broken-off piton. Since we didn't bring a hammer and piton that would be necessary to remove the old pin, there was little hope of being able to free climb past this initial section. Out of curiosity, I tried to make a few moves in the flaring dihedral higher up. I was so tired and discouraged at that point, I could barely find a way to brace myself in this corner, much less make any progress upward. Both Simon and I were jaded by fatigue and hunger and our spirits withered away with each additional effort. We had only a few hours of daylight left. Since we wanted to make it to the top then descend via the East Ledges before dark, we decided to abandon the all-free effort and continue climbing to the summit. Although we had made a valiant effort to free climb this route in the best style possible, our objective had been foiled by a mere ten foot expanse of rock.

There was no question that we did our best to free climb every move on the route. Yet, as I drove out of Yosemite on my way to a family reunion in Idaho, I began to wonder if it would actually be possible to free climb up this dihedral above Camp Six. I had hoped that it might be possible to find some kind of opposition using body contortions to allow progress up this shallow corner. Perhaps it would be worth going back up and giving it another try.

I thought about the conversation that I had the day before with one of my sponsors. When I called the U.S. distributor for Boreal and recounted my experiences on the route, he was happy to hear that I had managed to free climb the Great Roof. He felt that it would be an ideal subject for an up-coming advertisement and suggested that I return for some photos of the Great Roof. The idea of going back up for photos was just enough incentive to renew my interest in going back up and explore the possibility of free climbing the pitch above Camp Six.

I called my friend Brooke Sandahl whom I knew was keen on free climbing the Nose. The year before, Brooke and his partner had found a free, but circuitous variant up the last pitch, which crossed back and forth on either side of the original bolt ladder. Brooke had also bolted the proposed face variation to the left of the dihedral above Camp Six.

The timing was perfect. Brooke had the free time and was more than motivated to give the Nose another try. Our plan was to hike in to the top of El Capitan, rappel down to the Great Roof for the photo shoot and spend a few extra days checking out the free climbing possibilities on the pitch above Camp Six.

Brooke and I met the following week, hiked the nine miles to the summit of El Capitan, set up camp and began exploring different free climbing possibilities on the Camp Six pitch. The first task was to remove the old piton in the dihedral that was essentially a piece of trash in the crack. Certainly this, the numerous piton scars on other sections of the route, and the fact that there are a few chipped holds on the Jardine Traverse, detracted from the purity of this route as a "free climb." These elements were all part of history, evidence of damage inflicted by humans, as I had done with Simon.

The morning of our final mid-September day, I woke up on Camp Five, staring straight up the giant dihedral to the pitch above Camp Six. I dreamt that I had free climbed this pitch and felt a strong sense of excitement about what was about to unfold. Sure enough, just as in my dream, everything seemed to flow together perfectly. The weather was cool and I felt we concentrated as I linked together every move on my first try.

Brooke gave his own variant a couple of tries, but he didn't feel close to linking it, and the weather began to look ominous, so we decided to continue climbing to the top. The last pitch before the summit was perhaps one of the most exciting pitches I've ever done. With nearly 3,000 feet of exposure to the ground and some spectacular 5.12c face climbing over a couple of overhanging bulges, this was an ideal way to conclude such a monumental climb.

Arriving at the summit of El Capitan, Brooke and I celebrated the evening by camping next to our friend, "Mister Captain": a several hundred year old Juniper tree. The evening sky was illuminated by an awesome display of stars, while the moon traced its course through the immense skyscape. One after another, we added naturally sculpted pieces of wood into the dancing flames of our campfire. We huddled around its warmth, exchanging stories, laughing and reliving the most powerful moments of our climb. The final realization of this ascent was a culmination of eighteen years of climbing experience and a refreshing return to my origins and spirit as a rock climber.

ALL FREE IN TWENTY THREE HOURS

After having succeeded in making the first free ascent of the Nose, many people asked me why I wanted to free climb it again in a day. To free climb the Nose in one day, as opposed to the four days it took the previous summer, would offer a completely new challenge unlike anything I had ever done before. It not only represented a kind of "marathon linkage" of this monumental route, but provided a means of sharing my passion and experiences. I had long since wanted to make a film about climbing, and this would be one of the most challenging I had ever attempted. If I failed in this effort, this would be a story worth sharing with others.

The process of prepping for this ascent inspired a whole new sense of consciousness in my climbing. Throughout several months of preparation for this ascent, I practiced maintaining an attitude of acceptance; no matter what the situation presented, I made an effort to be patient and stay relaxed. My intent was simply to adapt my personal dimensions to be in harmony with the features of the rock by respecting the natural intelligence of my body. I wanted to go the furthest with the least amount of energy expended at each step of the way. When I made this shift in emphasis, my whole approach changed.

Through I knew this ascent would require a monumental effort, I underestimated just how involved it would be. In addition to the imminent challenges of the climb itself, I took on the responsibility of organizing and co-producing a documentary film about this ascent. I had no idea how much effort would be required to deal with the numerous technical, personal, and logistical issues involved in this project. Just about everything that could go wrong did go wrong and I kept having to say to myself, "It's all part of the climb and I must carry on."

In retrospect, it's not surprising that my fist attempt was unsuccessful. It came painfully evident when I arrived under the Great Roof at 12:30 in the afternoon, that I had made a few crucial errors. After twenty-two pitches of climbing, I had completely run out of chalk, was nearly out of water and the intense heat of the mid-day sun had all but drained my energy. Feeling tired and stressed by the whole affair, my hopes and dreams of free climbing the Nose in a day faded rapidly, as I spent the next five and a half hours trying to free climb past the Great Roof. After my fifth attempt, I had spent nearly every bit of strength I had left. At 6:00 P.M., with only one climbing rope and my body trembling with fatigue, Steve and I were forced to abandon the "all free" ascent and continue climbing to the summit. At that point, even free climbing between points of aid required a major effort and I began to question my chances of ever realizing this goal. Nonetheless, I knew that whether I would be successful or not, I had to pursue this vision.

After spending the next several days finishing the last few scenes for the film, I prepared myself to try the route again, without the responsibility of accommodating the needs of the film crew. I could now reclaim my freedom and simply climb.

On September 19th at 10:00 P.M., I started up the route again. Guided by the invigorating radiance of a full moon, I climbed pitch after pitch through the peaceful hours of the night. After arriving at Camp Four around 8:30 in the morning, I dozed off for what seemed like about ten minutes. I woke up suddenly to notice the sun had just began to peek around the corner. I decided to resume climbing while it was still cool under the Great Roof.

I felt strong and fluid on the lower section of this pitch. I felt at the limit of my capacity as soon as I began the crux series of moves, but I was confident, I had faith in something coming from deep within me, so I kept moving. At 10:25 A.M., I found myself standing at the belay feeling quite relieved and happy to have succeeded on this critical section of the route.

The difficulties of the climb were far from over. As it turns out, the "Glowering Spot" (5.12d) pitch was the scene of some of the most intense moments of my ascent. I started up this pitch at 12:00 P.M., during the peak heat of the day. When I arrived just below the crux section, I placed a crucial wired stopper in the crack. Unfortunately, just before I was able to set it in place, it fell out. Looking down at the ledge within striking range below, it was obvious that to continue climbing without this piece of protection would not be a reasonable choice. Nor did I want to down climb to the security of my last piece of protection and thereby forfeit my effort to make a "no falls" ascent. Fortunately, I found an appropriate spot to place one of my two remaining pieces of gear and managed to continue climbing to the belay.

By 1:00 P.M., Steve and I had arrived at Camp Six. I knew that if I could make it past this pitch, I would almost certainly be able to realize my goal of free climbing the Nose in a day. Since this crucial 5.13 pitch involves climbing up a shallow dihedral with many tenuous friction moves, I decided to rest on the Camp Six ledge, for nearly 5½ hours, until the pitch was under the shade.

At 5:30 P.M., as soon as the sun turned the corner I gave it a try. Being a bit anxious and impatient to get started, I resumed climbing before the rock had enough of a chance to cool down. Unfortunately, this costly error resulted in my first fall of the day. Due to a crucial error in my complicated sequence of moves, I fell again on my second attempt. While resting at the belay, I knew this third attempt would probably be any last chance. As I began the difficult opening moves, my foot slipped off its marginal purchase and I fell. Concerned that my free ascent might be foiled once again, I made a conscious effort to give my whole heart, and commitment, on this last attempt.

As I rested at the belay. I glanced out across the Valley to Middle Cathedral and noticed the same heart shaped shadow that had inspired my successful ascent of the Great Roof of the previous year. The shade line had risen up the wall, underlining the point of the heart. This was the ideal moment to give it my last full-hearted effort. After making it past the crux section, I nearly rushed into one of the last moves that I called the "Houdini." It involved a bizarre contortionist movement using a double arm bar technique to make a 180 degree turn in the shallow dihedral I needed to make one more insecure move while pinching the smooth arete and frictioning my feet on its edge. This time, I remained patient in following through on this precarious move and continued up to the belay.

Though I was extremely happy to have free climbed past the most difficult sections of the route, I still had four pitches to climb to the summit. After cruising-up the new two pitches of brilliant crack climbing, I found myself below the last two pitches at nightfall. Having made past the first airy 5.12a pitch with greater ease than I had anticipated, I was confident that, even in my current tired condition, I would be able to muster up the necessary energy to climb the past strenuous pitch of 5.12c climbing.

As soon as I reached out to the flake on the edge of the first overhanging bulge my feet cut loose from the face below, and I felt an alarming sense of fatigue in my arms. Without hesitation, I focused my attention on a tiny, two-fingertip edge on the face above. After barely making this move and traversing across a few more delicate face moves, I arrived at the last major overhanging bulge. Too tired to stop and recover any of my rapidly waning strength, I quickly proceeded over this bulge. I knew I could access the necessary energy to keep going all the way to the top.

With only one more passage to negotiate, the ascent would be complete.

Knowing that I might not be able to repeat the last pitch again if I failed on this move, I reviewed my strategy by climbing up and down a few times. Since I no longer had the strength to do this move in a static, controlled fashion, I needed to commit to an insecure dynamic thrust to the last key hold. Illuminated by the dwindling light of my headlamp, I proceeded with determination and faith and finally made it!

When I arrived at the summit after twenty-three hours of climbing, I had achieved a surreal state of consciousness. This was one of those special moments in life when I felt a sense of complete peace and serenity. In the twenty years that led to this summit I had never made an effort so great.

HILL, LYNN (1961-) The foremost American female rock climber for a decade, and the world's leading female competition climber in the latter 1980s, Hill was co-winner (with Isabelle Pattissier) of the 1990 World Cup title and was first in the 1989 ASCI (Association of Sport Climbers International) rankings. She has FLASHED hundreds of 5.12s, and some 5.13a routes. Her achievements include risky FIRST ASCENTS and BIG WALL CLIMBS in YOSEMITE, but she is best known for being the first woman to climb 5.14, in 1990, with her ascent of Masse Critique (8b+ or 5.14a) at CIMAI, France. The 75-ft (22.8-m) route took her nine days to RED POINT. She also made the hardest first ascent by a woman, Running Man, 5.13d, in the SHAWANGUNKS in 1989, and in 1980 did the first ascent of Ophir Broke (5.12d/5.13a) in OPHIR.*

*Biographical credits as was written by one of the best rock climber-mountaineers of the Twenty Century, Greg Child on "Climbing: The Complete reference to Rock, Ice and Indoor Climbing." Facts on File, publishers, 1995.

THE SCARFERS' HANDBOOK

ALISON OSIUS

"So go get it," she mocked.

"Maybe I will," I said. "So shut up."

I pushed back my chair suddenly, and started across the tile floor. Back rigid and imagining I looked as if I had every right, I swooped up the plate of pancakes with one bite missing.

Two bright knowing eyes met mine. A young man six feet from me, his chin on both hands, broke into a huge smile. Utterly flustered, I scuttled back to my own seat, and to my climbing partner Catherine.

Only a moment ago I had exclaimed indignantly: "Would you look at what someone's wasting?" Now the young man and his companion smirked at us, as if THEY were from respectable families and would never do such a thing. Suddenly, Catherine's eyes stretched wide and her jaw dropped.

"They're doing the same thing we are!" she exclaimed. "And they just took two perfectly good breakfasts out from under our noses!"

Thunk. Two plates of cold sausage banged down in front of us, and the two lanky youths dropped into chairs beside us.

"Your technique," intoned Blake slowly, inclining his head toward me, "really needs improving."

Thus we met our mentors, and began a short-lived but brilliant career in the Yosemite Lodge Cafeteria, otherwise known as the Scarfeteria. Blake and Bill were veteran scarfers, highly skilled technicians in the field. Easterners like us, they were part of a group from Dartmouth. They pointed out another of their number, John, a tall fellow in green-and-white striped shorts, quietly tucking into a vacant table and its toast. Rin—short for Catherine—and I were traveling together after being roommates at Middlebury College in Vermont. I had graduated a year before; she, scant months earlier. Like many climbers, we were trying to string out our meager means. Rin had also had the grave misfortune to lose her wallet, containing a large sum, somewhere along a highway in Nevada when she opened her car door to a policeman. (Minor velocity miscalculations.)

"For starters," instructed the guileless, charming Blake, "we all share everything. That makes it fun. Now, there are several ways of doing this. You can sit down when the people leave. Or you can politely clear their trays over to the conveyor belt for them, and take what you want before you set them down. Or you can sit by the conveyor belt and lift things off it." Under that arrangement, he said, one person would watch and alert the second when something good came into sight. The second would casually turn around, placing an empty plate on the belt and taking the full one off in one smooth motion. Wearing dark clothing, Blake added sagely, was best.

He continued. "Sometimes the idea is kind of gross, or somebody sees you and you feel weird, but so much goes to waste here. And face it, it's fun." We soon learned to be intensely aware of the competition. "You'll get ten climbers sitting around in here, all watching the same cold scrambled eggs," said Bill.

Who were the best people to watch for? Children, they told us, and Japanese tourists. Two Norwegian lads, one with long streaming red hair, one with a flattop, slid into the seats behind us the instant the diners vacated them.

"Now that is not cool," said Blake. "Not when people see it. That's when you get complaints to the manager."

"We have more than we need. Here," said Bill, turning around and passing a plate to the Norwegians. "Have this."

They stared back, suspiciously. "Go on, have it," he repeated, waving, and resumed his conversation with us. Silently, they accepted.

Blake was the master. But Rin and I got good, adding variations to his basic themes. We tried to be discreet, and soon learned to piously scorn the obvious prowlers, those with no finesse.

We preferred the conveyor-belt technique. Bussers would load the trays on to the belt; from a ringside table we watched with discerning eyes all that went past. I was astounded at what people leave untouched. You would think they would at least carry off whole bananas and apples. But these treasures headed down the chute—until we gallantly rescued them. We would buy newspapers in the mornings to read, and hold them up at the table. They were effective shields.

A symphony in scarfing, a game. We were still thrown into paroxysms of shame when greeted by an accusatory stare, but we also got many amused, conspiratorial smiles. Growing accustomed to the bill of fare, we learned to scorn the dinner rolls, of which there was always an abundance. Sometimes, sated, we would ignore entire trout or chicken legs; WE were waiting for dessert.

Coldly calculating, we watched our subjects. Of several elderly ladies, I observed hopefully, "They don't look like they eat much."

"Yes, but they look very frugal," Rin replied ruefully.

Bussers, who are no fools, were eventually aware, and highly amused. "Over here! Over here!" Art would whisper. Vince gathered us yogurt and fruit, which Rin put in her knapsack for breakfast. Bruce would approach us, silently holding up a tray for inspection. After a second's scrutiny, we would nod or shake our heads.

"Whaddaya want tonight?" another busser, Mike, would ask in the jovial manner of a host. "Chicken or veal?"

"But it'll cost you," he sometimes added, to our consternation. "You're going to have to take me climbing." Rin agreed, until he, a beginner, began campaigning for a several-day jaunt. Then he switched to a guilt trick: "I've been having to go a lot by myself lately," he emphasized darkly, "without a rope."

By far the worst thing that happened was the time a lovely older woman stepped up to our table, poured $3.50 in quarters in the center, and said, "Here. You kids go buy yourselves some lasagna. I was going to call my mother with this tonight, but I know she'll be happier when she hears what I've done instead." Scarlet-faced, we tried to protest.

"Oh, no," she insisted, adding gently, "I saw you take something off the conveyor belt, and I said to my husband, 'Those kids are hungry.'" Sometimes when I was young, it used to seem like so long between paychecks," she went on understandingly. (Yes, it HAD been a long time since a paycheck; we hadn't worked in two months.) "Keep it!" she said, bustling off. I chased her to her table, the money out-thrust. She turned, and with sincere finality said, "God bless you."

It was late evening, and we weren't even hungry anymore; we'd done well that night.

"We've got to buy something," I said in panic. Rin agreed, and reported that the woman's whole face lit up as she watched the plate of tuna borne back to the table.

"Wonder what she'd say if she saw us buying drinks in the bar later?" Rin remarked.

Side benefits, however, were multiple. Rin and I often climbed with other people, so the "Caf" had the benefit of being a good rendezvous place. There's also a lot to be said for living on a dollar a day, for although we always bought a token something in the Caf—fruit, or tea—scarfing is spectacular economizing (although I must own that we regularly blew our budget with indulgences at the Four Seasons Restaurant—and we knew enough never to skimp on tips). And, as Blake had said; " face it, it's fun." Once a climbing partner offered to treat Rin to a meal elsewhere. She said that she was on her way to the Caf.

"I've got to keep my hand in," she explained.

"Why do you do that'?" he asked, irritated.

"You don't understand. It's the thrill ."

"What thrill?" groused Alan. "Cold pancakes?"

Other climbers began to want to join our table, hoping to capitalize on our efforts. One we had to scold. Stiff and alert, Mark would stalk a tray as it came down the line, then pounce, his entire upper body vanishing into the conveyor tunnel.

Horror stories exist in the trade, of course. One scarfer gratefully seated himself at an abundant table, only to have the burly owner return from the men's room.

"That guy was cool," the scarfer said. "He just looked at me, then walked on by."

Then a security crackdown threatened us all. Many were apprehended. Intimidated, I quit cold turkey.

"Where are your guts?" Mark taunted as, reformed now, I righteously purchased my meals. Once after my dropout he did entice me, using a whole bowl of hot vegetables. Junkie-like, I could not resist. That time almost did me in.

We had long had the Caf managers identified, their movements calculated. One manager was dubbed "cool," the other "Little Hitler." Mark reported tersely that Little Hitler had just called in security on him. A kindly busser seconded the warning.

"I don't want to get in trouble!" I said. "Let's bail!"

"Relax, relax, we're not in trouble unless they SEE it," Mark said confidently. Suddenly he burst out laughing. "Look at 'em! They're all behind that little wall, spying ! They peek up, then they duck down !" "Stop laughing in their faces," I whispered fiercely, but I had to admit it was a hilarious sight: grown policemen and managers, bobbing up and down. I might add that Mark was apprehended shortly thereafter, and given a choice between a $15 fine and four hours of cleaning latrines. Last I saw, he was at the bathrooms of our mutual home of Camp 4, carrying a mop and pail.

That was the end of it for me. Rin and I went down to Joshua Tree to work for a climbing school. One day, she was chatting to our employer, Don, about the Yosemite lifestyle.

"You know what I used to do?" he admitted, smiling. "You're going to think this is pretty terrible, but when I was low on money, I used to go to that cafeteria, and look for leftovers."

Rin burst into unseemly laughter.

Stung, he argued, "It isn't stealing! You wouldn't believe what gets left in there—whole dinners! Come you, you don't think that's so bad, do you?"

"No," she replied: smiling, urbane, tolerant, "I suppose it's not so bad."

* * *

Some people's Yosemite is the Vortex, the P.O. Wall, Astroman; I look back several years and see that my Yosemite, as much as anything on El Cap or the Cookie, is scarfing. The other day a gorgeous score presented itself to me on a nearby restaurant table. I couldn't scarf it: no guts, and I haven't kept my hand in.

It was like coming back with a rope to a climb you once soloed, and not even being able to get up it anymore.

Alison Osius lives in Carbondale, Colorado, where she works as senior editor for Climbing Magazine. She is an author and the president of the American Alpine Club. Catherine Harris is an anesthesiologist in Utah.

The Naked Edge

Alison Osius

Muttering in exasperation, Coral Bowman set up a rappel. She and Sue Giller were a couple hundred feet up a climb they'd been planning to do all summer, and the thin nine-millimeter rope they were using to haul a day pack had snagged. Coral planned to rappel down her 11-millimeter climbing rope, free the other, and ascend again with Sue reeling in the 11-mil from above. She leaned back—and then she was falling through the air. The 11-mil had unclipped from the carabiner she'd attached it to. Sue's eyes met Coral's for an instant, saw surprise and disbelief. She's dead, Sue thought. I'm dead, Cora thought.

Just then Coral stretched out her arms, clutched, and caught the skinny haul rope in her hands. As she tried to hang on, Sue saw no slowdown. Coral slid and slid, burning trenches into her palms. Then her speed began to decrease. Fifty feet down, she stopped. Before her hands stiffened into useless hooks, she swung to a ledge, and clipped into some slings that were there.

Coral's was a supernatural feat—like a mother lifting a car off her child. Sue rappelled down, and pitch by pitch, lowered her friend to the ground. "I almost died!" Coral said when Sue first reached her, but neither said it again.

When Coral, possibly then the best woman climber in the world, and Sue had started on The Naked Edge in Colorado, they hoped to become the first female team up a route the climbing community virtually exalted. That was in 1979, six years after Jim Erickson and Duncan Ferguson first free climbed (ascended without using mechanical aids) The Edge. Their ascent of what had once been an unthinkable line opened up a new realm in climbing in the 1970s, a golden era of hard first ascents.

The Edge, which begins several hundred feet off the ground and ends 750 feet up, saw little traffic that decade. If you'd done it, you'd arrived in the climbing world.

I first heard of The Edge the year after Erickson and Ferguson's feat. It was my first real season of rock climbing and I was in North Wales, teaching at the Plas y Brenin mountaineering center, and so I was virtually an alien to American climbing. There was one route name I, like other foreign climbers, knew. More than the Nose Route of El Capitan, more than Astroman in Yosemite, we knew The Naked Edge. The name, and the shape, captivated us. The Edge flew upward in a rising prow, sailed and lifted above the world, above ordinary, earthly things.

And it was the film. That's where I, transfixed, first saw the Naked Edge. "Break On Through" was very dramatic, if overly body-beautiful as far as the luxurious flexing of the principals went. The film captured the dizzying height and steepness, the exotic raw presence of The Edge.

I sat next to my friend Charlie, who'd seen the film before; at one point he warned in a whisper, "This part's horrific." The lead climber, noisy and panting, wildly stuffed his fists into the final crack, which leaned out over bottomless air. Here, the film went a lurid, filtered red—well, maybe green, but my memory thinks red—just in time to show him arcing into midair. I felt a sick gladness that it was him out there and not me. The film showed the guy falling again and again, bouncing on his rope each time.

I remember with acute clarity my awestruck and sinking realization: I will never be able to climb that. There are some things in life I know and accept I can never do. I will never be able to climb that.

It was 1980, and I was 21, just out of college and used to the optimistic idea of physical things as possibilities. But not this thing.

I had learned to climb during spring of my freshman year at Middlebury College in Vermont. But the only steady, rather than scattered, climbing I had done was during a junior year in Scotland. After graduation, when I went to Wales, I told myself, I'll just have this one full season of climbing before I look for a real job on a newspaper. On the rock climbing scale, whose technical difficulty then went from 5.0 to 5.12 (according to a route's steepness and the size of its holds, not its length) I hoped to "get solid leading 5.9." Three of the Naked Edge's five pitches (150-foot ropelengths) were 5.11. That meant their grade was just below the scale's ceiling (only a few American climbers could climb 5.12 then). As my friend Becky termed the grade 5.11, "That's you and God."

That summer in Wales I climbed almost every day, and was ever more intrigued by the sport's movements and situations. And while one reason for the headiness was that things unexpectedly became possible—my leading went a grade farther than I'd thought it could—I never dared think about The Edge.

Before that season ended, I'd decided I'd take just one more summer to climb, got a job instructing in southern California, and paid a visit to that climbers' mecca, Yosemite. There I heard (incorrect) talk that Coral's rope had been covered with blood from her hands. Neil, a climber who had to leave Yosemite for back-East obligations, mentioned that he was going by way of Colorado. "There's a climb I want to do there," he said.

"The Edge," someone instantly concluded, correctly.

A week or two later, Neil wrote me a long, thrilled letter; he obviously wanted to record the experience. His childish exclamations were meant to be funny, but his exuberance rang true. "The Naked Edge! That's THE EDGE, reindeer! It's the neatest, coolest, greatest climb ever!"

I also remember that a month or two later when another climber, coolly asking about Neil and assessing him as up-and-coming, said "Neil's done The Edge, right?"

"Right," I said.

"He take any falls?" Only two, I replied, on the fourth pitch, on the overhang above the chimney, because he didn't know which way to go. The questioner nodded sagely, though like me he'd never done the route. We knew about it play-by-play.

By winter I figured I'd need just one more summer to climb, and so warm weather '82 found me instructing in Washington State. That fall, I joined a women's climbing exchange to France. Sue Giller was one of our group of five.

She told me the Edge story. I asked about why Coral had quit climbing after that day, and Sue said she had called the experience a "wake-up call" and that it had made her question her reasons for climbing. For Sue, the experience was a watershed. As an extremely conservative climber, she had felt herself immune to such accidents. After that incident—which would have not happened had Coral backed-up her rappel carabiner with another—Sue decided to be as safe as humanly possible about things she could control, and to simply accept those things she couldn't. She went on to climb extensively in the Himalayas.

By that time I'd also heard about Jimmy Collins, who had a fight with his girlfriend and then soloed—climbed without a rope—the Naked Edge. The previous five times he'd done the route, he'd always fallen on the fifth pitch.

I spent the next three of my "just one more" climbing summers in New Hampshire, also teaching climbing. One June, driving through Colorado after a winter newspaper job in Salt Lake City, I stopped and visited Sue in Boulder. I saw the Naked Edge for the first time, and actually felt a pang of disappointment—it wasn't as big as I'd imagined.

I went climbing with an old college friend, Dave, who lived in Boulder. Surprisingly, he hadn't yet done the Edge, and we talked of that as an option. By now I had climbed enough at its grade to know, rationally, I should do OK on it. But I was oddly, furtively glad when it rained the next two days, and then I had to leave. I had a sense of wanting to be really ready for the route, of wanting to climb in the area more first. Stronger yet, I suspect, was this: if you don't try, you can't fail. Or thrash.

A year ago this month I went back to Boulder. And one of the hot, sunny days that otherwise blend hazily in my mind was Edge Day, partly made such because for once no one else was on the route. Over the years, as the number and skills of climbers increased, the climb became well-traveled. It was on many a climber's Hit List.

Actually, this didn't start out to be the big day. Neil and I arrived at the cliffs late, having first done a long errand. In the parking lot we found our friend Dan, "burned out" on climbing after several weeks at it. He was annoyed that we were late. I countered that the last he'd said the night before was that he probably wouldn't join us. He disagreed.

Along came blond Brooks, whom I didn't know well. Plans of action batted back and forth, and The Edge was one. But Neil had blitzed up the thing again only the week before, Dan also had done it twice, and Brooks had tried once, and doubted he was fit enough to fare better.

Last summer, Dan had raved about The Edge. It had been the goal of his whole season, he and his partner had diligently trained for it; when the time came, they met with perfect weather and no other parties. Psyched up, concentrating fabulously, each climbed better than he ever had. "We transcended ourselves," Dan later said with surprise.

Today, my three cohorts said they'd come along, but didn't want to do any leading. (The leader inserts metal wedges called "protection" into cracks in the wall; if he falls, the rope catches on the last one he placed. At the end of each pitch, he pulls in the rope for his partner, who risks no sizeable fall.) I was getting irritated. A big group of four would be slower than two pairs.

"You've never done it," Neil pointed out. "You should lead every pitch." What he also meant was, "You should want to." But Edge intimidation had intruded. Leading every pitch on a climb means you carry the whole ascent's momentum. "Well, how about swinging (alternating leads) a couple of times?" I said, and it was agreed.

We all started hiking to the base of the Redgarden Wall, whose upper reaches are The Edge. It was understood that, leaving the parking lot at about 3:00 and traveling so heavy, we'd have to motor. We hurried up three moderate pitches on another climb that led to The Edge's start, and then we were there. I stood at the base, putting together my rack (collection of protection) for the first lead, placing the pieces smallest-to-largest on their shoulder sling. I felt as I did the first time I had submerged with a scuba tank: Hold on, let me think about this a minute. But as I had then, I simultaneously moved along. I pulled into the first open-book corner and stood on a ledge, arranging my protection in the crack, and my plan for where feet and fingers would go. Plotting the moves is one of the biggest joys of climbing. Then it was time to roll, to force the final act of carrying out the strategy. I pulled on finger locks, walked my feet up on holds I seemed to see with great clarity, reached and made myself crank on a shallow finger slot, and then, just when I started shaking, I was at the top ledge. Done, surveying the first hurdle, I was exhilarated—the realization of where I was sunk in.

I pulled in rope as Dan moved up, extracting the hardware piece by piece, to join me at the stance. Ropework would be complicated among four, but someone decided that Neil would now lead on by to the next belay. He came efficiently along and joined us. Pleased to have done a workmanlike job, I thought he'd toss out the customary, "Nice lead," or some pleasantry.

He just said, "Why didn't you rack up?"

I hadn't put the hardware back into order. Neil pulled the gear sling off me, impatiently snapped and unsnapped carabiners, and pushed past. I hesitated, then said to Dan with a little laugh, "Thought he'd have said something more."

"We should have racked up," Dan said shortly.

We raced up two more pitches, finding steep but manageable rock. Somewhere in there Brooks must have offered to lead the fourth, the chimney pitch.

The experience felt like New Year's Eve. I used to think New Year's was supposed to be a really, really great time. But the fun usually felt forced. New Years' weren't the wild times I was supposed to have, and I ended up thinking I must be socially lame.

So it was now. I plastered smiles on my face, which must have been unsettling for everybody else, who didn't think to affect geniality. Then I shrugged and just joined into the hustling, terse mode of our ascent.

In fading light, I was going last up the bell-shaped chimney when I got stuck. Butt and back against one wall, feet and hands against the rock in front of me, I wasn't close to falling, it was just that somebody put the brakes on me. Go, go, I thought . . . then: I would, but I can't figure out how. After long minutes during which everyone must have wanted to shoot me, I moved rightwards on pinch holds, then up the overhang, forearms beginning to flame. Go right here or straight up? I wondered. Even as my eyes flickered back and forth, "Go right!" the peanut gallery shouted.

I had been slated to lead the fierce final pitch, but now the light was really draining. I'm a slow-to-middling climber; Neil is very fast, he knew the terrain, and when he asked if I wanted him to lead it, I said a relieved, disappointed yes. I tied in to the belay that Erickson had described as "a sloping doormat, suspended in space," surrounded by overhanging rock. Neil moved 10 feet up, then with a quick, deliberate jerkiness, around a corner. When my turn came, I had no time to plan. I bolted up to the smooth and awkward bulging corner, slick from many hands, and with luck hit a sequence that worked. To my vexation, Neil hauled on the rope from way above to speed things, and the tension pulled one piece of protection sideways so that I couldn't remove it. As I bellowed for slack, I wondered how Jimmy Collins had felt here looking between his legs at acres of air.

Dan, thinking I wanted to back down and re-plan a move, snapped, "No, just do it!" I had no breath to explain, but I thought, "Fuck you, you've already done it."

I moved up to the final crack, where Erickson, at the end of his strength, made a "lunge forever" that prevented a long fall. Hurry, I reminded myself. Panting, I karate-chopped my hands to the top of the crack, then clambered up as the angle slackened to horizontal. I was at the very top of The Naked Edge. I sat down. I said nothing.

At the Shawangunks cliffs in New York the locals have a name for a day of blasting up a number of very hard climbs they've got wired, even doing repeated laps on some. They call it a Rape Day. The first time I heard that term I recoiled. But the phrase was used in innocent tones, had become generic, part of the extensive 'Gunks slang. Eventually, I actually stopped noticing it. That night on The Edge, I thought of this term that I'd never used. And I thought, what a Rape Day. This ascent was demeaning to the route and all around.

Dan followed, then Brooks. And Brooks, who'd been so quiet all day, whooped. Bless his heart.

Alison Osius

I told myself, well now, be real;. The rock doesn't care how you climb it. We just did The Edge! I joined him in shouting. I also thought about how it was actually pretty nice of Neil and Dan to retread a route they'd just repeated.

Then we all stumbled, crawled, and clambered down in the dark to the canyon floor.

Today, I work as a magazine editor. I can't climb every day any more, but I often boulder in the evenings and climb on weekends and vacations. A poster of the Naked Edge hangs above my desk, a powerful black-and-white showing two climbers, the rock kicking out above them, ropes whipping sideways in the wind, and birds swooping beneath. Recently, the climb came back to me. A writer had put together a nice slice-of-history piece on Jimmy Collins' free solo of The Edge. Editing it, I read of how Collins, then 20, did not consciously plan to do the solo that day. He did, however, head up a route that led to its start. At The Edge's base, he moved abruptly on to it. Then he just switched into auto pilot.

Only on the fourth pitch, when Collins had to commit to the intricacies of the chimney and overhang, did he finally admit to himself what he was doing. On the fifth, he took four deep breaths, then, not allowing himself to hesitate, cruised the bulge that had pushed him off so often.

I still had questions. So, glad but nervous to be contacting this legendary person, I phoned Jim to ask about just how the solo related to the famed argument. And why he'd since stopped climbing. The voice that answered the phone was friendly, animated, pleased to be talking about that long-ago day. Jim said that, contrary to rumor, he hadn't previously fallen off the last pitch every other time he had done the Edge. Just . . . four out of five. And it wasn't exactly his girlfriend with whom he'd had the argument . . . it was his ex-girlfriend.

One reason the pair had split, Jim said, was climbing's priority. He claimed that his solo act was not revengeful—not she'll be sorry—but an affirmation. "It was, 'This is what I do,'" he explained. Climbing was all he cared about, and he decided he could accept anything as long as it happened doing that.

"Why did you quit?" I asked. Jim said slowly that after a while he no longer wanted to put out the high intensity that climbing at the highest levels takes. And he decided that if he wasn't to climb at the top level, he didn't want to climb.

We chatted, and I said I'd done The Edge the summer before. Most of my friends would show faint or polite interest over that, but Jim exclaimed,

"You did? Congratulations!" Pleasure stirred in me, but so did a rueful sense of anachronism. Yes, once people must have congratulated each other over it.

I laughed. "Well, it's kind of a sad story," I said. I explained the build-up, then the action as anticlimax, and tried to make it funny. Jim didn't really respond. I sensed he didn't understand or want to absorb my disappointment.

So I threw in what seemed like a chestnut about how happy I was at the top. He asked kind of wistfully, "So is it still a big deal for people to do it?" I hesitated, then said, "Yes."

Walls Without Balls

Sibylle C. Hechtel

Memories of a California climber

When asked to write about women climbing in California during the 1970's, I thought, "Aha, another chance to use this title." I used it for an article I wrote for the American Alpine Journal in 1974. Ad Carter, the editor, wrote that he loved the title, but that the board of directors would not permit its use. They preferred "Keeping Abreast on El Cap." I sent back an indignant letter on the suitability of female body parts in a title, while male body parts were taboo. Insistence on my title resulted in the publication of "Untitled" (*AAJ*, 1974).

This censorship indicates the prevailing attitudes at that time. The climbing power elite fifteen years ago were officious, pompous men who weren't about to tolerate irreverence toward the established institutions, especially from a woman.

The attitudes of women climbers, and their expectations, have also changed tremendously from 1970 to the 80's. The high standard at which women are climbing today demonstrates that we have the ability to do hard routes. If few women were doing these twenty years prior, it was ideas which were the limiting factor, not physical ability.

Why So Few Women?

There were always isolated instances of women climbing with men, usually husbands or guides. There were rare instances of all-female ascents throughout the history of mountaineering. Until recently, however, women climbers were rare and all-female ascents an even greater anomaly.

There were many reasons for this. Social barriers were significant. In *Climbing In North America*, Chris Jones notes that in 1909 women had to be far from camp before they were permitted to "unhitch their voluminous skirts and reveal the racy climbing knickerbockers underneath." Prior to the women's liberation movement of the 1960's and the accompanying loosening of sexual mores, it was difficult for women to go on climbs with men that involved overnight trips (and they certainly couldn't live in Camp 4).

Psychological barriers were a second problem. Monica Jackson, in the *Book Of Modern Mountaineering* (1968), says that "the myth persists that women who mountaineer seriously must be over-masculine or sexually frustrated . . . . There is still a good deal of remarkably reactionary suspicion of woman mountaineers floating around among male climbers, which makes any breakthrough by the women considerably more difficult." She concludes that women should be included on international expeditions because "there is no reason why they should not have done as well as their male colleagues, (and) think how much more amusing the subsequent books about the expeditions would have been."

A third reason there were few women climbing was that few women before the 1980's participated in any sport whatsoever. Many women who have taken up climbing recently have athletic backgrounds—downhill ski racing, swimming, running, and cross country skiing. Lynn Hill and Bev Johnson were both former gymnasts. Before the mid-1960's, few women had participated in another sport long enough to retire from it to rock climbing.

On the Lead

Before 1980, a woman leading hard climbs was so rare that when she led 5.10, it was recorded in the climbing journals. Historically, men didn't lead climbs either - guides did. At an 1870 Alpine Club meeting, it was decided that "neglect to take guides on difficult expeditions . . . is totally unjustifiable and calculated to produce the most lamentable results." "Guideless" climbing constituted a minor revolution, occurring between 1880 and 1930. The first "manless ascents" followed soon thereafter. However, women climbers and female teams remained rare until 1960.

The small number of women climbing is a factor often overlooked when explaining why so few women led 5.10 in 1970. By 1971 I climbed in Oregon, Washington, Canada, New Hampshire and California, as well as climbing in Europe as a child. My parents were both climbers. Since they had no son, it was obvious that I would follow in my father's boot-prints. My father, who still climbs hard 5.10 at 73, had done many first ascents in the Alps and led expeditions to South America and the Himalayas. In his weekends at home, he took me climbing.

I saw no other women climbing until I went to Yosemite in September, 1971. There, I met three women climbers-Bev Johnson, Anne Marie Rizzi, and Judy Sterner, and heard about a fourth-Elaine Matthews. Of the four, two led 5.10. What a change -for a year and a half I never saw another female climber. Now that I had met some, they all seemed to be superwomen. It was both inspiring and intimidating.

Originally a southern debutante, Beverly Johnson had gone to Kent State on a gymnastics scholarship and then transferred to USC in Los Angeles. When I met her, she was the temporary park ranger in charge of fee collection at Camp 4 - a job the park service didn't usually hire climbers for. Bev was leading some very difficult routes, including New Dimensions, the first 5.11 in Yosemite. She had also done the NW Face of Half Dome and the Chouinard-Herbert Route on Sentinel Dome. She was particularly strong in off-width cracks and flaring, awkward chimneys, as I was sorry to learn (I wasn't).

Elaine Matthews was a legend. She had led the hardest climbs of any woman, including the West Face of Sentinel. In 1970, she and Chuck Ostin swung leads up to Camp VI on the Nose, where they were rescued due to a blizzard. They would have reached the top with better weather: they had completed all the difficult free climbing, the hardest aid pitches, all the pendulums, and hauled the hardest part of the route. Elaine was infamous for her appearance as a nude cover girl for the Vulgarian Digest. She lived in New York, so I didn't meet her until a 1972 trip to the Wind Rivers, but the tales of her hard climbs were endless.

In fall 1972, I met one more female climber; Barbara Devine, who led 5.11, and I started leading my first few 5.10's (unknowingly, as they were still rated 5.9 at the time). It is difficult to pinpoint the precise moment when women began climbing 5.11, or even 5.10, because often we didn't realize we were doing it. I led my first 5.10's, and followed and led my first 5.11's all without realizing I had ever done so. Ratings in the 5.10 range were rather tenuous after the establishment of the first 5.11 in 1970. Bev remarked, "Bridwell likes to take me along on first ascents. If I get up, it's 5.10, and if I don't it's 5.11."

The first 5.11, New Dimensions, was put up in 1970 by Jim Bridwell and Mark Klemens. By 1974, four women I knew led 5.11 (Johnson, Devine,

Despite this, the prejudices against women still existed, and they consisted of more than mild disapproval. Some men just would not relinquish the lead. In September 1971, I went to Yosemite and met a German climber, Heinrich. We decided to try Point Beyond, a 5.7. I was intimidated by Yosemite and expected 5.7's here to be harder than elsewhere. Heinrich assured me that he would lead everything. Despite this I was surprised when he insisted on leading the two 5.1 pitches up Monday Morning Slab. When I offered to lead, he said that he was the leader.

He continued up the first two pitches of Point Beyond. After failing on the third pitch, he decided we would have to rappel. I asked again if I could try the pitch. He finally agreed, though he was convinced I had no chance of getting up it. Unable to second the pitch, he pendulumed across the crux traverse. After this, he let me swing leads on our climbs.

A year later, my father asked me to climb with his German friend Bruno Friedrich, who spoke no English and was heading to the Valley. I'd just been snowed on in the Wind Rivers, so September in Yosemite seemed a pleasant alternative. I wasn't ready for Bruno's enthusiasm: I flailed up a number of hard off-widths and 5.10 chimneys with him, and by mid-September we were on the NW Face of Half Dome.

This was not something I planned on. I hadn't led much aid, jumared much, and had never hauled. I also didn't have any choice in the matter. Bruno was in Yosemite for four weeks, spoke no English, had no climbing partner, and was determined to be the first German up Half Dome (by default, I became the second German up it).

Bruno led the hard pitches, I led the easy ones, and I learned a lot about walls. Best of all, I discovered that I enjoyed doing walls. Half Dome is a great place to start, because there are lovely, flat ledges spaced at the right intervals. I loved waking up in the morning, watching the sunrise from my bag, and turning my head enough to peek over the edge, 2000' straight down at tiny trees and rivers, the glory of the Valley spread out before me.

BIG WALLS

1973 was an auspicious year for women climbers in Yosemite. We began to reach critical mass and activity fermented. Women from Washington, Julie Brugger, Catherine Freer, Carla Firey, passed through the Valley and Barbara Devine from the Gunks had paid a visit. In 1973 we had the strongest and most numerous resident contingent ever. In addition to Bev, Anne

Marie, and myself, Diana Hunter from Colorado and Ellie Hawkins, also from Washington, were living in the Valley.

Bev Johnson began the year on an appropriate note by soloing the South Face of Washington Column. Diana Hunter burst into fervent free climbing. My second route of the year was Stone Groove, with Diana and Jim Donini. Diana then swung leads on the DNB, presaging the brilliant face climbing she later put to use in leading Wide Country (5.11) in Eldorado Canyon. Her tragic death in 1975 was not only a personal loss but a setback for the climbing community as a whole.

Anne-Marie Rizzi and I took off a weekend from our busy college schedule to climb Washington Column. Everything that could go wrong did—severe lightning storms, heat, illness, general incompetence—so we didn't quite make it in a weekend.

I spent the summer climbing in the Bugaboos and Canadian Rockies. When I returned I learned that Bev had climbed the Nose with Dan Asay. Anne Marie had a horrible time on Half Dome (brilliantly described in her article) and had sold or given away her climbing gear. I did various short routes with both Bev and Ellie and noticed that Bev was sending me up on hard leads and carefully interrogating my climbing partners. When she suggested that I climb the Leaning Tower to get used to overhanging aid, I began to suspect her motives. Slowly it dawned on me that Bev was looking for an El Cap accomplice.

At the time, I was dubious about this, being a relative novice at climbing and also a busy student. Bev however had her plans firmly in mind and only needed an accomplice. Once again, by elimination, I was it. Anne Marie had quit climbing, Ellie had prior plans with her husband, and I was the only other woman with any wall experience. I took her advice and climbed the Leaning Tower with Roy Naasz. We made it up in the usual time and manner. After quizzing Roy carefully, she decided we were ready for El Cap.

There were other reasons for us to get off the Valley floor. Climbers tend to move around. Bev had lived in Squaw Valley for the winter, and had two boy friends, one of whom was usually in the East Coast and the second in Mammoth. By an unfortunate coincidence, they both arrived in the Valley simultaneously.

I had the opposite problem. I was madly infatuated with Walter Rosenthal, whose tent I had been inhabiting part-time. Walter decided that he would solo the Dihedral Wall and had no time for female distractions. He replaced me with a large rack of hardware and bivvy food, spread about the tent floor, and explained that he needed to concentrate on his impending solo. I decided that if he wouldn't see me because he was climbing El Cap, then I'd show him and go climb it myself. Bev and I set out on the Triple Direct on the same day that Walter started up the Dihedral.

We chose the Triple Direct because it was the easiest route. Robbins described it as a "bastard route" lacking in personality, but our first priority was to get to the top. We both lived in Camp 4, Bev was on the rescue squad, and we knew that a failure of the first women's attempt on El Cap would be a fiasco we could never live down. With this firmly in mind we took equipment for all contingencies: extra water, , storm gear, and an extra hammer in the bottom of the haul bag. No wonder the damn thing weighed over a hundred pounds.

At Mammoth Terrace, we left the Salathe route and headed up and right to join the Muir. This was as far as our topographical map went, and we got lost off of Block Ledge. Bev tried going straight up, plus up and left, and then started yelling for Charlie Porter at the top of her lungs. I was rather surprised until she explained that Charlie's van was right down below, that Charlie had just done the Shield, and that he could tell us which way to go. Charlie heard us, but we could never hear him. Luckily the one remaining direction, up and right, got us on route.

Climbing proceeded well up to the top of the Muir corners. Leading out right onto the prow on an easy bolt ladder was spectacular. We had been inside huge corners, protected from wind and exposure. Suddenly I was out on the prow. Wind rushed by me, and I could see around to the other side of the immense wall we were inching up. It was one of the most incredible sights I had ever seen. Then the bolts ended. Mystified, I looked up for cracks, pin holes, anything—was I supposed to hook across this?

"Bev, the bolts end. I don't have any hooks." An evil cackling came from behind the corner.

"Pendulum!"

Oh, of course, pendulum. This was a good place to learn.

"I've never done a pendulum before!" I wailed.

Bev was as reassuring as usual. "It's easy. I'll lower you. Just run back and forth. Be careful nailing at the end, that's an expanding flake."

I was clearly headed to my doom. Here I was, 2000' off the ground, about to run back and forth to nail my first "expanding flake." I wasn't ready for this, but penduluming actually turned out to be fun, once I got over being scared. I made it past the dread flake using nuts.

We soon reached Camp 4 on the Nose, decided it looked uncomfortable, and headed off towards Camp 5. We reached Camp 5 in the dark, Bev un-

Sibylle C. Hechtel

packing the haul bag and eating by headlamp while I cleaned in the dark. What an oversight not to borrow a second headlamp - we'd already borrowed pins, biners, jumars, hardware slings, a sit harness, bivvy gear, hammer, and pulleys.

I've always loved bivvies on walls; watching headlamps twinkling on Middle Cathedral, watching the moon rise over Half Dome and looking at the sculptured beauty of El Cap. It's just as well I liked them, because we had one more. The next day, we equivocated on reaching Camp 6 and then decided to go for the top. We didn't make it. We sat on small footholds, until I discovered that one can sleep by putting one's butt in a belay seat, head in one ertrier, and feet in the second ertrier. In the morning, Bev complained bitterly that whenever she tried to talk to me, I was asleep. A little stiff, we stuffed our gear in the bag and took off for the top, just a few pitches away.

That same month, Ellie Hawkins climbed the Salathe Wall with her husband Bruce and Keith Nannery. I sat in El Cap meadows, watching her lead the third pitch - the hardest nailing on the route. The story was that she went up because she was 100 pounds lighter than her partners and had fewer chances of pulling the pins. It was an impressive accomplishment. Ellie was lucky though—she didn't have to do any hauling. In October, 1973, Bev went back up on El Cap with Charlie Porter to do the first ascent of Grape Race. Altogether, 1973 saw a total of 5 woman-ascents of El Cap, three of them by the indomitable Beverly Johnson.

After a lull in 1974, I climbed the Salathe in fall 1975, with Tom Dunwiddie and Alec Sharp. In 1976, Molly Higgins from Colorado climbed the Nose with Barb Eastman. This was the first all-woman ascent of the Nose and the second of El Cap. By now there had been nine attempts by women to climb El Cap, eight of which were successful. Ironically, the only failed attempt was the first, that by Elaine Matthews.

Perhaps my friend Dave Evans remembered these statistics in September 1977. I was in Orange County, working on my Ph.D. when he drove down from Yosemite and insisted that I return with him to climb the Nose. As always, I was a pushover for being talked into anyone else's insane climbing ideas. This one was ok, except that Dave insisted that we under no circumstances use hammers. To avoid temptation we would leave them on the ground. My protest that hammers were useful for testing fixed pins, and that the party of three which had recently fallen off of Dolt Tower was rumored to have pulled a bolt were of no avail.

It seemed that I got all the pitches that were hard to do without pins. The offwidth before Dolt Tower was mine. Bridwell had said, "Don't worry, it's a piece of cake. Just layback it." Easy for him to say. I remembered something vague about Charles Cole having leapfrogged #10 hexes. I tried that method and it worked. My next ordeal was leading Boot Flake with just a few of the correct size of hexentrics and stoppers (Friends hadn't been invented). Dave berated me for being too slow and suggested that I get off my ertriers and free-climb the rest. Somehow Dave was uninclined to follow his own free-climbing advice on Pancake Flake.

I led one more horrific pitch, a slimy slit that is utterly unprotectable with nuts. It wasn't mentioned as being difficult on any topo, I'd never heard of it, so I assumed it must be an easy free section and went for it. When we got down, Kevin and Tim Powell told us they'd thought Boot Flake was the hardest aid pitch on nuts and that Tim had backed off the slimy slot. I wondered, Tim aiding Boot Flake? He'd led 5.11's I couldn't follow. Dave decided I was possibly an acceptable climbing partner after all - we had gotten to the top in 3 ½ days and without hammers. I decided I would never again listen to advice from any of my friends.

In 1978, Bev pulled off the ultimate coup: she soloed the Dihedral Wall. Now she had done it all: the first female ascent, the first all-female ascent, the first woman on a first ascent, and the first woman to solo El Cap. There's not much left except an all-female new route and a female solo first ascent.

Changing Attitudes: Version 2

Women's expectations of themselves and their predominantly male climbing partners changed as much as men's expectations of women climbers. Goals have changed greatly. My goals at the beginning of summer 1971 were to lead 5.6 and follow 5.7. I doubt any woman who starts climbing today would have such modest ambitions. Today many women lead 5.11, some lead 5.12, and it is widely publicized.

As women accomplished more, men's attitudes toward and expectations of, women change concommitantly. Today, if I go to a climbing area alone and ask a man if he'll climb with me, he usually asks what I can lead. Fifteen years ago a more likely response was the question, "I guess, what can you follow?"

Most of the changes in women's climbing over the last fifteen years have been positive. There are more women climbing, they are accepted as equals and are in an environment more conducive to their success. No longer is their right to lead climbs questioned.

Sibylle C. Hechtel

Along with the benefits of a more supportive atmosphere comes one disadvantage: there is much more pressure today for women to push their limits, and to raise the standard of their climbing. This pressure is no different from that facing serious male climbers, but it is a pressure we didn't feel for a long time. In 1971 it never occurred to me that leading 5.7 was inadequate, and I had tremendous fun doing it. Today women start climbing 5.8's and advance to harder climbs within weeks. As this happens, they are suffering more stress-related injuries such as tendinitis and ligament problems (just like men). To most, it is a price worth paying.

Are the changes for the better? Is women's climbing today better than it was ten years ago? I don't think women had it better then, or now, just that our experiences are different. It was difficult for a woman climber to become accepted then, but once we were, it was terrific. I was able to climb almost everything I wanted, despite being female. I miss some older attitudes. I liked never feeling any pressure to perform.

Many of the changes have benefitted both sexes. Today, men don't have to choose between staying home with their wives versus going climbing. They can go on a climbing trip together. I personally just realized an enormous benefit from the current focus on including women: I was invited on a climbing exchange to the U.S.S.R. The last exchange, in 1976, included no women. This trip, organized by the same person, was given a mandate that they must take women. I asked to go on the last one and they wouldn't consider it.

This year, they called me.

Sibylle C. Hechtell name is one of the first to appear on the pages of history of women rock climbers. She, along with the likes of Beverly Johnson, Lynn Hill, Beth Bennett, Carla Firey and Julie Brugger, is responsible for pushing women's climbing standards past the 5.10 range. This group was also instrumental in leading the way for all female routes in Yosemite, Joshua Tree and El Dorado, not to mention many female solo ascents. Sibylle has climbed extensively in the western U.S., Mexico and Canada.
An immigrant from Germany, she received a B.A. in zoology from U.C. Berkeley and a Ph.D. in biology from U.C. Irvine. She has taught at both Irvine and University of Michigan. Sibylle has also held a faculty research fellowship at the California Institute of Technology.

Sibylle C. Hechtel

Glimpses of Truth

Sally Moser

Some say that climbers have a death wish. No, it's a wish to live I always tell them. But after reflecting on the subject, it seems to me that part of the attraction of the sport may be that death is but a single mistake away. Given the fact that climbing and other high-risk activities entail making life-and-death decisions, perhaps climbers do have a death wish, or at least a desire to come a little closer to the void, to peer into that which is normally obscured.

While having a close encounter with death is not normally what we seek out; it is often necessary to put the gift of life in perspective. Over the years, several incidents have made me realize that at any time we are seconds away from death no matter where we are. It's never too soon to be thinking about what's important in life.

Moonlight glinted off Yosemite's water-polished walls, illuminating the valley floor. I punched the Ahwahnee Dining Room time clock at 11:33 P.M. and hurried to my packed-up truck. The shiny, fire-engine red pick-up's odometer read almost 1,000 miles. The maiden voyage for my first new vehicle, the journey led me to my brother's wedding in the Midwest some 20 hours down the highway.

The road to Wawona to pick up my passenger, Robyn, passed in a rush of shadows and curves. Upon my arrival, she threw her duffel bag in the open back.

"I'm fine to drive," I said. "Let's get outta here."

As she dozed, I drove, over Tioga Pass and down the East Side, following Highway 120. I stopped for gas around 5 AM in Tonopah, Nevada. She stirred.

"How ya doing, Sally?'

"Great, a little tired but I can keep on going."

An hour later the ghostly shadows lurking on the horizon settled into finite shapes. As the sun rose, the smoky hills of Nevada shadow-danced in the distance. Miles of desert highway rolled by, shimmering, mesmerizing, glimmering, hypnotizing, until suddenly . . . WHAM!

Hot sand kissed my face, feeling like the three-day-old stubble on a big-wall climber's cheek. Purple mountains framed the yucca bush at eye level. As I struggled to get up, Robyn's face appeared in my line of sight.

"Are you OK? Some people stopped and they're calling for help."

Nothing could be done. The sand welcomed me. I drifted off.

"Wow—I have to move. This hurts!" My tailbone protested at the hard, unyielding surface. Tied down to a backboard in an ambulance bound for Tonopah, I struggled to release my bonds.

"Let me move!"

"Now you can't do that," said a placating voice from above, "this is for your protection."

A five-minute plea to loosen the tethers finally paid off. The pain eased after I rolled on my side. Thankfully, the hour-long ride passed in a blur. An exam in the hospital which included a blood sample assessed my injuries as a small scrape on my wrist and a bruised tailbone; Robyn sported a neck collar.

The local magistrate spared us a ticket, mainly because alcohol had nothing to do with the incident. For if it had, his secretary told us, we'd be in jail as he had had a relative killed by a drunk driver. A trip to the towing company which had retrieved my truck proved illuminating.

Robyn and I stared at the once-new truck, its cab now peaked due to the rollover, the windshield smashed and doors askew. Joe the mechanic had it all figured out.

"Yeah, you drifted to the right when you fell asleep and the tires caught in the sand. It rolled four times; you came out on the second roll, and she came out on the third. You ladies are lucky; 95% of the time, if a person is thrown out of the car, it'll roll on him! If I were you, I'd go play the slot machines."

I eyed my prized possession for the last time. "What will you do with it?"

"Well, we'll sell the engine for sure and whatever parts we can. The frame is bent, so that's no good."

I shook my head and walked away.

Luck stayed with us until we found a cheap hotel room. After hunkering down for a day, we chartered a four-seater airplane to Las Vegas where a commercial flight to Milwaukee awaited.

We had come close, too close but had been spared, barely hurt. I felt blessed, cursed and puzzled. Why am I not dead? I wondered. It's not my time. What mission am I to do? What is important in life? The only question of these I could honestly answer was the last. People. That's what's important. Not my new truck, not the amount of money I had in the bank, not my job, the climbs I planned to do or new clothes.

Robyn and I got off the plane in Milwaukee and were greeted by our parents. Her family grabbed her and shuttled her away.

"Well, they certainly weren't very friendly," my mother observed.

"Geez, Mom, I almost killed their daughter. Do you blame them?"

They knew what was important: People.

* * *

After earning my degree in Economics from the University of Colorado in 1981, my goal was to lead 5.10. To accomplish that, I pilgrimage to Yosemite, the place where I had learned to climb. It seemed like a logical career move at the time.

My ability to do 10 pull-ups combined with my desire to push my leading skills would hopefully translate into a successful climbing summer. On the first day I followed a couple of hard 5.10s without falling. I hoped that following 5.10 would translate into leading 5.8 without too many problems.

My test piece was Surprise, a recommended 5.8, one of the Five Open Books near the base of Yosemite Falls. To up the commitment, I recruited Dianne, also an aspiring leader. The day began auspiciously enough, with Dianne backing off the 5.6 lead. I motored through, then embarked on the crux. A challenge yes, but not beyond my honed abilities.

After bringing her up, only the last pitch remained to be deciphered. Confident by this time, I moved upward, no protection between me and the belay. But where was the exit? The topo said 5.7. I went up, then traversed right; no, that wasn't the way. I returned left. . . .

EEYAH!

A mini-boulder I had used as a handhold liberated itself from the munge and became airborne. It flew, and I flew. Time extended as I bounced down the rock for 30 feet before landing in a large manzanita on a ledge. Stunned, I wrestled with the bush, cursing and not appreciating the fact that it had saved me from several broken bones. I threw in a piece, belayed Diane up and tossed the rack at her.

"Get us out of here. Go left, I went right and that's not the way."

Eyeing my bleeding knees and elbows, she had no choice but to suck it up and tough it out. Placing gear every few feet, she hesitantly led the final section and set a belay. I followed, a ripping pain in my side every time I tried to pull myself up. After limping down the descent, I headed immediately to a shower.

Blood and dirt mingled with soap and water as Diane, a registered nurse, inspected and sponged off my cuts and scrapes. "I think you'll be okay," she said, "Do you want to go to the clinic?"

My lack of health insurance as well as my plan to live in Camp 4 and Tuolumne for the summer precluded me from paying any expensive medical bills. I slunk into the Mountain Room Bar and proceeded to order all the white wine I could drink. One of the guides entered.

"Surprised on Surprised, Sal? Well, you aren't the first."

I barely looked up from my glass of liquid anesthetic to acknowledge that comment. Friends who had heard of my humbling stopped by, and at midnight I left the bar and stumbled to my tent.

The next day dawned harsh and clear. A pitbull hangover conspired with my injuries to make leaving the tent the hardest move I'd ever contemplated. Eventually, the necessity of relieving bodily functions compelled me to commit. I contorted my stiffened body through the tent door, then lurched the 50 yards to the Camp 4 bathroom.

For the next few days, I rued my existence. My right leg ballooned to elephantine proportions; wearing shoes or socks was impossible. It hurt to breathe, laugh or sneeze. Each morning I had to peel the sleeping bag off my oozing wounds. I finally received some medical attention when a third-year med-student in camp practiced his diagnostic skills on me.

"Your leg? A subdermal hematoma, that will recover in time. Watch those lacerations for signs of infection—the one on your elbow is deep and could have used a couple of stitches. Your ribs are bruised and not cracked, otherwise you'd have black-and-blue marks where the blood seeped out."

"Hey, Jeremy," he called to his friend, "come over here and see what rock climbing will do for you!"

I contemplated what climbing had done for me as I watched my friends from my lawn chair in Camp 4. What's important in life? My climbing goals that I had trained for and now couldn't accomplish? Would I climb again? Of course, everyone said, yes, you have to climb. Inwardly, I recoiled at the thought.

One of my climbing partners came by my tent and off-handedly said, "This is good for you. What doesn't kill you, keeps you alive."

My dander rose immediately. "Bull Shit. There's nothing good about this, my climbing summer is ruined, I'll never lead 5.10."

But after he left, the second part of what he said stuck in my head. Lessons, lessons are what's important in life, especially in climbing, because what doesn't kill you, keeps you alive. I, should I climb again, would be more cautious, put in more pro, test the holds for looseness. Fear of falling was now impressed upon my brain cells, my ribs, my leg, my elbows. To make this experience worthwhile, I had to learn its lesson and apply it. It was a gift to me which presented, on some level, what I needed to know.

Fourteen years later, my red four-wheel-drive gamboled up the dirt road to my Saturday rigging job. Women's Crying Climbing I called it, and half of the female climbers in Boulder had set up top ropes at a scruffy little cliff that June Blanding used for her feminist healing and trust-building weekends. I had made a cool hundred dollars cash working for her a few weeks before: set up the ropes, get a tan and watch the tears flow. Piece of cake.

Today the group numbered seven, rather large, and as they got acquainted, I hauled five ropes and assorted pieces of gear over to the 70-foot mini-crag. Not being a climber, Jane believed in overkill as far as safety was concerned, and this was the most redundant system I had ever seen: one person belayed by four people, with two on a rope, one with a Sticht plate and one with a hip belay, each rope hanging from a separate three-bolt anchor. (Later in my tenure, I discovered that this overkill was warranted—one woman fainted from the mental strain of belaying and other belayers rushed to her side, leaving the person climbing protected by one slightly shaky hip belay.)

As a bonus activity for the class, another line was rigged so that participants could try rappelling. After tying the rope into a tree at the top, I tossed it off only to have it hang up on a bush. I clipped into the old Goldline™ and began to head down to clear it for the students. Easing my weight onto the rope, I mentally noted that this was a bad rappel for beginners because of the overhang at the start.

POP!

I was flying and instinctively my right hand clamped onto the rope. I came to a stop on a small ledge a good 15 feet down from the overhang. What the. . .? My belay plate and locking carabiner dangled above me, still attached to the rope. Disbelief, shock and bewilderment flooded my being. My hand throbbed, having stopped my rapid descent to the talus 50 feet below. I knew not what had happened, and simply had to get down. Taking a single carabiner and rigging it into the rope, somehow I arrived on the ground.

Dumfounded, I hiked to the top of the cliff. I knew I had clipped into the rope, the plate and the biner still there were proof of that. Searching for the answer, I discovered the broken gear loop on my harness. Not meant to hold anything more than a few quick draws or nuts, the gear loop had given away under the pressure of body weight. In my haste to straighten out the rope, I had not taken enough time to check what I had clipped into nor had I given this seemingly innocuous cliff the respect it deserved.

My hand had turned into a near useless claw, the burn fully blistered across my fingers and palm. What to do? I needed the work so I had to continue on as if nothing had happened. Before returning to class, I stopped to bathe my hand in the cold creek water.

As I taught them to belay, one woman noticed the prominent blisters. "Look," she said, "she has calluses from belaying!" I smiled, nodded, and continued to keep my right hand palm down as much as possible.

June appeared from the main cabin as I wrapped up the belay lesson and said, "OK, everyone must sign the waiver before continuing."

I barely contained my laughter.

"Now, is there anything that anyone wants to share before we get started?"

I almost died, I wanted to say. I'm here and I don't know why. Yes, this is totally safe, but I almost didn't make it. Operator error. Mental meltdown.

The day passed. I kept my hand low profile and concentrated on the job. My adrenalin-flushed state gradually ebbed.

Finally I took my little secret home. I had planned to go to a party, but it paled in comparison to the day. I couldn't go and make social chatter to a room full of strangers. I made a totally avoidable, boneheaded mistake! Why was I still here?

Marveling at my good fortune, I sat on the back porch, drinking in the sky, the trees, the grass, the earth. It was alive, I was alive. What's important? The fact that I'm here and not mush on the talus at the bottom of the cliff. The fact that I can climb again, see my loved ones, learn this lesson and continue playing the game. Life, that's the most important thing.

Yes, I've been lucky. I've survived to climb and to live and to love and to laugh again. These days my goal is to come closer to the truth without getting too near the void. But by getting closer to death, I've gotten closer to life and am thankful for these glimpses of truth.

Sally Moser, the Executive Director of Access Fund, an organization dedicated to obtain, protect and maintain climbing crags access for climbers and others.

Sally—BA, Economics, CU-Boulder—has been involved with the Access Fund since 1989 in various capacities, including Development Director and Media & Marketing Director. She served as managing editor for Rock & Ice magazine for four years, and editorial director of Summit magazine for one year. She's co-author of three guidebooks to California's Southern Sierra, and worked as a climbing guide for Boulder Rock Club in Colorado.

Sally started to climb in Yosemite in the late '70s and still loves to climb any size crack.

The Two Old Bats:
A Climbing Partnership That Works

Susan Edwards

I came here today to run on the flanks of Mount Diablo—this mountain I know so well—where I must have run hundreds of miles and spent many hours, trying to sort my life out. I try to come here without expectations but sometimes, like today, I come for consolation.

Earlier this morning my body was screaming. It was so out of synch—struggling to go its own way, with its own muddled thoughts. Anguished thoughts about Inez. Tomorrow she goes to be tested for what could be a very deadly form of cancer. I can't bear the thought of losing my closest and dearest woman climbing partner and so I'm here to run.

It's warm and spring-like as I jog along the rutted trails that skirt Shell Ridge. Wildflowers are in abundance and red-winged blackbirds screech as they move along on their migration south. I wish I could join them in their flight! Instead I feel an urge to run hard, fast and long—until the thoughts recede and the pain goes away. But gradually, as I lope along at an easy pace, I become aligned with the rhythm and my mind and body began to calm down. Thoughts, ideas and feelings, when they do come, are clearer and I can begin to look them in the eye.

There was a feeling in the pit of my stomach, the pain of being connected. I can almost feel the rope tied to my waist—the one that connects us as we climb. I think it will always be there.

I feel helpless because, on this occasion, there appears to be nothing I can physically do to help my friend and partner. Yet this running—this moving meditation—is my own form of prayer for her, and reminds me of a more powerful connection that exists between us as a result of our climbing. As I think of our times together, I have a sense that I am beside her.

We are an "odd" pair really. These two "old bats," as we secretly call ourselves, continue to want to challenge themselves on the rock, even as they head into their mid-fifties. You would think we had sorted it all out by now and wouldn't need to do this risky sort of stuff any more—but somehow that hasn't happened. We did start late though. I was maybe 36 when I was first smitten by the Sierras and decided that rope skills might be useful for crossing some of the more difficult passes. I am a slow and cautious learner so it has taken me as many years to arrive at the level that Inez reached, starting a decade later. I admire her for that.

I have to admit there was a connection between us before we even had a chance to climb together. I recognized it by the first pangs of jealousy! The people I care for the most—the ones I particularly admire—are frequently those of opposite character to myself and even though I try hard to be content with who I am, and with who they are, I generally can't avoid some jealousy! So there you have it! And I hate it!

Inez, to my mind, is the vivacious one. She is outgoing and funny—her comments or imitations of people, even though harsh at times, caricature them in such a way that one can't help but be amused. She's a colorful personality and people have a sense, right away, of who she is. I, on the other hand, am the quiet, intense, rather introverted and somewhat stolid one—unless of course you give me a few whiskeys, and then my more "Inez-side" comes out! Inez lightens me up and I calm her down. Together we have fun, gossip, are silly, and generally enjoy ourselves.

It might sound as if we climb together on a regular basis, but in fact that's not the case. Somehow though, we seem to do many of the "more important" climbs together—the ones that have left an impact on my soul.

Ever since that first "expedition" we made to climb the South Face of Charlotte Dome, one of and Roper's Fifty Classics, we have been inspired by each other and dreamt of greater things together.

That climb, which Inez had suggested, was the first time either of us had attempted a long backcountry climb, but somehow we treated it like a Sunday jaunt—we could handle it—no problem! In truth we didn't know what we were letting ourselves in for; but there seemed no reason we couldn't do it, as long as we took it one step at a time. So it was then that, on a beautiful sunny day in June of 1972 we began the 10-mile hike in to the base of the Dome. We gossiped, as women will do, as we steadily made our way up the trail that follows the sparkling, crashing, waters of Bubbs creek, eastwards into the heart of the Sierras. It was the first time we had carried both camping and climbing gear, so the packs felt particularly heavy. We were carrying five days worth of food as well because our plans were big! After Charlotte Dome we would cross the pass behind it, to the northwest, and hike over to bag Mount Clarence King.

After eight miles we took our last break. As we nibbled on snacks and took a quick dip in the creek we could look north and see our Dome, two miles above us. It was awesome! And looked incredibly steep and difficult—worse than the already terrifying photo I had stared unbelievingly at in Fifty Classics—how on earth were we going to make it! In my usual way I kept these thoughts to myself and calmly hefted my pack on my back, hopefully for the last time. With a reminder to myself that perspectives can change, I continued the slow drudge upwards. Not only did I miss the faint trail as it disappeared behind some bushes but scrambling up steep scree, with packs that constantly threw us off balance, became increasingly wearing. It was late in the day when, with little patience left, we found ourselves battling through manzanita bushes on brief and discontinuous animal trails not far from the base of the Dome. I was feeling frustrated with my route finding abilities—they needed considerable honing! I would have staggered on to try and find the small seasonal stream hoping it would still be running down the back of the dome. This time Inez suggested we stop. She had spotted the only small flat area suitable for a tent. Our sleeping quarters would be nestled up against manzanita bushes. There were some large slabs of rock in front where we could set up our kitchen; and a tall tree from which we could hang food, far from the paws of hungry bears—we had everything we needed for a comfortable base camp!

To stop was such a relief! I was totally knackered! My back was aching and my energy was totally spent—the thought of getting up early to go and climb this huge ugly mound of granite, now in front of us, was so repulsive I didn't even want to think about it. Inez, not so inclined as I to spiral into despondency, suggested a day off. I couldn't believe how much brighter the outlook seemed—what a great idea! Lets bask in the sun, find some water, check out the route and rest our bodies! Maybe we could have fun after all!

Rolling out of bed the next morning I lit up the stove for some hot water—before I knew it there were flames leaping up from around the base of the plastic plunger. Memories of a previous disaster flooded into my mind as I grabbed a handful of gravel and doused the flames. But it was too late—the plunger had melted in a number of areas and would no longer "plunge!" Great! Perhaps all that freeze-dried food wasn't such a good idea after all! Just the thought of trying to eat it in cold water gave me major indigestion! Inez came to the rescue again when she rummaged in her "beauty bag"—the one that, yesterday, I had scorned her for bringing. "What the heck do you want to bring lipstick for? It only adds more weight, something we can do without up here!" "It makes me feel better about myself and that way I'll climb better" was her response. Not very understandingly I decided I didn't really care, as long as I didn't have to carry extra weight as a consequence. This time she took out a nail file and with careful strokes managed to file the lumps of melted plastic down sufficiently, so that the plunger would go at least two thirds of the way into the cylinder. We were able, in time, to build up enough pressure to light up the stove as usual—what a relief! Another problem solved and the "beauty bag" concept was beginning to seem OK after all. It felt good each time we were able to sort something out whether it be finding water, hanging our food, finding the base of the climb, route finding on the climb or surviving our first bivvy. Yes, that was a surprise! Not something we had exactly planned for. It had been my role to gather together all the route information and nothing I had read really explained the descent as anything other than a walk off. So I wasn't worried—we were moving steadily and it seemed as if our timing would be just right—to reach the summit before dark that is. Neither of us had concerns about descending in the dark, in fact I for one rather enjoy it. I suppose it comes down to the fact that both of us would rather climb deliberately and at our own pace. We are not into timing pitches, and dislike feeling pressured. This may sound a dangerous habit to those who live in colder climes, or to those who hate to be caught out in the dark and under no circumstances wish to bivvy. In fact there are those who scorn anyone unable to climb in a hurry and to some, bivying is looked on as failure. To those people we say, "Smell the roses!" and that's exactly what we did on Charlotte Dome. As a consequence, or perhaps I should say reward, we reached the top of the climb just as the sun went down. I belayed Inez up to the summit ridge, which had a steep drop-off behind. To this day she laughs at the seriousness of my tone when I said, "Sit down, we have something to discuss!" Ahead of us was the narrow ridge and beyond that, although we didn't realize it at the time, was a series of rappels down the back of the dome. One of our headlamps was out of commission which made the prospect of continuing, out of the question. Inez, in sprightly tone said, "Well, I noticed a great place just below us for a bivvy!" I was surprised because I hadn't even been thinking along those lines. But what else was there to do. So, we lowered ourselves onto a narrow ledge behind a large block. Pulling everything out of the daypack, we used as much of it as we could, to help ourselves keep warm. I couldn't contain my laughter when Inez pulled over her head, a netting bag full of slings. In this homemade hat of sorts, she reminded me of women in my native Britain, who go to the shops in their curlers with a scarf tied tightly over the whole shebang. My mother once told me they were advertising the fact that they had a date that evening. This particular evening we had a date with the stars! The night rapidly grew cold, as did the rock around us. I had my knees drawn up under my parka and I sat facing the big block, which separated us from the vast black chasm beyond. I couldn't sleep—I was too cold. But occasionally I had the illusion I was about to nod off—for a glorious second I lost consciousness—but as my muscles relaxed I would promptly fall forwards, hitting my head against the block! Getting frustrated and stiff, I would get up and jump around to warm up. Beside me Inez seemed quiet and still. She lay curled up in a fetal position on top of a rope, with her feet in our small pack. I couldn't believe that hypothermia wasn't creeping into her bones. In all the stories I had read about "unplanned" bivvies people either sat wrapped around each other all night, or at least needed to sit and rub their hands and feet together occasionally. Suddenly, worried to death that Inez might go to sleep permanently, I felt a need to check her. "You're still OK? Still alive?" I blurted out. She murmured a response and snuggled back into her cozy snakelike coil. I was envious! At times like these I become frustratingly aware of my ability to worry, about anything and everything! "What will the morning bring; why can't I just relax and sleep; is Inez OK; am I OK? If I stop worrying is that a sign I'm dead? Oh for God's sake! Just STOP IT! SHUT UP!" Maybe this is why I climb! To stop these endless thoughts! When I'm on the ground or resting like this, I worry about every stupid little thing, including why I climb. At least when I'm climbing I just climb!

We were like lizards in the morning. I remember opening one eye and seeing an orange line on the horizon—gradually it crept up until much of the sky was illuminated with a warm glow. But it wasn't on us yet. Finally it arrived and we let it seep into our bodies for a while before we began to move. It was heaven sauntering along the ridge, my body relaxing in the warmth, my mind distracted by the task at hand. Before long, and after a number of rappels, we were down on the granite slabs. Suddenly, with the need to concentrate over, we felt sapped of our strength and sleepily wandered along, dreaming of cool water. Finally we reached the stream and after imbibing our fill, there was nothing else to do but dive into our sleeping bags for an afternoon siesta. Inez, now relatively perky, was propped up, pen and notebook in hand, wanting to reconstruct the climb pitch by pitch.

Susan Edwards

"That fourth pitch you lead, didn't it have a lieback on it and what do you think the rating was?"

"Well, I think it was um, maybe a, under. . . , you know I don't think I can do it. . . ."

My jaw dropped permanently open and my head fell back onto my pillow—what a sweet slumber!

We were so satisfied with the success of our climb that we just wanted to bask in it. The idea of rushing over to do another climb, and one we weren't so interested in, seemed all too much. The day was beautiful—why not just take it easy again! And then head down to the Kings River in the evening. We seemed to have the same ideas and wanted to go at the same pace. It was relaxing and I was having fun—no need for any macho posturing!

We camped close to the river that evening. Our awareness of the fact that bears were sharing our territory was increased only because we were in a small campground that had a bear box. I needed to get up for a pee in the night and fumbled in the pocket beside me for some TP, trying to be as quiet as possible. Suddenly I received a sharp dig from Inez. She sat up abruptly, "Did you hear that?" I giggled, "It's only me!" She was terrified that some bear was sniffing around the edges of our tent looking for a tasty morsel.

The next day we traipsed on down the trail with the sun shining and the vivid yellows and blues of the wild flowers exploding in front of our eyes at every turn in the trail. We were chattering on about how wonderful we were at climbing and how well we handled everything. The climb had been downrated from a 5.8 to a 5.7 because it was apparently felt that the first ascenders overrated it. We thought it was more like 5.8 in many places and were convinced that we had even done a couple of 5.9 moves! Because of its sustained nature we certainly wouldn't have recommended it to any new 5.7 leaders. We were learning what classic backcountry routes were like! The overall ratings seemed harder when one added in the route finding, being out in the backcountry and the exposure. Nothing on Charlotte Dome had felt like a single, low level of commitment, pitch of 5.7 might. We were also finding out that "classic" climbs are not going to be "giveaway ratings." Five sevens are not going to be a pitch of 5.5 with one move of 5.7 in them. They are sustained, solid 5.7 ratings all the way.

So we were loudly expounding the fact that this climb had to be much harder than a "rinky dink" 5.7, when around the next corner came a rather good looking renegade climber-type. With chests puffed out we chatted quietly and pleasantly with this compatriot, hoping he would ask about the amazing climb we had just done. He told us he was on his way south to a family wedding in LA. But that he couldn't resist nipping up to do a quick climb on the way there, so that he would have enough room to eat his heart out at the reception. Then he told us the name of the route he was on his way to solo. It was the one we had just done! I was stunned and somewhat embarrassed as Inez gave him some beta, and he very graciously thanked her. He had no additional questions or concerns and I knew he must be someone really good! It truly was a Sunday jaunt for him whereas, for us, it had been one of the most challenging adventures we had yet undertaken. We weren't about to let this news burst our bubble however, and so, after saying good-bye to this stranger, we continued to expound! We became convinced that we were probably the first pair of women to have ever climbed this route and most definitely were the only ones in their 40's. The records certainly didn't disprove this but, as Inez found out from the rangers, accounts from climbers were minimal. Oh well, we would just have to be content with the inner rewards the climb had given us! Like the bond that was beginning to build between us.

Climbing partnerships are a strange thing really. Climbers rave about how intense the partnership is, how deeply we must trust each other and how intimate it all is and yet, very few of these intense, trusting and intimate relationships last more than a few climbs. It's true, I believe, that climbers thrive on intensity but at the same time they find out very quickly who they can or can't trust, whose habits they can live with, who has similar ethics and many other issues. Decisions about partners matter little, or at least have less impact, for a day at the crags—in fact it's a great time to try people out as it were. I'm not necessarily suggesting that people aren't selective about whom they spend time with on shorter climbs but somehow the decision becomes far more important when dealing with longer, more committing adventures. Of course this is individual but, for me, I need to trust, admire and have confidence in my partner. To me the best person is one I hardly notice is there and yet I always know is there, if you know what I mean. Similarities in philosophy and approaches to climbing are great and yet a complimentary nature of personalities and skills seems to work well. This is the combination Inez and I have and it works well—on the rocks at least.

I don't want to be pie-eyed and unrealistic about it all. We've had our difficulties.

And that's why I want to tell you about another climb we did in July of 1997.

This one was dedicated to the healing of our relationship. It had been fractured for over a year and I believe we both thought that if we could just get back on the rock together—preferably on a long and challenging climb—then the wounds might finally be closed.

I have found it tremendously powerful to dedicate runs or climbs to a particular person or for a particular purpose. I first dedicated an 18-mile run to Bruce, a young mountain guide who died of pulmonary edema on Huascaran in Peru. A few months previously I had climbed on the same roped team as him, a number of times, in Ecuador. I wanted to spend some quality time "being" with him. Then I dedicated a climb of Arrowhead Arete, in Yosemite, to my father who was sick and dying of prostate cancer. I told him about it on his deathbed, and how he had been there with me. He and I had taken a trip to Yosemite together and he had fallen in love with the Valley—I saw from his eyes that he understood.

Now there was a climb that I had wanted to do for a number of years. I had tried to find a suitable partner but nothing had come to fruition. It was the perfect climb for Inez and I and when I mentioned it to her she jumped at the opportunity. Plans were underway pretty quickly and we began to get tremendously excited. It had been five years since we had made the trip to Charlotte Dome. We were considerably more experienced and yet we still desired the same quality of adventure.

It began on Saturday July 19th 1997. Neither of us had slept much and Inez had been hassled in the wee hours by a pair of bobcats, maybe trying to alert her to the fact that the alarm had already gone off (or had it?)! We lurched awkwardly up the boulders noticing that it was already quite warm—the only sounds, our huffing and the crackling of leaves and branches underfoot.

We were in Yosemite and heading for the N. Buttress of Middle Cathedral (5.10a or 5.7 A2)—a misnomer since it's way to the right of the true buttress and in fact runs up the left side of the sweepingly smooth and gigantic north face. Earlier in the year we had checked out the route with binoculars, had read one party's account of their ascent and had studied the several route descriptions. This must have seemed sufficient since we didn't appear at all fazed when the topo didn't show up while sorting gear. . . .

Never mind. . . . "Between us I'm sure we can remember the details don't you think?" Our confidence was overwhelming. . . and maybe a bit misguided!

We stashed our large packs taking only a small one, now bulging with bivvy gear, cameras, shoes and four and a half quarts of Gatorade—sufficient we thought for what we anticipated to be a day and a half ascent.

Allen Sanderson, a friend of Inez's from the Net, had come up with us the night before and would be climbing the more popular three starred DNB just around the corner from us. Our climb—the first long route to be put up in 1954, by none other than Warren Harding and cronies, receives one star in the current guidebook. Even though not climbed very often this ranks it with other excellent Yosemite climbs of the same rating such as the Kor-Beck, the Prow, the regular route on lower Cathedral Spire and shorter routes like Peruvian Flake and Y-Crack.

We set off—glad to be moving and having something to focus on other than our sleepiness and our stiffness.

The first few pitches went easily, the only concern being loose blocks and getting used to the deadweight of the pack. I found myself lulled into thinking this might be the way the whole climb would go. Then I lead up some grungy cracks to a huge pedestal and a dead end. This must be the "Right Rabbit Ear" and this bunny has to be mighty big because the left ear is nowhere in sight! Admittedly I didn't look too hard, that wasn't our current concern. We were looking out across the great North face and the only possible way seemed to be a small ledge leading out towards it. This must be the "hidden chimney pitch" because as far out on the ear as we could go, we were still unable to see what was around the corner. This is where Steve Roper says the climbing becomes "serious" and, with the area feeling sinister and my negative thoughts getting the upper hand, I pictured some horrible, dark, bottomless bombay chimney.

"Well, I guess I'll just go and investigate" Inez said boldly. "Thank God she's leading it!" I was thinking, and continued to think for the majority of pitches Inez would lead beyond this. For my own pitches I would just think, "Why did I get THIS ONE!"

"It's not so bad!" Came the retort from round the corner, and for a short while I could see Inez climbing the bottom of the chimney then came the grunting! Hauling the pack, as was planned for chimneys, wasn't so easy on this one, and as the chimney closed up near it's top I found myself fighting my helmet, the pack and the gear all at once. Exiting the chimney there's a 5.9 lieback (gimme a major break! as Inez would say) that takes you around another corner to a tree—an abyss dropping away below!

This was the first time we used aid and it wasn't to be our last. If I'm right we had to aid on 6 of the 18 pitches. "We can climb 5.9 and this ain't no frigging 5.9!"

More chimneys, bulges, roofs, corners and face finally took us, late in the afternoon, to what might be called a broken ledge system. It looked like a great bivy spot and, although not yet dark, we decided to stop. The anchors, a couple of rusty pitons,were par for the course on this climb and we backed them up!

There was no way I would have considered descending off any but the lowest anchors. One of the rappel anchors, marked on the topo as "stump" was a dead tree stump held up by a sling, which in turn was attached to one old piton! What craziness would bring a person to lower their life off such precariousness!

"I'm great at setting up wall bivies!" Inez announced perkily as she set about rigging up a line that connected all the ledges and allowed us to remain tied in. The bivy was palatial compared to the 4" ledges we had sat on all night on Higher Cathedral a few years back. It was warm, in fact balmy, and after a substantial snack we settled down for the night.

We had figured and refigured the number of pitches we thought we had done, and settled for the highest possible estimate, which was 12—this meant only 6 more pitches. However, looking around, the reality of our position was maybe just over 1/3rd of the way up this great hulk of rock.

Never mind. . .it was a full moon night, and although we were unable to see it rise, the glow crept up El Capitan directly opposite us. It was so beautiful and as I listened to the yelps and howls from the wall rats, I fell into my first ever bivy slumber.

Time to climb some more! While it's cool! Inez went up a nice face pitch and then, "Oh no! It's the 10a pitch and it's mine!" "See that white sling over there?" Inez said, "It has to be a bail sling, it can't be that way." It was of course. . . so up I went, hands out in front exploring, feet inching up one after the other. It's a series of small books, and as the crack runs out in one I have to move into another. Finally they all run out and I'm left with a minimal number of small placements. I switch the gear around a little in order to make the last vital placement before some face moves to the belay. My mouth is dry and I can't wait for Inez to arrive with the liquid.

For a second time Inez traverses off into a chimney—she loves those dark, dank flues! "They'd be a lot easier with kneepads!" I find it tantalizing to listen to the strange noises and not be able to see what's going on! Finally it's my turn. As I traverse around the corner I gasp—there's a red helmet quietly dangling upside down in the chimney! As you may have gathered chimneys freak me out a bit anyway, but this one looks extra spooky! As I creep way back inside the chimney to unclip a pin I realize why the helmet was abandoned. Quickly removing mine and slinging the two of them between my legs I hurriedly crash my way out of this slimy hole and eventually arrive beneath a small chockstone. Climbing up behind it I practically get a mouthful of bird feathers. Once again I gasp—in front of me are the remains of quite a large bird. "Thought you might find that interesting, so I left it there" says Inez. This young lady is full of practical jokes!

I won't bore you with further blow by blow details of the climb. We continued with a steady regularity—never questioning our ability to complete this adventure. Inside we were proud of how well it was going and how well we compliment one another. The pitches continued to be interesting and it wasn't long before we emerged into the baking sunshine. We were to find out later that it was in the 90's that day. We rarely looked at the watch, but it was still light, and seemed like late afternoon, when we reached the catwalk.

There were a number of possibilities for getting off this climb and since it was tempting to remain at the same elevation, or start going down, we searched for the continuation of this narrow ledge, the catwalk. . .to no avail.

It was getting dark again. . .what to do?

Reluctantly we settled down for another bivy, and tried to squeeze the last drops of water out of our bottles. The food bag was so smelly, from the remains in the sardine can, that I moved it way up beyond my head. That night I was restless. With the lack of water we hadn't felt like eating much, and my body seemed to be churning. I watched the moonrise, then tossed and turned, picturing how it would feel to drink, and immerse my body in, the water at Bridalveil Creek.

Our morning plan was to climb the 200ft or so of rock above us and hike over the top of Middle Cathedral down to the water. Once we were sufficiently hydrated we would return to the Valley via the Gunsight.

As light crept over the horizon I heard what sounded like a pack sliding down the rock.

"What's that?"

"Huh? Nothing" said Inez. "Better get going, the sun is going to be on us as soon as it's up"—we were now on the Eastside, and it was going to be warm. We packed up and it was then that I realized what the noise must

Susan Edwards

have been—the food bag had disappeared! Some little critter must have made off with it!

Never mind . . . we couldn't stomach dry food anyway!

The climbing was under our belt in 3 pitches but there was still quite a hike to get to the top of the rock. I was beginning to look at the plants-were there any that might be holding onto some water that could provide us a little relief? We staggered up the slope in the blazing heat, occasionally resting under a tree.

Our conversation concerned the things of survival; where to go, how to go and how to relieve our stress. On one occasion we sucked on stones—we were having a hard time salivating and although this didn't really help, the stones were cool and were a distraction. The only plants with any hope were ferns and the succulent, Stonecrop. I pulled at a fern and its long stem broke loose—the base was cool and moist & I rubbed it across my lips, but it was no relief.

Stonecrop, on the other hand, had fat juicy leaves, but I had no idea if it was edible. How stupid I thought! How stupid it would be if we died here beside clumps of plants that could have saved our lives! I vowed to find out more about them. But we could last, or so I hoped. Inez was getting tingling sensations all over her body and I secretly monitored our conversations for signs of incoherence—nothing worse than usual on that front!

We bushwhacked and crept down slabs forever, with the sounds of waterfalls rushing against our ears. Finally we were on the last stretch and I rushed headlong through shoulder-high bushes, to the brink of the cliff above the water. There was no obvious way down so I veered off to the right and after 10 minutes, managed to find a passage through. I knelt down, my lips practically touching the water and, with my hand cupped, I swept water into my mouth and over my head. The water tasted slightly bitter and relief didn't come immediately, but sitting surrounded by an endless supply of water was the most wonderful feeling in the world!

"Inez! Over here!". . . . "What the heck is keeping her!". . ."Inez!"

Another few swigs and I retraced my steps back to the bushes. I yelled over and over again but there was no reply. I was stunned! How could I have lost her in the last few minutes! I returned to the river, eyeing its banks along the way—the silence was eerie. My mind began to go crazy! What if she is in a coma back in the bushes! Why did I leave her at the last minute!

After a number of unsuccessful reconnoiters I decided the only solution was to head out via the Gunsight and get help. As I walked back up the slope, for the final time, Inez called out—she had found a way down through the cliff, had been sunbathing and sleeping, assuming I was further upstream! My relief and joy was overwhelming, but it was tinged with hurt. Why hadn't she also seen a need to come and search for me or have the thought that I might have come to some harm. Never mind, it's not worth getting all upset when here we are alive and well. More importantly it's time to get going! People will be wondering where we are!

Back in the gunsight we were on the last rappel when a loud and familiar noise heralded the sight of a helicopter circling high on Middle Cathedral. "Oh no! They're looking for us!". . . "Wave, let's wave!". . . . "Here we are! Over here! We're OK!". . . . "They must have seen us that time!". . . "Oh no! Here they come again! We're OK! Go away!" This continues until they finally spot us and on a couple of occasions come in really close. This insect-like object looks like a menacing, yet curious, craft from another world. It hovers, observing us, trying to interpret our language and we are desperately using the same words and hand signals over and over again, apparently making no impression.

They are yelling to us with a loudspeaker, something like "Nod your heads if. . .you are OK" or was it, "if you need assistance." Inez starts nodding her head and I follow suit. They immediately come in a little closer. "No! No! We're OK! Go away! GO AWAY!"

And. . .they finally do! As they leave I feel as if I want to know who those people were.

Allen had become worried. He and Kent had a difficult time on the DNB, having to deal with a bivy and dehydration. When we were twenty-four hours late he began to picture all sorts of gruesome scenarios and finally went to discuss them with Search and Rescue. It was their decision to send the "copter" and, back at SAR Cache, after we wrote down accounts of our movements and strategies they let us go—no charge. Apparently, had we made some stupid mistakes, we would have been stuck with a hefty bill for their thorough reconnaissance of the area.

We would have done the same as Allen under the circumstances and we're grateful for the concern of our companion. Under conditions of such extreme temperatures and exertion a person may only last two days.

The many events of the last few days had thrown all superficialities aside. I realized how much understanding there was between Inez and I, how tight the rope still felt, and that the healing was well on its way.

Now with the run completed I know that I can face whatever is meant to be, and that the best thing I can do is forget my own worries and be there for my partner.

Susan Edwards

THE CAMMILA CONNECTION

MOIRA VIGGERS

"One is stuck."

My heart sank as the plaintive cry wafted upwards. If one really was stuck, then heads would roll, and mine would probably be the first.

It was entirely my mother's fault. Feminist, flower power child of the sixties, she had insisted on flouting convention to the extent of refusing to marry my father, even when the product of their union was born, and only reluctantly agreed that I should take both surnames. For Christian names she had reverted to her Liverpool roots mixed with San Francisco influences—hence, here I stand, Tracey Dawnfeather Parker-Bowles.

It might have been easier if I had favored my mother in looks, but unfortunately I took after my father, being rather more Rubenesque than waif-like. A Tracey I might be, but a Dawnfeather! Never. Life was made more difficult by the fact of my mother proudly using my full name at every opportunity. There was no hiding from it. Suffice it to say that "A Boy Named Sue" had it easy.

It therefore came as no surprise when the visitor to the BMC Office where I work, as an administrator seemed exceedingly interested in the name displayed on my desk. The surprise was that his interest was in the latter half.

"Miss Parker Bowles . . . it is Miss Parker Bowles?"

I agreed that it was.

"Mendlessohn's the name, Alasdair Mendlessohn. Your boss has told me all about you. Could we have a talk?"

This was interesting. From an initial vague feeling that I recognized his face, but I now knew whom my visitor was. It had been some months since his face had been splashed all over the popular press, credited with changing the image of the new Prime Minister. They called him the "Spin Doctor" and said that he had won the Election for New Labor. A PR man to the core, trained by Bill Clinton aides. Since then, he had rather dropped out of sight. What on earth could he want with me?

I was soon to find out. My boss, unusually sycophantic, agreed instantly to Mendlessohn's request to take me to lunch, saying that we should go "somewhere nice" and that I shouldn't hurry back, which of course had the effect of making me extremely nervous. However, Mendlessohn— "lease, call me Alasdair"—was charm itself, ordering in fluent French, and pouring Chardonnay with a liberal hand, while he explained his mission to the BMC office.

I must admit that initially I thought he was pulling my leg. I know lots of people think that climbing is "character building", but climbing as an image builder, it seems unlikely. But Alasdair was persuasive talker, painting the picture of the climber, silhouetted against a stormy sky—I tried to tell him no-one climbs in the rain, but he wouldn't listen—battling and triumphing against nature. A man at peace with the environment and himself, confident in his judgement and physical capabilities, self reliant, capable, a leader of men. . . a prince, as a matter of fact.

"A prince? You can't mean . . . surely, you don't mean . . . Charles?" To say I was flabbergasted would be an understatement. Did he really mean he wanted Prince Charles to go climbing to improve his image?

He certainly did. Not only that, he wanted me to teach him.

I was struggling to hold on to reality.

"Me? Why me? I'm not even a guide... or an instructor . . . or anything. I'm just a weekend climber."

And here it was again—my wretched name. Alasdair was convinced that it was time that Charles was seen in a new light by the tabloid press. Climbing would provide the right sort of image, and if he were seen to be climbing with a young, attractive (his words, not mine), woman whose name just happened to be Parker Bowles, then how much better the great British Public would feel about that particular name. And how much easier for Charles to introduce that name again, in a different context... "We could even put it about that you're distantly related..."

I can't say that I was keen, but brandy suspends judgement, and Alasdair was VERY persuasive, and before I really knew what I was doing I'd agreed to take the heir to the throne climbing.

"It won't be for long", assured Alasdair, "A couple of weeks or so, until he knows the ropes, so to speak, a photocall for the press, and then you can go back to your job. And of course there will be . . . ahem . . . a reasonable remuneration, plus the eternal gratitude of the future King of England... maybe an OBE, or the like."

It was the start of a very difficult period of my life.

Alasdair had arranged for us to meet informally, at the crag. "But you must remember to curtsey—he'll expect the protocol. And call him "Sir", or "Your Highness." I'd dithered about where to take him, and eventually decided on the Wye Valley in the south west—suitably obscure, sheltered, and easy. North Wales seemed rather too high profile. He arrived in a stretch limousine, with bodyguards times two, and a shy smile. He was shorter than I'd realized. You can take it from me that it's not easy curtseying when you're wearing a rucksack loaded with hardware, climbing ropes, abseil ropes, Uncle Tom Cobley and all. It's not so much the curtseying as the coming back up again. HRH was gracious enough to instruct a bodyguard (even their muscles had muscles) to carry the sack, and we strolled down to the crag, while he enlightened me as to his previous experience.

"One did a little bit at Gordonstoun of course. Just the basics. Good for one's personal development. One's father went to the same school you know."

One may well have learnt the basics, but one had certainly forgotten them. One had also learnt to belay around the waist, and had never heard of new-fangled sticht-plates and ATCs. We spent an hour perusing the subject and learning to tie a figure-eight knot, while the bodyguards drank tea. Finally, we were on the rock. I top-roped him up a moderate - he was not a natural climber, but brute force and ignorance triumphed in the end, and he topped out successfully, to a small round of applause from the bodyguards. I suspected they were taking the mick, but he seemed quite happy.

We moved on to a Diff. but unfortunately at this stage, a group of Scouts came wandering along the bottom of the crag, intent on exploring the nearby caves. None of the little blighters recognized him, thank heaven, but his outfit of heavy woolen breeches, Norfolk Grenfell jacket, check shirt, thick socks and boots caused such hilarity that HRH became a little miffed, and I decided to end the session before the bodyguards intervened on his behalf.

The next few days passed in a blur. It had been agreed that I had three weeks to turn HRH into what could pass for a climber, at the end of which Alasdair would "leak" to the press the hint of a Royal photo opportunity at a given location. Unfortunately, it became clear very quickly that HRH and limestone did not get on. It was too polished, too subtle. I decided on a change of venue—Cornish granite. Rather more friction, and a photographer's gift, with windblown skies and crashing waves. Terrier's Tooth at V Diff held the makings of success, but it was not to be. I virtually had to drag HRH off the first stance, after he lost concentration, and started talking to the cliff plants. On the final pitch he wandered off route and, despite my shouted warnings, insisted on pulling up on a ledge already occupied by a fulmar chick, receiving the inevitable regurgitation of evil- smelling vomit full in the royal face. My best efforts with tissues were a dismal failure, and even the bodyguards kept their distance. Needless to say, one is not used to this sort of thing and traumatized by this incident, HRH put his royal foot down, and demanded a different crag, one well away from the sea.

So we turned to grit—Stagnate in fact. Not exactly the quietest crag in the country, but it certainly had plenty of routes for novices. Time was running out, so I decided we'd concentrate on one route, practicing to perfection, but which one? Several Diffs later HRH had still not managed to complete an entire route—he appeared to be unable to grasp the technique of jamming. The crag was spattered with blue blood, and the Royal Signet Ring, worn by the heir to the throne since the days of the Black Prince, and never to be removed from the royal finger had disintegrated into three pieces, and had to be repaired with "Evostick" by the bodyguards.

Finally, in desperation, we tried Grotto Slab (without the chimney at the top, of course), and HRH managed to top out, to near hysterical acclaim from the bodyguards. We did it again. He looked better.

We only had one more day before the photocall, but at least we now had our route. The atmosphere of celebration was such that, as we drove away from the crag HRH spotted The Scotsman and his pack, and suddenly exclaimed. "One could murder a pint of ale." The next thing I knew we were in the bar, with HRH and the bodyguards, challenging the locals to a game of darts, while I bought the drinks. It's not that I mind buying my future king a drink, and it's well known that the royals don't carry cash, but you'd think the bodyguards could have taken their turn. However, a convivial evening was spent by all, to the detriment of our heads the following morning, the dawn of The Big Day.

I'd insisted that we were up with the lark to allow time for a few practice runs before the press arrived. Alaschir had only told them that there would be "a royal photo opportunity" at Stannage at midday, and we were just practicing for the final time when disaster struck. Well, I say it struck, but to be honest it was self-inflicted. HRH, perhaps a little overconfident with repeated success, decided that he wanted to have a go at the top chimney, and when one wants to have a go at something, one expects to be allowed to do so. Knowing, as I do, that it's a nasty, thrutchy little chimney, and that HRH's jamming left a lot to be desired, it came as no great surprise when the rope ceased to move. As one correctly surmised, one was stuck—well and truly stuck.

As I started to heave frantically at the rope and shout advice, I could see way below me the assorted transport of the gutter press arriving, bang on cue. As they climbed slowly towards the crag, HRH's flounderings became more frantic, but served only to wedge him still further in the chimney. We were doomed. I could imagine the headlines in the tabloid press the following day:

"Charles Takes 'Clown Prince' Title" (The Express)

"Charles Is Stuck-Up" (The Mirror)

"Oh My Orb and Sceptre!" (The Sun)

However, just as I'd resigned myself to complete ignominy, I noticed a very strange thing. The press weren't heading towards us, but further along the crag. I looked across to Manchester Buttress, possibly one of the most photogenic climbs on Stannage, but much too hard for HRH, at Severe. At the top sat a well-known Himalayan mountaineer, and halfway up the route, clad in skimpy "Lycra" and bikini top despite the chill wind was . . . Diana! As I watched, stunned, the press arrived and Diana started to pose the most dramatic moves. She topped out easily as the flashbulbs popped, and started a series of 'impromptu' interviews. I decided, rather churlishly that she was probably auctioning her "Lycra" for charity.

But at least we were reprieved. Desperation lent me strength, and I finally managed to heave HRH out of the chimney and up to the top. No one paid us any attention whatsoever as I hastily packed up and we made our way gloomily off the crag. Even the bodyguards were too busy watching Diana to see us go.

So that was the end of my attempt to improve HRH's image. Although thoroughly upstaged, he had at least escaped with his dignity intact, a point I made to Alasdair, who was inconsolable at having lost his royal contract, and faced with the options of becoming a Minister Without Portmanteau in the Government, or complete obscurity with Saatchi and Saatchi.

Me ? I ended up back at the BMC, sans OBE, and in bed with Alasdair.

Well, I did say he was VERY persuasive. . .

Unfortunate enough to be brought up in Norfolk, one of the flattest counties of the UK, Moira Viggers discovered climbing relatively late after a move to the southwest of England, where she still makes her home. Early forays onto the local highly polished limestone founded a climbing technique which, although sadly lacking in power, laybacking and jamming abilities, does merit some neat footwork, a degree of neck, and a certain ability to levitate over loose blocks. This technique has taken her, with varying degrees of success, up mid-grade routes throughout France, Spain, the Balearics, Ireland, Australia and New Zealand, as well as the UK. Qualified as a climbing and kayak instructor she now works in outdoor-based management training, as well as leading treks to the Himalayas once or twice a year. Married to Dave, a climber and guidebook writer, both were involved in the early development of Range West crags in Pembroke, South Wales, probably her favorite climbing area, combining as it does the essential ingredients of towering white limestone crags above a crashing blue-green sea. Moira has had various stories and articles published in UK climbing magazines and the Climbers Club journal, and is a regular contributor and former prizewinner at the National Festival for Mountaineering Literature.

Ingleborough Base Camp

Sally Zigmond

Dear Muriel:

I hope you're feeding the rabbits and keeping my matchbox collection free of dust. You know how I like to maintain standards. I've tried to impress that on the others here, but I'm finding it an uphill strugglee—excuse the pun, dear. I don't think they're treating this expedition with the seriousness Mr. Braithwaite envisaged when I suggested it to him.

Mr. Braithwaite deserves respect. After all, he built up the Braithwaite Paperclip Company single-handedly. Ninety and still pushes his zimmer frame about with the energy of a teenager. Remarkable. He introduced me to his niece, Pamela, the other day. I think he said niece, only all the Braithwaites are dark-haired and hers is very fair. Nevertheless, I digress.

Respect is important. The accounts department owes it to him to take this exercise seriously. Which is why when I found three bottles of whisky under George's sleeping-bag I judiciously tipped them away and declared there and then that Ingleborough Base Camp was an alcohol-free zone, as I believe is the current parlance.

You find out a lot about one's fellow man on one of these character building exercises. I never knew George had such a violent temper. You'll have to sew back the buttons on my shirt when I get home.

Fred had to put his oar in, didn't he? 'Look, Arthur,' he said in what I considered a most imperious manner - after all I have been at Braithwaites for over thirty years - and he should call me Mr. Clegg. 'Everybody else wanted a weekend in Scarborough, but you had to twist old Braithwaite's arm. We're only here taking a stroll up Ingleborough, you know. This isn't bloody Everest base camp.' I suppose he was referring to the way I've set up a roster and organized forays in groups of two into the neighbouring hills, to acclimatize and to test my altimeter. By the way, I still disagree with Dr

Abbot. Diamox would have been most useful. Poor Jim and Stewart seem permanently light-headed and need to lie down a lot.

As you know, dear, I've read a lot about these character-building excursions in all the management literature. As well as honing our bodies into efficient machines, the idea is to 'bond.' Talking together is one way. So, I have organized a roster for us each to give a lecture on our favourite pastime. I got the ball rolling last night by telling them about my collection of three thousand matchboxes. (You are keeping them dust-free, aren't you dear?) Tony and Des were attentive throughout, and said afterwards that they hadn't had such a good time since they went on a tour of Bradford sewers. It was a pity the others didn't share their enthusiasm. They went down to Ingleton. I told them we were quite self-sufficient for supplies and didn't need to barter with the locals, nor were late nights wise in view of the need to keep our bodies in peak condition. Sorry about another pun, dear. I'm feeling so relaxed and motivated.

They ignored me as usual, like they did when I told them they should staple of floe memos together if they consist of more than two pages, which mine invariably do. The other week my five-page note to Mr. Braithwaite, about the disappearance of soap in the men's washroom lost its last page. He promised to read it when he'd finished teaching his niece Pamela to use the photocopying machine. I told her it wasn't necessary to lean over it quite so far. She said she'd bear it in mind.

You know, Muriel, I'm feeling very invigorated by the thought of tomorrow s assault on the mighty Ingleborough. George laughed when I said this. He said it was a pimple. Therefore, I reminded him that at 2415 feet (or 736 metros, using the standard conversion rate); Ingleborough was the one of the mightiest peaks in Yorkshire. He sniggered when I said that, but what can you expect from a Lancastrian?

I have drawn up a list of the equipment we shall require for tomorrow's assault. Which reminds me. You are following the menu sheet I left for the rabbits. I have allowed four hours for the ascent and three for return. That Alan told me he could run up it in less than half the time with lead boots on, but I discreetly reminded him of the time he allowed too little time for the annual audit. He thought we could get away with counting the number of boxes of paperclips in the warehouse and multiplying that with the average contents of each box. Slap-dash, I call it.

I've also made sure that all our rucksacks are suitably equipped. I organized an inspection at 1600 hours. The others grumbled, I can tell you, but I was glad I did. Do you know that none of them had suitable clothing? This is not a Sunday-School picnic, I told them. 'Could have fooled me,' said George. I ignored him. He s only jealous Mr. Braithwaite didn't put him in charge. I found one of those magazines in his pocket? I was so concerned that I made the not inconsiderable trek across inhospitable terrain to the nearest telephone box to speak to Mr. Braithwaite personally. His wife said he d gone on a weekend trip with the accounts department to climb Ingleborough. Very odd!

Must close for the present, Muriel, as I need my beauty sleep. Summit day tomorrow and I can't wait to air my trusty boots and Venture Scout shorts again. I hope the others return soon. I've heard the nightlife in Ingleton can be pretty wild.

I don't know how to tell you this, Muriel. My heart is heavy as I write. Our attempt on the summit failed. A great cloud of disappointment has settled over our little camp of plucky chaps, as we pack up the tents and prepare to return to Cleckmondthwaite. The others mutter in whispers and cannot bring themselves to speak to me. I know they do not want to upset me further. It wasn't their fault. It was mine. I had planned for every emergency, but not this.

I sounded reveille at 0500 hours. When no one emerged to partake in the hearty breakfast I had prepared, (I believe that the stomach should be lined with a healthy layer of fat) I went to investigate. Moreover, what a sorry picture assailed my eyes. George was face down in his sleeping bag, groaning loudly. Stewart was being violently sick into his crash helmet. (He insisted on bringing his motorbike.) Des and Tony were complaining of violent headaches. I couldn't find Fred anywhere. I hope he hadn't decided to emulate my hero, Captain Oates. At first, I put it down to my failure to bring Diamox, but George told me through his pain that there was a plague raging in Ingleton and they had all caught it.

As you might expect, I was bitterly disappointed at this turn of events. My morale was very low, but the honour of the Braithwaite Paperclip Company was at stake. After ensuring that my team-members were comfortable, (they nobly agreed they could manage for a few hours without my ministrations), I set off alone for the summit. After a great deal of trials and tribulations—some involving a particularly persistent ram—I achieved my aim.

I proudly staked my Union Jack into what I calculated to be the absolute peak (still not quite got the hang of the altimeter) I felt I deserved a moment or two's rest, so I settled down in one of the quadrants of the four-way shelter. I was just unscrewing the stopper of my trusty Thermos and looking forward to a well-earned brew when I became aware of some rustling and giggling behind me. I turned and what a pleasant surprise I had. It was Mr. Braithwaite—without his zimmer frame—and that young Pamela.

I felt honoured that he had decided to witness my triumph. And how understanding he was about the misfortunes of the others. I was dreading having to tell the shareholders about our failure, but Mr. Braithwaite waived a gnarled hand with an airy, 'Let's forget about the whole thing shall we? We don't want to upset Mrs. Braithwaite. Such a kind man. Young Pamela didn't look too pleased to see me. I thinks she was cold, so I told her a woolly jumper and a thick tweed skirt (like you wear, dear) would be more sensible than that skimpy top and frilly lampshade thing round her waist. I may be wrong, Muriel, but I thought she stuck her tongue out. Perhaps a midge had flown in. Anyway, I've never seen Mr. Braithwaite looking so well. It must be the prune juice I recommended. He winked.

In fact he looked so well that I've invited him and Pamela to view my matchbox collection. You have remembered to dust it, haven't you Muriel?

Best wishes

Arthur.

"Sally Zigmond is 48 and lives in Harrogate, Yorkshire, England with husband, Jon, and two teenaged sons. She graduated from London University with a degree in English Literature and once worked as a translator for Interpol. Although she has been writing for publications for many years, during which she has won several major UK short story awards, the only time she ever reached the summit of any mountain was via a cablecar (and that made her giddy). However, since Jon took up climbing, she has got to know and admire many men and women who are gripped by the compulsion to pit themselves against rock and altitude. Through them she has learned, if not to fully comprehend, at least to recognize their obsession and to observe it with great affection from the safe distance of her word processor."

Teaching Mr. Hokey-Nokey the Lambada

Sally Zigmond

Dear Sharon

Do you remember the other week in the pub I said I fancied that tall bloke with the tan and the muscles and you said I'd never stand a chance 'cos you overheard him saying he'd been to university and I only got GCSE Art?

Well, I've got news for you. After you left, he started to chat me up. Turned out he's some sort of tour rep. Said he could get me a free holiday. Talk about lucky. I'm right off Majorca. Too many foreigners, for one thing. Anyway, he said 'How does six weeks in Tibet sound? I said, 'Great! Is it anywhere near Tenerife?' In addition, he said I was priceless. Isn't that lovely?

He guides people up mountains for a living. Someone has to do it, he said. 'That's a co-incidence,' I said and told him about that school trip to Wales. You know. When it rained, so when we were at the top we couldn't see anything and you ate three ice creams while we waited for the train to take us down again, then threw up on the platform?

The flight was a bit slow and the bus-ride was awful, but I m here now. Base Camp, it's called. Only when Andy said that, I had in mind Pontins in Clacton. Not this. I think they're still building it. There's piles of rubbish everywhere and bits of tatty rags hung from bits of string. (They could do with a launderette.) And there's lots of blokes hanging around, waiting for something to happen. I thought they'd be a bit more responsive to having a woman about the place. They're all so dull. I told them all my Essex girl jokes the other day. All thirty-seven of them. Nobody laughed, even at the 'what's the difference between a supermarket trolley and an Essex girl?' one. I don't think any of them have ever been to Romford.

Actually, I'm not the only woman here, I've discovered. At first I thought she was a bloke. She's Australian with cropped hair and a ring through her nose and no chest. She calls herself Steve. Andy seems to like her. Can't think why. He says she's done lots of climbs on her own all round the world. Don't suppose anyone would go with her. I told her her eyebrows needed plucking.

Did you know the cows here are called yaks? That Steve's a yak. She told me Andy only asked me here because I make him laugh. I gave her one of my looks, which made her laugh more, so I got on with washing Andy's socks in a bucket. There's no plumbing here yet. I'm telling you, Shaz, I'm complaining to the tour operator when I get back. I asked Andy if it was Thomsons or Lunn Polly. He laughed.

I've got this tiny little tent. It's quite cozy, but there's nowhere to plug in my heated rollers. And I wish it had a better view. Seen one mountain, seen them all. Andy said he'll be taking some guys up one of them. I said I'd go if they had one of them little trains with a caff on the top.

I tell you, Shaz, I'm bored silly. There's nothing to do except file my nails. Andy spends most of his time with the other blokes (who are all anoraks, if you ask me), playing cards and telling faddish jokes. He talks to Steve a lot. She's a guide, too. Andy says she's got a P H D. Is that a skin condition, I asked him. She's very spotty.

I found this lovely little shower in a hut the other day. I'd just taken off all my clothes, right? When suddenly, this little Japanese bloke is standing there with his mouth open, his face as red as a traffic light.

Anyway, it turns out it's for his private use. And he's got this big swanky tent all to himself. And his own cook. Very posh. When I asked Andy why we hadn't got all those mod cons, he said this Japanese bloke wasn't a proper climber. Paid pots of money to be pulled on ropes all the way to the top of the mountain. I think that's sensible, don't you?

Steve was there when I said this. She gave me a look, so I told her lemon juice bleaches facial hair. Andy laughed. I think he finds her as awful as I do. She's always pestering him. 'Root planning,' she calls it. Which reminded me my roots need doing. But when I ask Andy where the nearest hairdressers is, he laughed. His laugh is beginning to get on my nerves. It's not as if I ever say anything funny.

Anyway, he doesn't do it as much now. I blame Steve. Miserable yak. They both went off before dawn yesterday with Andy's group of anoraks and the little Japanese man. His name s Mr. Hokey-Nokey, or something like that. He waved to me.

I got a bit bored when they'd gone, so I thought I'd tidy things up a bit. Well, if there's going to be a party on Friday, I thought I'd better. At least, I think there's going to be a party. Andy keeps talking about a 'bilay.' I

Sally Zigmond

think that's Spanish for party. And he said the other day he and Steve were going to organize some practice rappelling for the anoraks. Sounds like fun. Wonder if it's like karaoke? They always have karoake at Pontins. Helps break the ice. Which reminds me, there was ice on the tent last night. It's a silly place to build a camp, if you ask me. They should have put it nearer the beach.

Anyway, I worked very hard unfastening all the bits of rope from those loops of metal and straightening them out. I broke four nails. I though Andy would be pleased with me. He wasn't. He didn't laugh. Wonder what they call a male yak'? Steve laughed. I thought her face would split. Apparently, the ropes are supposed to be attached to the bits of old metal. How was I supposed to know that?

They're a funny bunch here. They wouldn't know a good time if it slapped them in the face. I mean. Apart from Mr. Hokey-Nokey, who wears Calvin Klein, the others campers have never heard of fashion. They've got all the right names on their gear, but they're hardly colour-co-ordinated. And they've got funny ideas. They hang those great big loops of metal from their waists. Even Andy. I suppose it s ethnic.

The food's ethnic. too. I asked the bloke that does the cooking whether he could do me a pizza instead of lentils. With pineapple topping. That night, while the rest stuffed their faces with roast chicken, I got a plate full of peas. The others thought it was hilarious. Especially Steve. She s beginning to get on my nerves.

In fact, I'm pretty pissed off with all of them, except Mr. Hokey-Nokey. They're not taking this party seriously at all. Although I think Andy's had enough because he and Steve and the other anoraks went off to another camp this morning.

I'm staying put. So's Mr. Hokey-Nokey. Apparently he gets vertigo. I'll ask him to help me plan the party. He should know all about karaoke, what with him being Japanese. The others will be back on Friday. They said there'll be a bit of a celebration then. I expect that' s why Andy and Steve want to get to grips with the 'Duma.' I wonder if it s as tricky as the Lambada we learned last year in Torremolinos?

I've promised to teach Mr. Hokey-Nokey the Lambada. He said he was looking forward to it. He owns a car factory and says I can use his personal shower any time I like. Things are looking up.

Ciao, as they say in Japan.

Luv, Tracy.

Climbing and The Art of Peeing

Dorcas S. Miller

I was working as a river guide on the Penobscot and Kennebec rivers in Maine. My butt was wet so much that I got diaper rash, so on my days off I headed for the mountains. One of my co-workers was married to a ranger at Baxter State Park and I often visited Jean and John at their cabin at Chimney Pond, on the flank of Katahdin.

I'm not sure why I was looking for a challenge that summer. The Penobscot had a stretch of Class 5 water that was reputed to be the hardest commercially run white water on the east coast. That should have used up my adrenaline for the year. But I had pleasant (and, truth to tell, some not so pleasant) memories of rock climbing when I worked for Outward Bound in the early 1970s, and something about climbing attracted me that summer. One day in early September I hiked into Chimney Pond and asked the other ranger, who was a climber, if he would be interested in going out with me.

"Sure," Ben said, his face brightening. "I have tomorrow off. We could go over into the North Basin and climb Hanta Yo. Do you have shoes?"

"Oh, yes," I assured him. I'd brought along my climbing shoes: medium-weight Fabiano klettershoes. Ben was kind enough not to point out that they were classics.

The next morning we hiked into the North Basin. Autumn had arrived at this mountain of early winters. The mountain ash, birch, and blueberry had turned brilliant colors. The mountain cranberry and bearberry were heavy with fruit. Sun poured into the cirque and we basked in the warmth of an Indian summer day.

Hanta Yo is an eight-pitch climb that follows a long corner system to the right edge of the thousand-foot North Basin Wall. If Hanta Yo were in Yosemite or in Cannon, it would be a favorite beginner/intermediate climb. Tucked away in the North Basin, a six-hour drive and two-hour hike from

Boston, the climb sees little activity. That day, Ben and I did the third or fourth ascent.

Ben fitted me out in a Whillans harness, which I had never worn before, and showed me how to remove protection. My climbing before that day had been limited to top-roping; climbing in most outdoor programs is used as a challenge rather than as a skills development activity.

We started up the wall, alone in that golden universe. The higher we got, the more world lay at our feet. Red and yellow mountains and dazzling lakes stretched beyond the lip of the basin.

About half way up, we had a bite to eat. I was so excited that I'd forgotten my lunch, so I shared Ben's gorp and water. I began thinking how nice it would be to take a leak, but I was much too shy to ask how to go about doing it. Clearly, I couldn't take off the Whillans—I wasn't sure I could get it buckled up right—and I didn't know how to rig up an alternate harness. I decided to wait until he was at the next belay, scrunch my shorts to one side, and pee down the pantleg. The system had worked well enough with a one-piece bathing suit when I was guiding.

It didn't work at all. I peed in my pants.

I turned my butt to the sun and hung out to dry when I was alone and backed into the rock when we shared the belay. At the top, Ben suggested changing to long pants because we had to bushwack to the trail. I enthusiastically agreed.

Hanta Yo was so exhilarating that we went out the next day and climbed Pamola Four, a ridge in the South Basin. Pamola Four is mostly fourth class, but we roped up because I was feeling the exposure and the stiff wind. That day, I asked how one could take a leak. Ben showed me how to use a chest harness: he became fascinated with the activity on Baxter Peak while I peed (this time not in my pants). Still it was all too cumbersome. I wanted an easy way.

We climbed at Acadia and then again at the Gunks. By this time, it was clear to both of us that we were interested in more than climbing together.

Ben loaned me a book, "Learning to Rock Climb" by Michael Loughman. It had lots of helpful tips for getting started, but the best part was the photographs of Amy Loughman. It was inspiring to see a woman about my size doing graceful, balanced moves on rock. In the dozen years I'd been guiding and teaching, there had been few women role models. I'd missed them.

As he gave me the book, Ben commented, "It's hard for people to climb together and be romantically involved. Issues in the relationship tend to interfere with climbing well together. I know several climbing couples who have gotten divorced. Loughman advises against climbing with your girlfriend, boyfriend, or spouse because it can strain the relationship. He ought to know. He and Amy are divorced."

Wonderful, I thought. I'm having a great time climbing and I'm excited about this new relationship, but chances are that I'll have to give up one or the other.

I'd been noticing that no one else was wearing klettershoes. In fact, on our last day at the Gunks, I overheard someone say, "Look at the funny shoes that girl has." I wanted to tell him that I'd been climbing in these funny shoes when he was in grade school, and that climbers had done first ascents of many of the climbs at the Gunks wearing these funny shoes. Have the weeners no sense of history? Besides, I'd whipped up Easy Overhang in my outdated shoes, while the fellow ahead of me whined and trembled and sweated in his E.B.s. State-of-the-art shoes aren't everything.

But they are something. If I wanted to improve, I should get a new pair of shoes. Ben suggested that we stop at Rock and Snow in New Paltz.

"OK, but you have to stay in the car," I said. I was extremely sensitive about being a woman in a world populated by men. So far, I'd seen one female climber—or rather, I'd seen her brand new E.B.s flapping in the breeze as she put both knees on a ledge. I did not want to be a "girlfriend," someone who knew nothing about the sport, someone who got dragged up routes her partner wanted to climb. I was fiercely independent and staked out my territory.

I wanted to go into the store, ask a lot of questions, and make my own decision. So I went into the store, asked a lot of questions, and decided I couldn't afford any of the shoes on the shelf. I also found out that Ben, who memorizes every equipment catalog and who used to work at REI, knew more about shoes than the salesman.

(Several months later, Ben's previous girlfriend returned a pair of P.A.s and a Whillans harness. Not a bad deal for me; she was my size.) It was November and the climbing season in New England was drawing to a close. "If you love climbing so much, don't you get frustrated when winter rolls around?" I asked Ben.

"Oh, it'll be ice climbing season soon," he said. "Want to come?"

"Forget it," I answered. "Too cold."

It was too cold, but I went anyway. I borrowed a pair of ancient hinged crampons with extra-long front points (which held me out from the ice) and put them on my three-quarter shank hiking boots (so the whole thing was pretty flexible) and used an old ice ax (which weighed twice as much as a new one). Since I'd never climbed ice before, I thought everything was just fine, except that I lost sensation in my feet and hands every time I went out.

"More clothes," Ben said.

I layered on poly, pile, wool, and nylon until I looked like the Pillsbury dough boy. I still didn't stay warm, but the excitement and challenge of this new activity balanced the excruciating pain of warming numb appendages—at least for the first two years. Then I began serious complaining.

Ben didn't understand. He thought I was kidding. Once, on a spring climb, my hands went dead; Ben was stripped down to a single layer and was still sweating. It wasn't just the wrist loops or the fact that I was gripping the handles tightly. My hands could go numb anywhere, any time. We started doing comparison testing and sure enough, my hands were always colder. Feet and nose, too, though the nose wasn't as crucial to climbing.

My experience rock climbing and ice climbing have shown me that Ben and I are so different that I really can't take many cues from him. Ben has a wide range of comfort; I get hot and cold easily and am constantly taking off and putting on clothing. He's six feet and four inches, while I'm five feet and five inches, so I have to make two delicate moves to get to the bucket he reaches easily. Ben is strong and I'm not; I have to move quickly and smoothly so I don't drain my strength. And, of course, he can pee even in all those winter clothes and a harness, while I have to disrobe and bare my butt to the elements.

I couldn't change my anatomy but I could, perhaps, change my clothing. For the first two winters we climbed together, I used a swami, but I wasn't satisfied. It was too loose or too tight, the holsters slid around and sagged, and I always felt like a klutz. Although I could take a leak, it was still an act of bravery. I liked my Whillans, but there was the perennial problem: peeing.

I'd read an article by a woman in Alaska who had put zippers in her pants. I hauled out my sewing machine and experimented, putting a coil zipper along the crotch seam of my poly underwear (with the zipper on the outside), wool pants, and wind pants. Lo and behold, I could take a leak without removing my harness or pulling down my pants. I had to get used to peeing through my pants—at first I felt like I was going to pee in them—but after a time it felt pretty normal. Solving that problem actually improved my ability to deal with the cold, since I'd been drinking too little water and getting dehydrated, which made me even colder.

I also got better clothes and equipment. Plastic boots, for instance, are the ticket for toasty toes: I can cinch down on the crampon straps and not cut off the circulation. But I still haven't entirely resolved the cold problem. My Baltimore-born body simply doesn't deal well with the stop-and-start rhythm of ice climbing. Skiing and snowshoeing make more sense because I have more control over the pace of the activity.

(I solved the rock climbing dilemma, not with zippers but with elastic-waisted clothing. I found I could pull down shorts, sweats, or lycra, pee, and wiggle them back up under the harness. This maneuver is very difficult with zippers or buttons.)

My approach to peeing is like my approach to climbing. I can't do things the way that other people do them because the other people are usually taller, stronger, and male. Although I watch other people climb and pay attention to how they use their feet, how they balance off one smear to reach another, and how they lean off a bucket, I have to translate all that into my framework. I hate it when someone tries to tell me what to do; that person usually doesn't understand my reach and balance. On the other hand, if I see a person my size—usually that's a woman—do a hard climb, I'm more inclined to take a crack at it because there's a fairly direct translation from her to me. One spring I saw a woman leading Deception Crack at Stone Mountain and I thought, "I could do that." I later led it; it was my first 5.9.

For a long time, I wasn't interested in leading. The process of placing protection seemed to come between me and the rock. During my previous life, when I top-roped, it was just me and the rock. All the new gizmos inhibited my climbing.

Besides, I was always climbing at my limit when I followed Ben. The idea of leading those same climbs was terrifying. No thanks, I said to Ben's frequent encouragement to lead.

Two things changed my mind. I went to see Rosie Andrews and her slide show, "Women climbers in the 80's." I was inspired by her observations and slides of women climbers. After the show, someone asked her about starting to lead. "Choose something you've done a dozen times before, something on which you feel really comfortable," she said. It made perfect sense. If I tried leading something easy, then I'd learn about placing pro and build up my confidence.

She said something else that struck home. "Women are most limited by their attitudes. We're not brought up to be aggressive. Most women are not willing to risk falls. To be really good, you have to take some falls." That made sense, too, but I wasn't as sure I'd take that advice. I wasn't sure how good I wanted to be.

The second event was that Ben and I went to Stone Mountain, North Carolina, and I fell in love with friction. We had been doing mostly cracks: cracks at Katahdin, Acadia, Cathedral, and the Gunks. But we'd done very little friction.

I felt free on friction. On the easier climbs, I felt like I was walking, not climbing. Placing pro didn't get between me and the rock because there was little pro to place—many of the climbs at Stone Mountain are bolt-protected. Leading at Stone Mountain and later at Whitehorse Ledge bolstered my confidence on other kinds of rock, too.

Because I know few women climbers, I've enjoyed reading books and articles. I also pay attention to what sociologists would call the oral tradition. Ben has a stack of stories gleaned from years of reading climbing magazines.

He told me about Diana Hunter, who led a new climb when her partner—Henry Barber—backed off. I thought about her the day I led the Byzantine at Acadia. Neither Ben nor Dan could get started and I wanted to give it a try. Dan insisted I take the rack. I'd done almost no leads, so I said it was silly to take it along. I waltzed by the crux. When I got to a rest, Ben told me to put in the #6 hex. "What's that?" I answered.

I thought about Miriam Underhill one night when I helped on a rescue in Huntington Ravine. I'd just read the chapter in *Give Me the Hills* in which she describes an early trip to Tuckerman's Ravine on Mt. Washington. She and friends had spent a full day skiing and were so whipped they couldn't possibly take another step. Two of their party didn't return that evening; however, and she embarked on a rescue.

Ben and I had gotten up at 4:30 a.m. and hiked in to Huntington to do Pinnacle Gully, my first alpine ice climb. We did the route and then hiked back down to the car, arriving at sunset. There, we heard about an accident in the ravine and volunteered to help, as we are both emergency medical technicians. Secretly, I hoped I wouldn't be needed, but the director said he could use anyone who knew how to walk with crampons. Even I qualified.

The rescue went smoothly. I took my turn helping to pull the banana-boat sled. It was a quiet, still night on Mt. Washington. The clear sky shone with a million stars. I was the only woman there and I felt protective of the fellow in the sled who didn't even have a girlfriend to call from the hospital. We finished at midnight and got home at 3 a.m. I had relived Miriam's story, with my own cast of characters.

It would be a great end to this story if I could write, "My climbing blossomed and I became an extremely bold and talented climber. I did a first ascent of a 1,000-foot wall in the northern Rockies and led all of the hard pitches, and I was asked to join a 1995 Himalayan climbing expedition." Then I could describe how climbing has changed my life and opened new worlds to me.

But I haven't become an extremely bold and talented climber. I'm an intermediate, recreational climber who doesn't even aspire to do the desperates. I've dealt with some small challenges (like how to leak on a belay) and some big challenges (like how to be both a climbing partner and a spouse—Ben and I have managed to survive the odds). In between, I've climbed a lot of rock and had fun doing it.

Dorcas S. Miller, a former Outward Bound instructor and river guide, helped found and was a member of the board of directors of Women Outdoors, Incorporated, a National program that provides women opportunities to develop outdoor and leadership skills. She has written for *Canoe*, *Climbing*, and *Sea Kayaker Magazines* and published five books. "The Health Trail Cookbook," "The Maine Coast: A Nature Lover's Guide," "Track Finder," "Berry Finder," and "Winter Weed Finder." She is currently a free-lance writer and editor.

Rope Dancers

Lilace A. Mellin

Purposefully woven in such colors-blues and blacks
striped with green or pink winding up and around
what s winding-their beauty whispers what risk.
It helps to be comfortable with your equipment:
concentrate on the plaid umbilical rising from your belly ring
toward a carabiner atop the crux, through,
and then the slanting sloop into your partner's hand sworn
not to swat at bugs, pledged to stop any fall.
It's one step, two, a search for new handholds
and again short rest. If your fingers
bleed from fistjams you won't notice

till later. All that matters is the thrill
of their holding-the rope not needed
except as a reminder of route, kind distraction.
Like everyone, climbers scorn safety till unsure
of their next move. Know how far you can reach
before you start. At the top you must rappel
the sheer straightness down-red bright as an open heart
gels in knuckle gullies, toes wince on flat ground

only now complaining. Soon the rock will lie naked as a chest
we re desperate for, to lean against in passion, fear,
the two impossibly knotted.
This poem appeared in the Asheville Poetry Review, v.1.1

Lilace Mellin Guignard has an MFA from the University of California at Irvine. Most of her climbing has been in the friction-bliss of Western North Carolina, but she recently moved to Reno and now enjoys the western granite around Tahoe.

Leading Through

Rosemary Cohen

"It's your lead."

Secure as the second on the double rope, I have crossed a traverse line following the alternating loops of red and blue, both colours faded with use, which are fixed to the Lewsian gneiss by well-placed wedges and karabiners. Hers has been an exemplary lead, without rope-drag or snags, despite passing around two corners of the outcrop. She is well secured on the tiny belay, her red helmet at an odd angle, pushed out of place by the overhang. The climb thus far has been delicate, moderately technically demanding, and hard to protect.

Judy has led the lot. I am easy to persuade into seconding. I love the feel of the rock without the gut-gripping fear of a long fall. In particular I hate the first twenty feet off the ground, when imagination has my lifeless body spread on the deck, with a pile of ripped wedges beside me as a testament to my inability to place protection. I am that unfashionable thing, a leader who will not fall. Mostly I don't lead.

Judy has never fallen. She does not fear leading and she becomes cooler and more self-contained as the hazard increases. She loves very hard fingery slabs, and can find places to wedge runners in that most unpromising terrain.

We're on Fionn Buttress, the classic Scottish VS on Carnmore. The crag is twelve pitches tall, facing southwest, and seamed with classic lines. The approach is a ten-mile walk over bog, through someone's shooting country. The shooting lodge is below the crag, by the campsite and the bothy. A mooring for a motorboat on the lock shows how the stag-hunters reach the place. We walked here in the dark last night, four women, having stopped for chips at Gairloch and left it too late. Even in midsummer, sunset comes eventually to Scotland.

Pitching our tents, benighted in the pathless wastes of Letterewe, my sister remarked to me that she always seemed to be blundering about a bog in the dark when she went out with me and that was why she did not climb with me any more. Stella said, "I can tell you two are sisters."

In the fine morning, having pitched a new camp below the crag itself, my sister and Stella are attempting the Hard Rock classic of Dragon, while Judy and I try the easier, but no less perfect and longer route to the left of the crag. From time to time we can hear them shouting at one another around the other side of the buttress.

The rock is dry, except at the start, where the crag always weeps and there is green slime in the crack. Judy chose to lead up by an alternative route, outside the crack. I followed, bludgeoning up the crack itself, jamming my fists into the slime. I have little scabs all over the backs of my hands, where the jamming-injuries have failed to heal since the last time I climbed. A colleague once asked me what type of skin-rash that was; he was interested in dermatological rarities. We call it gritstone rash.

Four pitches up, the clouds roll in over the ridge opposite, bringing weather from the sea. We are climbing light, without packs, or foods, or waterproofs, because this is really just a large outcrop, not a mountain, and the summer weather was warm when we set out. Our tents, green and orange, sit neatly on the gentle lawn by the loch, a sheltered spot where the deer graze in spring, outside the shooting season.

As I complete my progress across the traverse, raindrops begin to land on my helmet. Judy's is dry, below the overhang.

"Your lead," she says, pointing skywards. She prefers not lead thuggy cracks through overhangs, even at VS 4c.

I have no excuse. The belay is complex, with five points of attachment, but the ledge is tiny. A hanging belay, with no chance of changing over the anchor without a good deal of hassle and a rope-salad in red and blue. The dead ends of the ropes hang in free space, in long U-shaped loops. I recall a similar occasion, climbing with my sister, when she came around the corner to find me suspended above the sea (it was at Pembroke), and asked me if I was sure I was securely belayed. She is as accustomed to my loose anchors as to the midnight bog-yomping.

I have to lead. A clap of thunder incites me. I have no excuse. We are much more than twenty feet up, and there is no chance of my hitting anything on the way down, before the rope grabs me.

I snatch the few spare chocks from Judy's gear-sling. Most of the gear I have already collected crossing the traverse or it is part of that magnificent

Rosemary Cohen

belay. I turn my face heavenwards, and receive a few more raindrops, and another clapping of thunder.

I am afraid, so afraid that I seize a pair of large handholds and propel myself upwards, grabbing everything in reach. I am boosted by each new rumble from the west.

I have stopped breathing. I usually hold my breath when I am afraid, and then I breathe too hard and get pins and needles in my fingers. There are lots of hand and footholds, but it is very steep. I ram fistfuls of fingers into the crack, because hand-jams are so much more relaxing. I try some foot-jams too, twisting the tow of my slithery rubber rock-boots into the vertical fissure. I am forced to take a breath and try to place a runner. A un-pulleyed fall from this height onto even so solid an anchor would lead to awkwardness.

The advantage of jamming-cracks is that they can be guaranteed to hold a wedge the size of one's hand. I put in tow. Then I clip them to the ropes, trying to avoid twists, and I lunge on.

My heartbeat has caught up with my breathing now, and my feet are beginning to shake. When I try to stop and clam down there is another thunderclap. I seem to be a magnet for mountain thunderstorms. Later that same season I was to comb a dome in the Sierra Nevada, creeping across holdless, protection-less, granite with electricity singing though my hair.

In my present ignorance I am trying to get to the top of the climb before I get wet. Up I go in record time, and my runner's tied in. Judy follows me even more quickly. She takes over for the delicate, white slab, now running with rainwater. I wait for my rushing heart and respiration to settle down, and for the abrupt onset of exhilaration, like the injection of a drug, which follows and escape from perceived danger. I feel safe with Judy leading again.

Away to the right, on Dragon, my sister and Stella are abseiling off. We cannot abseil, because of the traverse pitch. We get very wet.

Down below, a boat creeps across the lake and then drives up onto the land—a tiny amphibious vehicle—with two men aboard. Smoke begins to rise from the chimney in the shooting lodge.

Judy and I squelch down the descent route in treadless boots, slipping and sliding. We get into our sleeping bags, hoping our clothes will dry. We drink tea, and plan other routes, and my sister and Stella think they might try Gob tomorrow.

How do we know which was the best year? That summer, of Carnmore, and Pembroke, and Yosemite, was full of fine weather, and great routes, and great plans for more. I have never before or since set out to climb in Scotland with three other women, leaving the men behind.

Since the, Stella has become President of the Pinnacle Club, but the rest of us have fought against the slow drift away which is fuelled by work or family. We have none of us given up climbing, although opportunities are fewer. The desire is till there, between rainstorms, and the other hazards of life.

It is only looking back that I can say that was the moment. I cannot relinquish climbing, even though I will never be a master of the art. I need that sensation of being suspended above the earth, as in an Apollo module, looking back at the swirling blue planet. I felt it there, in the mossy groove above Carnmore, pursued by the thunderstorm.

Ten years afterwards, a tiny boy, dressed in a pale-blue boiler suit and wellies, points up the slope above the gentle green track and exclaims: "Climb mountain!" I hold his hand while he sets off up the hill. He'll have to do the leading next.

Since she first climbed on Harrison's Rocks in 1974, Rosemary Cohen has travelled in the Himalaya, and climber in Europe and America.
A medical doctor, she is married with two sons, and continues to combine climbing with family, a career and many others hazards of life.
She is the author of a novel entitled Above the Horizon.

THE TRAGIC MOUNTAIN

ARLENE BLUM

The Aeroflot jet is oppressively crowded, but I feel totally alone. I watch the sun set golden over the Atlantic with a feeling of fatality. I am in a space and time machine and do not know where I will come out. In my purse is a telegram: "Invite you International Alpine Camp Pamir '74. Sportkomitet USSR." I have only known for a few weeks that I was going to Russia to climb Peak Lenin, a mountain over 23,000 feet high.

Before I left New York, I called home for messages. There was a letter from Fay Kerr, a New Zealand friend. Her women's expedition to the Indian Himalayas was hit by an avalanche. Four climbers were killed. Again friends were killed in the mountains. I feel completely resigned, an automaton being propelled to an unknown fate.

Why am I flying to Moscow alone? Climbers usually go on expeditions together. I won't meet my climbing companions, Heidi Ludi, Eva Isenschmidt, and Margaret Munkle, until I get to Russia. They are Swiss women from "Rendez-vous Haute Montagne," an international women's climbing club to which I belong. I have Heidi's warm letters urging me to join them in the Pamirs, but still, I know nothing of their personalities, ambitions or even their climbing ability.

The Russians have invited 180 climbers from ten western countries to climb in the Pamirs, a range of high, rugged mountains near the Chinese border. Since it's the first time American climbers have been allowed to visit the Pamirs, there has been a great deal of excitement about it in the States. A dozen experienced women expeditionary climbers applied to be part of the American team. We were all turned down, which is why I'm going with the Swiss. Two strong women climbers without previous expedition experience were invited. The men climbers were selected from those who had applied and had previous expeditionary experience. I discussed this with a woman climbing friend who had also applied and been turned down.

"I heard a rumor that when the Americans chose their team," she said sweetly, "they wanted to make certain that any women along would be ladies."

A TYPICAL DAY AT LENIN BASE CAMP

The breakfast gong sounds. I yawn and stretch luxuriously on my thick foam mattress. Then I put on my tennis shoes and stroll out between row upon row of identical tents.

The Russians are staging this "sport scamp" to raise hard currency for a Himalayan expedition next year. They're charging us $750 each, and trying hard to give us our money's worth. There are hot showers, volleyball and soccer fields and movies at night. The accommodations are surprisingly—even amusingly—lavish. Everything lives up to the glossy full-color brochure with the invitation, "Well-known Soviet climber Vitaly Abalakov wishes you to conquer the Pamirs."

The Russians have put flagpoles with our national flags in front of the tents, so the camp has the air of a people's summit meeting. I smile as I pass the British tents. Abalakov and the other Russian "Masters of Sport" have been a bit scandalized by the casualness of the British climbers, especially their way of naming a new leader every day. Two nights ago in the middle of the night the British took down their own flag and raised a pair of lace panties. But when they straggled out at dawn, grinning broadly and ready to salute, another British flag was waving proudly.

In the mess tent, the tables are laden with smoked salmon, hot sweet Russian tea and beluga caviar. I smear a thick slice of dark Russian bread with sweet butter and then pile it high with caviar. Extravagant, but it seems to be plentiful here. (Later, when I priced caviar in Moscow, I found I'd been eating $30 worth every morning.)

I look for a place to sit and eat. In fact, finding a chair in the crowded mess tent is one of the few serious practical problems of the day. The Austrians and the Germans, who are assigned to the first sitting, like to linger on, so there's never quite enough room for the rest of us. The tent is jammed with climbers chatting in a complex mixture of languages. There are the three elderly Italians—one in his 70s. I don't see the French; they must be making an even better breakfast from the cases of pate, chestnut paste and pop-top cans of wine they brought along. Heidi and Eva are at a German-speaking table. I feel too sleepy for a German lesson. The Americans are here, but I'm shy of sitting with them since I wasn't invited to join the team.

I decide to sit with a group of English-speaking Russians. Elvira Schataeva, the leader of a group of nine Russian women, is talking animatedly about the problems of organizing an all-woman expedition. "Most Russian men just didn't think an all-woman party could climb a 7,000-meter peak," she says. Lenin has not yet been climbed by a group of women and either Elvira's party or ours my be the first. "What route do you plan to take?" I ask. "We plan to traverse the entire summit of Lenin climbing the East Ridge and descending the Razdelny route."

"We were planning to go up by the Razdelny route, but why don't we go together?"

"This is impossible." She doesn't say why, but I sense that the Russians want their women to make the first all-woman ascent without us.

She smiles. "We cannot climb together, but we can celebrate together. We'll have a great party after the climb." She is so confident of success. As we wander out of the mess tent toward the Russian encampment, she says, "Our group is very strong. We have strong collective spirits and will stay together no matter what happens." I wonder a bit as I look at the inadequate Russian equipment—the heavy cotton tents with button closures, the flimsy wooden tent poles, the clumsy, old-fashioned nailed boots. The light from the icy summit of Peak Lenin shines on Elvira's golden hair.

Today we're to begin carrying loads to Camp I. I'm eager to get started, but Heidi and Eva want to bathe first. The Swiss have brought an inflatable orange-and-yellow bathtub, and they spend a surprising amount of time keeping themselves and their clothes clean.

Our plans for the climb must be cleared with our Russian adviser. We stand in a large tent in front of a photomap of Lenin with the routes marked and painfully translate every word from English to German to Russian and back. The discussion seems interminable. He is dubious of the strength of a party of four women, but finally he acquiesces. Then forms with every detail of our daily plans and our expected time of return, must be filled out.

To Western climbers the Russian approach seems rigid and bureaucratic. We're not used to these mass ascents. Everything we want to do here has to be specified in detail and approved. The routes are so well-traveled they seem like highways. There are shortwave radios everywhere, spouting forth messages: "The weather is good. The weather will turn bad. Go up.

Go down." Half the time the radios don't work, and weather reports aren't reliable, which confuses things further.

Now that our plans have been cleared, our food and gear have to be organized and packed. An antlike army of climbers has been coming and going between camps on Lenin for several days now, patiently moving supplies up the mountain. At four in the afternoon, our little group finally manages to join their ranks. Big thunderclouds are forming for our daily storms. Our packs are light, so we'll have to make several trips over this terrain. Heidi and Eva and Margaret keep stopping to look at the flowers and chat with climbers coming down the mountain. Things are going so slowly, it seems like we're never going to climb anything. "Stop being an impatient American," I tell myself. I try to join in the conversation, but it's all in German. There's little point in waiting. I carry my load alone.

A Night at Base Camp

Back at base camp that evening, the climbers are sitting around drinking vodka and telling stories. The Russian women come down dancing and singing spirited folk songs. "We've made our second camp in a snow cave," they tell me.

Far into the night I discuss the merits of women's expeditions with some of the men. Half the groups here are all men. The British, who have no women among them, say flatly, "Most women climbers aren't first-rate. They're not really serious. They're so eager to succeed and prove their ability that they don't exercise good judgment."

"But attitudes like that are exactly what make it so difficult for women to GAIN experience and judgment."

"Besides, women can never get along with each other."

"That's ridiculous. I climbed McKinley with five other women. We got along well and made the climb without serious problems. There have even been physiological studies that show that women adapt to altitude more readily than men." They shake their heads and smile paternally.

Bruce Carson and Fred Stanley come bursting in. "We were caught in an avalanche below Krylenko Pass. We think seven people have been buried."

"Do not worry," the Russians say, "Abalakov, a Grand Master of Sport, is confident that no one has been killed."

Still we continue to worry, until some Japanese climbers come down with news that no one has died. Weary, I go back to my tent, turn off the electric light and crawl into my sleeping bag.

The Summit Day on Peak Lenin

A glorious morning. Nine climbers from Switzerland, Germany, Japan and the U.S. are preparing to leave Camp III at 20,000 feet for the summit. Margaret, who is in her 50s, isn't feeling well and has stayed behind, so Heidi and Eva and I are going on alone. But the Russian advisers tell us, "A storm is coming in. You shouldn't try for the top today."

I wonder if they're saying that because the Russian women have not reached the summit yet either. They must be climbing from the other side along the East Ridge today.

I'm worried about Eva. She has been feeling ill for several days. I've been trying to persuade her to eat and drink more, but neither of the Swiss seems convinced when I tell them dehydration causes altitude sickness. Yesterday they just lay in the tent all day. When I tried to get them to drink, they said, "Leave us alone."

They want to carry just enough gear for an emergency camp. I feel an emergency camp on the exposed summit ridge will be too dangerous. "Let's go light and try to get up and down quickly," I suggest. "If we run out of time we'll have to turn back without reaching the top."

We can't reach a consensus, so I decide to try for the top by myself, going light, with the intent of turning back at two in the afternoon. It seems quite safe: The weather is good, the route straightforward, and a trail from the footsteps of other climbers leads to the summit. Two other people are climbing alone; I can always join them.

I move steadily upward, stopping from time to time to drink some lemonade or eat a candy bar. The going is easy, with spectacular views of the high mountain ranges of Central Asia.

By noontime clouds are forming on the neighboring peaks, and the wind is rising. I have to fight my way against the gusts to the top of a steep section on the ridge. As I move along the level, it begins to snow heavily. I continue upward.

The storm is becoming more violent. Damn it. I have to go down. The summit can't be far above, but to go on alone would be stupid.

The storm has obliterated the tracks behind me, and the whiteout obscures everything. I go down a few hundred feet. The terrain doesn't look right. I retrace my steps hurriedly before they are blown away. I try again to find the right way down. And again. "You may really have blown it this time kid. You're really alone up here at 23,000 feet."

After a few minutes it clears up a bit. I see the way down. I start down, moving as fast as I can. Ahead of me I can see another figure fighting the storm, coming upward toward me. It's a Swiss climber. "Geben Sie mir Wasser." he gasps. "Oh, good," I think, as I give him my water, "someone to go down with." He drinks and then abruptly leaves, heading upward.

Another apparition in the storm—this time running down behind me. It's Jed Williamson, an American. "Did you get to the top?" I ask him. "No." We descend together in silence.

Farther down at about 3:00 we find Heidi, Eva and Anya, a German climber, huddled in the snow with the storm raging about them. "We are bivouacking here," Eva says. "Stay with us. We can surely reach the summit tomorrow."

In my faltering German, I say, "I am through with Peak Lenin. I am going down. Come with me, it is too dangerous to stay here without tents or stoves."

"No. We will be safe here. Stay." I try to convince them to leave, but my struggle alone in the storm has left me too tired to argue anything with anybody, especially in German.

I stumble down behind Jed. The wind blows me off my feet. I sit there. Finally I get up. Are we really going the right way?

The snow is up to my thighs and the wind is driving crystals of ice into my face. I am so tired. We seem to have been fighting our way down for an eternity.

We stumble into a break in the ridge. It's the break that leads to high camp. As we step down into the sheltered camp, there's sudden silence and relief from the storm.

I collapse outside the tent too tired to take off my crampons. A Dutch climber, Hans Bruyntjes, helps me. I crawl into my tent but can't sleep. Of the nine climbers who left our camp this morning, only Jed and I have returned. The other seven are somewhere above us on the summit ridge, exposed to the full fury of the storm without tents, stoves or sleeping bags. I pray that they are all right.

AGAIN, CAMP I ON PEAK LENIN

After the severity of the last few days, the rock and ice down here seem warm and soft. A stream of climbers files by on their way back to the luxuries of base camp. Among them are Molly Higgins and Marty Hoey, the two women on the American team, who both climbed strongly and reached the summit before the storm broke.

Arlene Blum

Somehow, I do not want to go down with the others to base camp, to leave the mountain for the last time. Things up here are still unresolved for me. Only six climbers came down to camp the morning after our summit attempt. Eva died of exposure in the storm that night on the exposed summit ridge. So senseless. If only I had tried harder to persuade her to come down with me. If only things had been different.

Why, oh, why could the weather not have been like this a couple of days ago? Today when no one is climbing, when it doesn't matter, it is perfectly still and beautiful. If only things had been different.

I keep seeing Eva bending over the flowers. She was such a slight person. She really didn't seem to belong on a harsh mountain. It didn't have to happen. But then I think, "Who are you to say where she belonged?"

I sit here piling rocks into unstable configurations, unable to summon energy to do anything more complicated than see if I can add one more rock to the tower without causing it to collapse.

Three Americans—Allen Steck, Christopher Wren and Jock Glidden—come down from a different side of the mountain. They say they reached the top of Lenin yesterday. As the storm raged they had been camped high on the summit ridge. "Our tent pole broke in the storm. We kept our clothes and boots on continuously for several days in case the tent was destroyed.

"When the storm finally ended, we started for the summit. Someone was lying in the snow. It was a body—Elvira Shataeva. We went farther and found another body, then the remnants of a tent and two more bodies."

The Americans think that some of the women were too weak to go farther and the others stayed with them instead of going for help. Their equipment was poor. Their stoves probably failed so they couldn't melt snow for water to drink or eat. Their cotton tents were blown apart as they huddled there for warmth. We hear that the women radioed the base camp that one woman had died and two others were sick. Then, on the third day of the storm, Elvira and another Russian must have decided to go down—too late.

People are sitting around speculating about why the Russians didn't radio the other climbers on the mountains to form a rescue party. There has been no official announcement at all, but we have heard that Elvira radioed, "Goodbye, we are going to die."

I can't think of anything but the irony of today's warm sunny weather. If only it had come a few days earlier. Everything would have been completely different. Right now we might all be down in base camp celebrating.

My rock tower crumbles. I think of this summer in the Pamirs. About 200 climbers attempted to reach the top of Peak Lenin; 100 succeeded, 13 died.

The sun shines. The top of Lenin seems so close above me I can touch it.

ARLENE BLUM is a well-known mountaineer, biochemist, lecturer, and author of "Annapurna, A Women's Place"(Sierra Club Books). She has taken part in climbs of Mt. Everest and Mt. McKinley, and led the first American ascent of Annapurna I, 1978.

Arlene did her undergraduate work at Reed College, and went on to the University of California at Berkeley were she complete her doctorate in biophysical chemistry (1971). Notable among her many awards are The Society of Woman Geographers Gold Medal for Outstanding Achievement (1984), the Sierra Club's Francis Farquhar Award for Mountaineering (1982) and Mazamas (1988).

Arlene Blum is a historian of women in mountaineering, is on the Board of Directors of Earth Island Institute, and presents motivational lectures and workshops on leadership.

Rock Climbing: The Lasting Love Affair

Beth Bennett

To understand the deep and long-lasting effect that climbing has had on me, my childhood history is of paramount importance. When other girls were reading Nancy Drew and the Bobsy Twins I was devouring Tarzan novels. I always envisioned myself as the hero (never the heroine), swinging from boughs, rescuing the underdog, and living as a Rousseau-an enfant savage. Although I don't believe that this literary menu led to my involvement with rock climbing *per se*, I do think that my early identification with the active role contributed to the approach I later took toward climbing.

When I had grown up somewhat (at least beyond the point where I was reading Tarzan by flashlight under the covers) I did attempt to undertake a more typical feminine activity: modern dance. While I never would have been invited to join the Martha Graham group (or even the local performing arts group), several years of plie and relevee and reckless jete did instill in me an appreciation of balance and grace and artistic technique. Whether or not I ever attained a mastery of any of these attributes as a dancer is another question. It was much easier for me to develop a sense of balance on a vertical face than on the dance floor, and I believe the grace of a good climber executing a difficult sequence rivals that of a world class ballerina. Having seen many 5.8 climbers who can leave me in the dust on the pull up bar, I am convinced of the value of good climbing technique. It took me years before I got past the one pull-up stage—which didn't stop me from leading 5.10 (although I was worthless on even easy overhangs until I developed some upper body strength).

When an aspiring boyfriend took me climbing for the first time these isolated events of my past were catalyzed and I fell in love with rock climbing, the longest lasting love affair of my life. Despite the fact that it's been over 15 years since that first 5.5 slab in the Linville Gorge area in North Carolina, vignettes of those (and many other) climbs still remain clear and vivid. Perhaps more than any other aspect of climbing, this is my most treasured, that I can recall with startling clarity favorite, isolated sequences from past climbs, as if I were picturing the face of a good friend. This playback procedure is probably similar to the process of visualization, encouraged by coaches of many sports in order to place athletes mentally in situations with which they will have to contend during competitive events. In my case, this re-enactment may not be as effective as a strict visualization, but on the other hand, I don't do it to improve my climbing, but rather because I enjoy the memory. I see that little edge, and the toe of my boot centered on it, rocking my knee over my foot and standing up. It's a little like seeing a favorite movie over and over, in that the suspense, the not-knowing is not there. I know I am not going to fall, that my foot does stay on that hold, there is a hidden handhold around the corner, that tenuous jam doesn't slip when I move the other hand up. One part of me enjoys the suspense while I'm climbing, but another, more bucolic part of my mind likes the rerun better.

So what are these vignettes like and what do I get out of them? Perhaps the best answer is to give a few illustrations.

Years later, I still tense up and get nervous when I think back to my first forty footer (fall). I had reached the top of a bulge on a 5.9+ route on the Bastille in Eldorado Springs called Blind Faith. Most people jam the crack through the bulge. At that point, I hadn't been exposed to many cracks, and I hadn't figured out how to jam. So I climbed the face. At that time, I was opposed to chalk, especially in Eldorado where the white blotches permanently marred the red rock. (I have since seen the error of my ways!) I can never forget the feeling of inevitability and awful resignation as my hands slimmed slowly off the rounded holds at the top of the bulge. In the days immediately following this debacle, I returned mentally to that bulge too often for comfort. Yet, I think this process of recall is beneficial in that it allows one to explore alternatives: Why didn't I lunge for the bucket?! Why didn't I climb the crack? Why didn't I put in another nut? These alternate scenarios might be more readily applied next time, and thus this process can afford a real learning experience.

The Naked Edge is arguably one of the most beautiful climbs anywhere, because of the quality of the climbing and the position, high on the Red Garden Wall overlooking all of Eldorado Canyon and the South Boulder Creek drainage. I'd wanted to climb the first pitch ever since I saw it: a steep finger crack in a shallow dihedral, which blanks out near the top of the pitch. I've done the route too many times to count now (having participated in a filmed

Beth Bennett

documentary with Lynn Hill in 1980 added at least 10 repeats to the grand total). My first foray (still without chalk) was memorable simply because my forearms were so exhausted ('pumped') that each move near the top of the pitch was fairly dynamic—when I reached the buckets I was still afraid I couldn't hold on.

Then there was the day bouldering on Flagstaff when I fell on my butt after sliming off the chalked and greasy holds of an easy problem. Now, chalk is funny stuff—one uses it to cut down on sweaty hands and fingers and augment the cohesiveness of hand to rock but when rock is overchalked, it becomes extremely slick, and virtually necessitates the use of chalk to overcome the lack of friction developed by the magnesium carbonate overlay. I had never believed this until that day on Flagstaff. Frustrated and humiliated by landing on my rear end in the dust in front of a crowd, I grabbed a chalkbag and proceeded to walk up a half a dozen boulder problems I had never succeeded at before. I've been an avid chalker ever since. (Although I must add, parenthetically, that I still disapprove of over-chalking—rubbing the chalk well into one's hands not only decreases the overload on the rock, but also results in a better friction.)

One really rewarding aspect of climbing is the potential for developing close friendships with a partner. One of my earliest partners is still a dear friend: Pat Adams. Together we did the third free ascent of the Yellow Wall on the Diamond, Long's Peak. The memories of many pitches of long, clean hand cracks run into one another, but the joy and closeness we felt when we topped out, just moments before the afternoon thunderstorm began are crystal clear. As is the memory of the long walk out and cramming into a small Peugeot with three other climbers from New York and all their gear who took mercy on us as we hitched back to Boulder. On many other occasions Pat and I used the old ploy of 'boy hide in bushes, girl stick out thumb'. The potency of these memories of friendship is only enhanced by the beauty of the experiences that were shared.

Another experience with Pat is still vivid in my memory but because I at least was absolutely terrified and physically miserable. We were trying to free climb the Diagonal Direct, a long line on the lower East Face of Long's Peak, leading up to the Diamond. A combination of free routes up the lower face and on the Diamond itself gave the possibility of a Grade VI, an exciting idea as it had not been done at that time. The first several pitches went well despite Pat's disdain for my use of a cheater rock to begin the first move (as the snow had melted more than usual that year, I couldn't reach the first holds!). We rapidly reached the point at which the regular Diagonal route rappels into a second corner system and began to climb past. Unfortunately for our dreams of glory, the runoff from above left the leaning crack system of the Diagonal Direct full of mud and running water. After several falls, we decided to rappel into the regular route, but the afternoon thundershower decided to gainsay us by appearing in midmorning after we had rappeled—an action which cannot be undone once the ropes were pulled. The climb back up the repel was frighteningly unprotected and involved using crack-n-ups (small, anchor shaped devices ranging from 1/8" to 1/4" in width) as points of aid. The sleet and howling wind added considerably to my tension and misery. The rappel down the diagonal crack system was a fitting culmination to an extremely unpleasant day as we careened across the wall, slipping on wet rock trying to make the necessary pendulums to reach the belays. Nonetheless, we could laugh and joke at ourselves and our plight—an important element of a good climbing partnership.

During an experiment with biofeedback I was asked to focus on an experience which I found relaxing, and then on another which I felt to be unpleasant. For a pleasant experience, I recalled a fine day's climb: the fall weather was lovely, the breeze pleasant, the sky clear and blue, the rock warm and friendly. Oddly, this memory generated more stress as perceived by the machines than did the recollection which I felt to be more stressful. My theory for this discrepancy is twofold. First, as I mentally reenact the moves of the climb, I probably tense the same set of muscles that I use while climbing and muscle tension is picked up by biofeedback machines. Second, climbing is a stressful activity. Apart from the obvious muscular exertion which is a form of stress, there are certain mental stresses associated with climbing engendered by fear of falling, failure, injury, and so on. The combination of mental and physical stresses which I had called up during the biofeedback session were much more apparent to the machines than to me. I think that this is an important point, and perhaps one which accounts for much of the popularity of climbing and other so-called high risk sports. I enjoy and need a certain amount of stress.

From an evolutionary perspective, this apparently harmful proclivity for stress can make sense. In order to stay fit and survive, our ancestors were exposed to high levels of stress incurred in a hunting and gathering lifestyle. I think it's very likely that humans evolved with high stress levels as a typical part of their environment and consequently still have the tendency to function best under some optimum stress level.

Climbing and other high risk sports are an ideal opportunity to expose oneself to stress, both physical and mental, for a number of reasons. First, the physical exercise of climbing is beneficial (although the tendon and joint injuries which accompany climbing at higher grades are clearly a result of this extreme level and are of dubious physical benefit). At times, climbing may be aerobic, though certainly the hikes to and from all but roadside attractions induce some level of aerobic capacity. The mental benefits from limited exposure to semi-controlled stress situations may be the most important benefit from climbing, although the pleasure derived from the actual experience is arguably the ultimate rationale for pursuing the activity. By routinely exposing oneself to high adrenaline levels, to situations in which one must think fast and act rapidly on the results of those thoughts, and accept the consequences of those actions, one can build up a capacity for dealing with this sort of situation in real life experiences. While situations of such seriousness may be few and far between (e.g. dealing with medical or psychological emergencies) self control and rapid action may be crucial and even life-saving. I would never say that I climb to exercise these mental muscles, but I think their development is a significant by-product of my climbing. But in the end, it's really the wind blowing in my hair, reaching for that little hold and feeling the smoothness of the moves that keep me climbing.

Beth Bennett has been at the forefront of women's climbing for many years and continued to climb at high level while pursuing her Ph.D. in biology and raising her child. She has published a number of professional papers in the field of molecular, cellular and developmental biology and thought in the department of biology at the University of Colorado, Boulder.

A Mountain Experience

Julie Brugger

When my parents asked me where I wanted to go to college, I said "Somewhere with mountains." I thought I really wanted to go to MIT and be a mathematician, but I may have been one of the smartest kids in my high school, but I had been too much of a nonconformist and troublemaker and I could never get the required recommendations from my teachers. I suppose they would shake their heads now and with knowing looks say; "We knew she would come to no good," and with a secret smile I would do nothing to undeceive them.

Why mountains? I had never lived anywhere there were mountains, hardly had seen any, and certainly had never climbed one. But mountains are the ultimate symbol of man's striving, and even then I must have known how strongly the struggle was to pervade and shape my own life.

I had always been the shy and quiet type, and assumed the role of not-so-impartial observer, wondering at the antics of my fellow creatures. I could find no meaning in their endless preoccupation with their appearance and the impression they made, and the cruel games they played with each other. I could never be sure whether it was them or me who was crazy. Of one thing I was sure, I did not belong, and I wondered if there was a place in this world that I would ever feel I did.

So I came out to Washington to go to college, away from the Midwest whose horizons were as empty as what life there seemed to offer. The University was large; I could remain anonymous and undisturbed while I searched for my own path.

One day I wandered into a Climbing Club meeting, and watched beautiful slides of rugged black mountains. They were pushing their way above the lush green forest and valley, above the corrugated white glaciers, and sprawling across the horizon under an intense blue sky, as I had never known existed. There was so much space, so much possibility. The mountains seized my imagination and I felt that I already knew more about them than I possibly could have, felt that hidden beyond some shadowy ridge or sparkling on some distant sun-touched summit maybe some kind of answer awaited me.

I wanted to go out into those mountains at once and signed up for a beginner outing for the very next weekend. I quickly learned that the mountains do not offer their possibilities to the unskilled and unknowledgeable. Their ways must be learned their weather, how to travel, how to be safe, how to overcome fear, how to respect. In order to do that I found a summer job in the city instead of returning home so that I could take the Basic Climbing Course from the University on the weekends. I never went back to the Midwest again except to visit.

That summer I learned how to tie knots and how to handle the ropes to belay my partner and travel safely on glaciers. I learned how to read maps and use a compass to navigate in unknown or obscured terrain. I learned how to employ the mountaineer's intimidating ice axe and crampons to ascend an icy slope or arrest a dangerous fall. I learned that with the right equipment and clothing it is possible to be safe and relatively comfortable in diverse weather conditions. I learned how to find the weaknesses in a sheer rock wall and use them to climb it. My excitement grew and with it my desire to learn more. With every small summit came a triumph out of proportion to its size. It came from a growing certainty that I had found my path and set my boot upon it, all of the signs pointed that way.

There was the beauty of the physical environment. Cool, shady forests with trees so straight, tall, silent and covered with moss that they gave me the impression of being as old and as wise as the earth. Wildflowers that exuberantly crowded the meadows stood proudly alone or hid shyly away, and each urged me to learn its name. Crystal clear water that tumbled noisily down rocky streambeds, or tapped a quiet rhythm as it melted from a protected pocket of the last winter's snow, and always invited me to drink. Snow in all of its forms, from the soft white blanket that quiets and blurs the winter landscape to the hard, metamorphosed, twisted forms that reared up or plunged down vertically all around me in the glaciers. Rocks of every hue and description. Rocks that were so solid they could support my weight on a sliver as thin as a dime and rocks that crumbled beneath my touch, and all gave off that distinctive odor of ozone when struck one against another. Mountains of all temperaments, some calm and majestic, some playful, some truculent, and some downright malevolent, and each offering me its own promise of adventure and challenge and reward. Above all that the piercing blue sky. It was a place big enough for me to breathe and not feel a constriction in my chest, a place where my heart could expand and never get too big to fit. The wildness of it spoke to the wildness in me.

And there was the delight in getting to know this body that I am living in. I had never been good at any athletic activities and I considered myself uncoordinated and inept, but my desire to be in the mountains made my determination strong and I discovered that with time, patience and practice, I could learn most anything, some people just learn faster. Then, when I have learned, there is the pure joy of the movement, hiking steadily for hours with a heavy pack, or executing a series of delicate maneuvers on the rock, or skidding dizzily down a steep snow slope at breakneck speed but in complete control. I am in tune with my body, fit, and free. The feel of my heart pounding in my chest, the smell and sting of my sweat, the strong, smooth flexion and expansion of my muscles and their satisfying and relaxing ache at day's end, all let me feel and rejoice in my aliveness. I can communicate with this human machine. I know when to listen to its murmurs and aches and pains and when to ignore them and exert my will and push it to its limits. I can respect those limits but I know how to expand them as well.

And there were the many challenges to face and the opportunity that each one offered for me to grow. The challenge of trying something I don't know if I can do and giving it the very best I have to give, to chart my depths by plumbing them. The challenge of admitting my fear, facing it, and overcoming it and in overcoming it finding I can stop avoiding having to face it again. The challenge of accepting failure as a possibility, inevitable sometime, and not due to personal deficiency, a chance to learn more about myself and what I can do differently the next time. The challenge of summoning total concentration for a difficult move, of tuning out the world and harnessing every muscle, every nerve, every brain cell, every heartbeat for the task at hand, to transcend, literally, to climb over.

For the first time in my life I found people I could relate to. My coursemates were a varied lot, young and old, students, couples, scientists, and carpenters. Yet we all shared this developing love for the mountains. Sitting around the campfire at night, their faces shining with firelight and the excitement of the day, their smiles and laughter felt real to me. Simple conversations became a pleasure instead of an inanity. Shared adversity built trust and stripped away pretensions and the other excess baggage people carry around to deal with their complicated world. These things have no use in the mountains. Apparent now, for me to see, was their sincerity, their enthusiasm, their sense of humor, their scrappiness, and I realized that, among people such as these, I could feel some sense of belonging.

Most of all there was the great laughter building inside of me, an urge to throw back my head and stretch out my arms and shout my happiness to the world.

At the end of the course two of the other students and I decided to climb Mt. Rainier although our instructor told us he did not think that Basic students were ready for such a climb. We went anyway and you never saw three more scared, sick, sunburned, tired, and exhilarated people as drug themselves down from the summit that day. It was our first climb all on our own and although now I know how easy it was, scarcely another has given me such satisfaction. By the end of the summer I was little different on the outside. A bit more tan in the face, more muscle's definition, and armed with a smile, but on the inside a small, slow flame had begun to burn and spread its warmth outward. An orphan child had discovered she had a home.

In the fall I took a Rock Climbing course and the flame leaped and crackled as I learned new techniques and expanded my skills and watched the colors change and felt the nights get colder and my friends gather closer around the campfire. When the course finished I continued to find other novice climbers and together we would attempt routes of increasing difficulty, sometimes scaring ourselves to death, sometimes failing miserably, and sometimes succeeding with remarkable ease, but always learning and increasing our confidence in our ability.

My first boyfriend was a climber, and when school was over we took up the lives of "climbing bums." We journeyed all over the West to different climbing areas—much to my parent's dismay—in a beat up red Volkswagen, living on granola and peanut butter sandwiches, wearing baggy green Army pants and heavy leather boots. The climber's uniform of the day.

We went to California and Canada, Washington and Wyoming, and everywhere could be found that unearthly blue sky. I learned to love the freedom of that life. It was life reduced to the bare essentials, no bills to pay and no schedules to meet. No decisions to make except what to have for dinner and what to climb the next day.

I learned self-reliance from bivouacking in snowstorms with no food and minimal equipment. From do it yourself Volkswagen repairs on the road, and making the money that most people spend in a weekend last the whole summer. I learned to choose which risks to take in the mountains and which to forego.

In the company of one so highly skilled, I quickly expanded my definition of the possible. How far it was possible to hike in a day, how much it was possible to carry, how hard a rock climbing move it was possible for me to do and learned that the limits of possibility are often self defined.

My joy at being in the mountains only grew. The future that middle class American society offered held no attraction for me. The things that I found were important health, freedom, love, and the continuation of the struggle could not be had for money. It became clear to me that I could never live a normal life, that there was too much living to be done than could fit into weekends and two weeks vacation a year.

More enlightening than all of these, I learned how to love someone and what it means to have a real friend. Always I had been so painfully aware of my separateness, I felt a yawning gap between my feelings and perceptions and those of other people, and now I became aware that it was possible to touch another person and be touched and momentarily bridge that gap. By sharing my love of the mountains I gained the courage to share other parts of me as well, and found that they could be accepted, and understood, and even loved. I learned the quiet happiness of sharing the rituals of everyday life, of getting to know someone's ways, of the superfluity of words.

So we stretched our money as far as it would go, and when it gave out we did whatever we could to make a little more, just enough to go on another climbing trip. For two years we lived this life of vagabonds, my dedication and enthusiasm never flagged, I felt I could live like that forever.

The mountains took my first love. It was in the fall and he was working on the apple harvest. I was on a rock climbing trip to Yosemite where he soon would join me. I had been working a nine-to-five job for six months in the city and was impatient for the outdoors. He had gone out climbing on a day off, there was a rockfall, my friend was suddenly and incomprehensibly and forever gone.

I knew where to run. I went to the city, stood numbly through the funeral, loaded up the old Volkswagen, mine now, and went to the mountains. The pain and the loss were so great, but climbing could take all my energy and concentration and let me forget for awhile. I cried on all the belay ledges. With tears streaming down my face I sang all the songs that reminded me of him and our life together, sang to the trees and streams and rocks and glaciers and summits while the sun poured down from the constant blue sky. There, in those places where we had shared so much, I was reminded too often of him. I was alone again and feared that I would always be alone. But the mountains were still there all around me, my love for the mountains was still there, it would always be there, could never be lost. It gave me the strength and courage to continue on the path I had chosen, knowing that there would always be beauty and joy in life. I became perhaps quieter and more reticent again, and although those around me thought I took it so well, I was dying inside. But I pushed on. California to Canada, Washington to Wyoming, always there was a challenge to be met, another mountain beyond the one just climbed, the sapphire sky, and the emptiness to be filled.

I did some of my best climbing then. I was on my own, the responsibility was all mine. I had no one of greater skill or experience to rely on. The only other thing that had been important to me was gone, so I had all of my energy for myself. And I had a manic amount of energy. I led my first 5.10 then and, I suppose, broke an important barrier for myself, though it didn't seem very significant to me at the time, since only part of me was there. I had never even dreamed of doing it; it was something that the best climbers I knew still spoke of with awe. But my partner and I had done all the 5.9's we could find in Yosemite, and all there was left was something harder. I tackled more difficult mountain climbs as well, and climbed some of the forbidding north faces in the Canadian Rockies. Eventually, days could go by when I didn't cry, and slowly, slowly, the pain went away.

The mountains brought my second love. I had seen him around for years, wearing the look that says stay away, and now I felt drawn toward him. I had looked out of those same eyes and knew the feelings they could be hiding. I felt a kindred spirit behind the walls, one to share my love of life and mountains with and it was time to share again. I had learned to lose and live and I was no more afraid of those adamantine walls than I was of those of granite on which we danced our intricate dance. I was used to challenges and I was not afraid of hard work. It was both of these. But, in time, like our mountain ranges, the peaks and valleys rolled out behind us and one day we could look back and see how far we'd come.

We grew even closer than I could have imagined. We shared so many of the same thoughts and feelings. Our sense of our differentness from the world and our similarity to each other strengthened the bond. Our love for the wild places and a need to continually seek challenges took us from climbing to skiing and kayaking and bicycling the backroads and running the trails.

Anything to be in the mountains! Skiing in the winter good, hard work climbing up and a chance to concentrate and improve my technique on the way down, or on a day when everything comes together, to really fly. Winter can be a friendly season for those who have the right equipment and can keep moving to keep warm, and there are many rewards it has to offer. My favorite days are when the sun is out and it's so cold the moisture in the air crystallizes and sparkles all around you like visible magic. I think the only thing that keeps me sane, working through the rainy Northwest winter, is knowing, that all that rain is making big piles of snow for me to play in, on the weekend. A big gulp of fresh air and realness will get me through another week.

Kayaking takes me to mountains that climbers would scarcely look at, too tame, but they have something to offer those who look other places than just upward. Water. Rivers each have their own color and personality and snow fed streams have the same magic sparkle as a cold winter day. In the winter I slide down it on my skis, in the summer in a boat, but it's the same leaping, laughing water spirit bearing me along.

Bicycling on the twisting mountain roads, the swiftness of my passage gives me a different perspective on the mountain environment and the flowing rhythm of the movement frees my mind to wander as it will and explore new possibilities.

When the now ubiquitous running shoe first appeared, climbers were quick to discard their clunky old boots and take to the trails in those wings of nylon. Hiking in the summer in shorts and running shoes with only a fanny pack, feeling the miles fly under my feet, watching the mountainscape unroll before me, stopping only for a cookie and a gulp of water, the feeling of lightness and freedom, this must be the closest feeling to heaven (where they are said to wear real wings) on earth.

I found a profession that allowed me plenty of free time to pursue these many activities. I could make good money while I was working, take off on a trip, and then find a new job when I returned. But climbing was still my first love. Because my boyfriend was more of a rock climber than a mountain climber, attracted by the athleticism and extreme difficulty of the moves, I too channeled most of my energy in that direction. I began to train, to lift weights to increase my strength for the most demanding moves. With so much practice, so much time spent on the rock, the tips wore off the ends of my fingers and the rubber wore off the toes of my shoes, and I could climb harder routes than I had ever done before. Yosemite Valley was my home every spring. The smell of the sun on my skin, of bay leaves, of tincture of benzoin that we use to toughen our hands, the formic acid smell of the sting-ing red ants that abound there, any of these can still evoke the feeling of the sun pouring down from a narrow, blue corridor bounded by walls of rear-ing granite, heating the rock, raising tiny beads of sweat on my fingertips as I gaze at the tiny seam of a crack splitting a flawless face ("We're going to climb this!?"), or of the life in dusty, crowded Camp IV where climbers' col-orful tents jostled against each other like a fistful of jellybeans, but the dis-comfort went unnoticed at the contented conclusion of a hard day's climb-ing.

But I missed the mountains, missed traveling with everything I needed on my back, secure in the knowledge that I could go wherever I wanted and handle any situation that arose, missed watching the sun set and rise again, while precariously perched in my tent, high on a ridge, miles from civiliza-tion, snug with all I needed to survive. After many seasons pursuing still higher numbers in the rock climbing arena, I wanted to explore new places and try new things. It took little to persuade my friend; he must have been getting more mellow as he got older. We went to Canada in the winter to climb on the frozen waterfalls, to the mountains of South America, the rivers of Idaho, and the canyon country of Utah. There, too, the dazzling blue sky overspread our adventures. It was like the feeling that I had, that in all of these different places, there was always something the same. We were the best of friends and traveling companions. Seeing the excitement in his eyes lifted my heart and fed my own.

It had been all too apparent for years, however, that we could not climb well together. This was a difficult lesson for me. He was too much better than I, too impatient, and not one to hold himself back. He always wanted to lead and I discovered that I could not get as much out of climbing if all I did was follow. It had to be me up there too, me taking the risks, me making the decisions, and me asking for what I needed. And so I had to do things on my own, share my mountains with people who did not mean nearly so much to me as he did, take myself away from the pleasure and security of his com-pany to pursue my own dreams; it was hard for both of us to accept, the dis-tance after so much closeness. But the distance offered a chance for survival of the love that closeness threatened to extinguish.

These are not any astounding revelations, but lessons that people must learn every day. In my case, it seemed that the mountains were always my schoolroom.

We spent many years together, living our lives as we pursued our climb-ing, always asking for the best from ourselves, never content with less. You might say that we were living in a dream world, avoiding growing up and facing reality. You might say that climbing isolated us from other people and other experiences that would have allowed us to grow in different ways. Still, there could be no price too high to pay for the love and the living and the learning that we shared. The spirit of striving finally led us to question our relationship. It could not work for us in the present as it had in the past and it was time for a change. Certainly we were not afraid of the challenge and the hard work, but could this be a case, as often happens in climbing, when better judgement will lead us to abandon our objective in the face of overwhelming difficulty? Or is it simply that we have gazed too long at the mountain from one perspective and have overlooked an approach on the other side? As I have done before, I know that I will again rely on the lessons I have learned and the strength I have gathered from the mountains to steady me and comfort me as I struggle with the most difficult challenge of my life. I will take my sorrow and my confusion there and be able to find some peace.

The things that brought me to the mountains are the things that keep me there. Their beauty I never cease to be delighted with sights so simple as a sunrise, tiny flowers greeting me from an unlikely niche they have found high on a windswept peak, a lively lizard scampering across the rock as I struggle for a handhold, a limpid pool reflecting craggy peaks and the cerulean sky. They rouse a voice in me that says "This is why I'm alive." Often, now, the feeling is not that of never failing astonishment at the beauty of a new prospect, but of welcome recognition and homecoming as I return to the same beloved places time and again.

My body, as I have used and abused it throughout the years, has remained a trusty friend. With good care, I find it can perform, with the benefit of experience, better than it did in its younger days. It is even more important now though, to stay in shape, and I have found city activities running, swimming, lifting weights, playing soccer, and bicycling that I enjoy for their own sake as well as for the conditioning I get from them. The feeling of living in a fit and energetic body is so wonderful that, even if I stopped climbing I could not keep a normal working schedule because I wouldn't have time to do all the things I love to do. This old body is always willing to try new things, usually will protest temporarily with sore muscles, but then settles in to its usual slow but steady pace. We have many miles yet to go together.

No matter how far or fast you travel, how many summits you climb, how difficult a move you make, there is always another challenge in climbing therein lies much of its allure. I am still seeking the challenges, overcoming fear, accepting the possibility of failure, concentrating all my resources on the undertaking, but more and more it seems that the stiffest ones take place, not in the mountains, but in my own life. The lessons I have learned in the mountains are standing me in good stead, but the growth often seems to come, not as it did there, with great joy, but with great pain. Still, each summit reached offers a glimpse of all the others there are to climb.

And still I find friends there aplenty. Some are those I have known for years. Some gray hairs have begun to make their appearance among them. To some I have grown closer throughout the years, and from some I have grown away. But we started climbing together, and though many of them don't climb anymore, we have shared adventures that forged bonds that can never be forgotten. We have belayed, yelled at, laughed with, hugged, competed with, worried about, bivouacked with, pissed off, cried with, and generally well used each other. What it was that brought them to the mountains, and what it was they got from the mountains they still have within them, and whatever else they do, this we will always have in common. Some are those I have met on my travels, gypsies all, we are bound to meet again. And so we do, in Yosemite or Huaras or Banff or Kathmandu, and share the adventures we've had since last we met. Some are gone forever. They lost their lives in the mountains pursuing their own personal dreams. They live in my memory, forever young, smiling against a backdrop of mountains, the wind ruffling their hair, and come to visit me at odd moments, summoned by an experience that is so like one I had shared with them. And still I find new friends to share my mountains with. I have learned to recognize them by the energy and enthusiasm they radiate, by their shining eyes and animated way of talking. They feel right there, real. They don't have to be climbers, but they usually have a love for the outdoors. These are the people I want to be with, who do what they do out of love. Among these people I can feel like I belong, like we are a small coven of sanity in an otherwise senseless world.

And the great laughter seems to have found permanent lodging in my soul. It bubbles out unexpectedly when I'm going about the business of being a normal person and those around me must wonder at my sudden silliness. It allows me to have a graceful sense of humor about any situation and keeps me from taking anything too seriously. Sometimes it comes on so strong it brings tears to my eyes. It's a little furnace in there, churning out energy that keeps me warm and glowing with life.

At times, feeling a need to accede to the expectations of a society I thought I had rejected, I have tried to use climbing as a means to gain recognition, to be considered a success. I have sometimes got caught up in the pursuit of routes or summits, as a collector pursues butterflies, to capture them, and take the life from them, and display them to the amazement and approval of his colleagues. But these attempts to take the mountains for ambition and not for love have all failed. Because it is not what I have done that ultimately brings me a feeling of peace and belonging, it is doing it. And it is not even what I am doing, but how I am doing it, if it is honestly, joyfully, whole heartedly then surely I am living as I was meant to live. Climbing, for me, is not a means to an end, nor is it an end in itself. It is a process, and the mountains are the perfect symbol of the process, arid summits, the human spirit in its isolation, mutely and everlastingly reaching for the sky.

If those smug teachers of mine had sent out glowing recommendations to the college of my choice, I could be a math professor now, determinedly writing equations on a dusty blackboard for the enlightenment of students whose faces would be erased and replaced every year. I could have secured my niche in the world and my claim on the American dream. Instead, all of the wealth I own I carry inside me. My security is knowing that what I have, nothing can take away. My ambition is just to get better at climbing, at understanding, at living. Instead of paying into Social Security for my old age, I pay into a plan that will keep me forever young. Climbing has brought so much into my life and helped to make me the person I am. Even my old die-hard father, who for the last fifteen years of my climbing career could only say, "Why don't you go back to school?", has finally recognized this. Upon returning from my first expedition to the Himalayas, a fairly complicated affair requiring fund raising by selling T-shirts and soliciting donations, in which my father, to my great surprise, heartily participated. I was touched when I learned that he had kept a scrapbook of the whole event, which he proudly displayed to me when I went to visit. He was more concerned than I was, I think, about the seriousness of the undertaking and congratulated me on a gallant attempt and a successful return. This from a man who never offered any praise that I can remember when I brought home all those report cards with A's, and for an endeavor that most of society would consider so useless. I am not looking for approval from my parents after all these years, I am just glad that they can recognize how much reward my own path has brought me.

Julie Brugger

I don't know where my life will lead me, but I know there will always be mountains in it. There is simply a sense of well being, that all is right with the world, that I get from being there and that I don't want to live without.

Someday the challenge will only be to see if I can hobble up a gentle trail to a sweeping vista to gaze at the mountains I once climbed. I will meet it with the same light in my eyes and lift in my heart, knowing that, as sure as that heart, rendingly blue sky, will always be found there, so also will be peace and joy.

Julie Brugger was born in Philadelphia. In 1967 Julie settled in Seattle, Washington as a student at the University of Washington and in 1970 graduated with a degree in math and a "terminal passion for the mountains." Since graduation, Julie has made her living as a freelance computer programmer, which allows her the freedom to pursue her avocation: climbing mountains.

Cholatse North Face

Catherine Freer

Kathmandu pummels the senses, challenging one to simply cope, after the immediate saturation that follows arrival. And yet the temples seep into consciousness, the beauty of this city strikes a cord within us, the dragon image echoes the adventurous spirit that brought us and moves us toward our objective: the unclimbed North Face of Cholatse. (21,130 ft.)

I lounged on the hotel balcony at dusk, absorbing the shock of my return to this dream place. As though on cue, wave after wave of fruit bats left their moorings, heading for their night roosts. They might have been birds except for the peculiar intensity of their whisper flight. Something in the stroke of their wings produced an eeriness, a palpable myster-force.

Pigeon's cooing woke Todd Bibler and me early the next day. We joined Renny Jackson and Sandy Steward, and set about our final preparations amid the rising hubbub in the marketplace. Accommodating our moves to the Nepalese bureaucracy, we juggled our way out of town after only two days. Thirty-seven porters and loads, sirdar, cook, kitchen boy, sahibs, all piled into a truck. The estimated six hour drive to Jiri found us there fourteen hours later. Extricating ourselves from the truck at midnight, we decided the worst was over, and Cholatse would be a breeze.

Next morning bed-tea heralded the beginning of a quieter mood. Life slowed down and came in manageable gulps. There is a rhythm to the days, trekking in. Eating, walking, looking, talking—plenty of time for the land to work its magic on us, for our interior landscapes to respond to the character and subtlety of the exterior landscape. The indigenous people too thrive in this huge, lush, terraced, God's country. They are as determined by the land as by their genes. Transplanted, I fear they would wilt, unsuccoured by the vastness, the beauty, the quiet. Soon we all succumb, the view fills our souls, the days obscure the future. We flow through this region coming closer to ourselves.

One afternoon, near the crest of the hill, an old wrinkled woman sat by the side of the trail. I greeted her as we passed. There were crows cawing, circling above. As we turned the next switch back I heard a cawing near her, and I looked back and she was cawing to the crows. She sounded just like them. It seemed that they called back. So there she was, this old woman on a hillside in the afternoon sun and shadow, talking to the birds, living out her life.

The land soothes us when we lay down at night, and resists our penetration by day, putting hills in our way. Yet beckoning. Smoothing off our rough western edges. The valleys open affirmatively towards the peaks. One noon-time we round a corner and there they are, pulling us towards them like a magnet. Unseen 'till now, they'd been pulling all the same. The desire to see our mountain rises to a more prominent place in us. More than before we go to sleep with our dream and it awakens us. We notice each other as partners and recognize the common urgency we feel. This summit is important.

Two weeks, a little less, and we're at base camp, above a glacial blue-green lake, in an idyllic meadow directly across from Cholatse. Taweche, Ama Dablam, and Lobuje rise in the distance. The face is riveting, the weather turning good, and we spend hours a day peering through the telescope, arguing the merits of different lines. It's no easy trick. The couloirs look dangerous, the buttresses slabby and crackless, the "ice runnels" are only plastered spindrift.

We could aid the rock, but gullies go fast. Scouring the face for bivy sites, we wonder if we should take hammocks. I-Tents are lighter. In 6,000 vertical feet there must be a few places to put them. Eventually we agree on a route that zig-zags up the face past a fearsome ice gully toward foreshortened final pitches. We can only speculate from this perspective.

Todd and I turn our attention to the East Ridge of Lobuje, rising dramatically from the town of the same name. A mere three hours approach gains us the familiar feeling—climbing again, looking down on the ravens and lamarghars, the landscape receding suddenly as the days pass with our effort. The climb is good. The jumbled rock is solid or frozen in place. Two pitches speak out: steep face climbing and a smooth dihedral lead me to a belay on the crest. Todd gets a long hand and fist crack up an otherwise blank slab. Two bivy ledges are hard won, and the third night finds us on the summit ridge.

Descending from their ascent of the Southwest Ridge, Sandy and Renny call to us, advising a rope for the summit jaunt. We follow their tracks down the snow shoulders, their curving lines a spectacular frame for the most beautiful views in the world. Back at base camp, we're met with big smiles from growing friendships. Phu Dorje, our superb cook, has baked fruit-nut bread for a celebration tea. We decide unanimously that a good cook is the most essential ingredient in a successful expedition.

The weather was with us on Lobuje. Anxious to take full advantage before a storm, Renny and Sandy leave for Cholatse the next day. We rest another day, reorganizing our food and gear, Todd stalking the summit, always watching. The current finally finds us on the lower slopes, unable to resist the upward directive. All parts of us become subservient to whatever moves us efficiently upward.

The neve that first day was rather good. Base camp hurried away beneath, and soon we were jumaring a rope fixed on a steep rockpitch. Afternoon found the four of us together, pooling our hopes and enthusiasm in anticipation of the climb ahead. Sandy and Renny had fixed three pitches above the bivy. From their highpoint we leapfrogged the lead up toward a vertical bulge of green ice that issued onto a long ramp splitting the upper face.

We avoided the considerable rockfall in the gully, keeping close to the wall, and hoped to be on the ramp above by nightfall. I led a traverse skirting the worst of the rotten snow that characterized these pitches. Renny led past. We neglected to move the belay to a safe corner in our rush to finish the gully and an ice chandelier broke off, crushing my hardhat, giving us a scare and me a terrific headache. Darkness forced us to retreat to sitting bivys.

Next morning, by the time we'd moved back into position to push the route round the corner, the rockfall was already beginning. Todd only had time to do the steepest section before whines too close for comfort forced him back to the belay. We made soup and fiddled away the next four hours, waiting for cooler temperatures to allow us to continue. Just after 2 p.m. Todd finished the pitch with a hanging belay and we were moving again. Renny ran out the next rope and a half, and three more mixed pitches took us to a pretty good ledge, with room for one tent.

By mid-afternoon the following day the character of the route revealed itself definitively. Steep rock, vertical ice, and too much steep, unpredictable, unconsolidated snow. No sunlight meant little thawing and refreezing at that altitude on a north face. We might've known.

Amid all the insecurity, somehow the anchors appeared on cue, a pocket of ice on the verge of despair, or a solid, friendly Friend crack. Before long, ropes were tied off and the troops were moving through, pushing the route until nightfall, sometimes beyond. We had to watch Sandy: the advent of darkness seemed to trigger his adrenaline. One twilight with fierce enthusiasm he threw himself on a vertical rock pitch, viciously hand-jamming against the ice oozing out of the crack. After tenuous aid moves on pins tapped into the ice, he finished the daring pitch and announced happily that he'd found a ledge to bivy on. His enthusiasm called to mind a different scene than reality made available to the rest of us. Renny jumared up and when I saw him lead off again above Sandy, it was as clear as when I saw it myself that the ledge was two foot square. Many hours later we fell exhausted into our tents. In the long night , images of friends and family came larger than memory. My thoughts wove understandings as the specter danced shadows on the tent walls.

The next days run together, the route finding relentlessly complicated as we moved up the ramp to a horizontal step before the steep ice bowl that led onto the summit ridge. A late-night bivy here seemed cozy until daylight revealed our position. I led off over steep rotten snow with hidden ice runnels. Renny moved through faster than a bear through uphill timber. His pitches always seemed cut from the same cloth—nothing we wouldn't gladly have given away. This time it was a treacherous steep snow pitch; no pro for 165 ft. Sandy tried an alternate path before leading on solid ice up into the steep bowl. Todd ran it out raz-mataz over the intimidating bulge above, and I did the next rope length on good ice and neve. Renny climbed the last pitch in the dark. I was the last to jug home that night with Renny shouting "We're saving you a place." Still gullible, I imagined a big-enough ledge, flat, ready-made. Well, ready-made it was, a curved porcelain space, too small for the four of us cradled miserably all night.

The moon was still shining close on Makalu's shoulder as bulging mushrooms yielded to the summit ridge early the next day. Seven days of struggle, and we were tired. Dreamlike white towers hung over our heads. The summit looked inaccessible, but over the top was the only way out. We climbed into the mist.

Finally, we were up! What a relief to get what we came for. We paused, surrounded by a dramatic panorama: Everest, Makalu, Cho Oyu, Gyachung Kang.

We didn't want to hurry away but our already rationed supplies made us uncomfortable with the descent still ahead. Two days of rappelling and down climbing the south ridge, a route climbed only once in 1982 by the Swiss, finished our food and fuel and we were met on the moraine by Ongchu Sherpa with tea and chapatis. Radiant smiles all around.

Our plan of lying in base camp savoring the line of the route vanished as afternoon clouds appeared, obscuring the peak, bringing a storm. We hastily decided to beat it down to Thyangboche for Mani Rimdu festival. The instantaneous arrival of the yaks indicated that our sirdar was one step ahead of us, as usual.

We all had different post climb ambitions, but when the time came it was difficult to summon the motivation let alone the necessary energy, and we found our feet trundling down the valleys toward Lukla and airport life.

Catherine Freer began climbing at age 19. At age 37 she was considered by most to be the best woman climber in America. Catherine was killed in 1987 while attempting the second ascent of the Hummingbird Ridge on Canada's Mount Logan. She was responsible for numerous first ascents in many of the major mountain ranges of the world.

Can This Trip Be Saved?

Wendy Roberts

Beyond the edges of Seattle stretches a vast wilderness where Espresso drinks cannot be found. I savored the totally beige foam in the bottom of my cup and consoled myself that this weekend's climbing at Squamish would really work out OK. After all, we had all made a commitment to really TALK about our differences, and women are great at making commitments, right?

Jean and Margaret were already arguing over who had gotten the #2 Friend permanently stuck on their last Joshua Tree trip. Alison and Harriet were becoming increasingly frustrated as they tried to sort out what they were going to climb. Harriet wanted to work on learning to lead, preferably in the 5.5 to 5.6 range and mostly on cracks. Alison wanted to climb face, 5.9 to 5.10d, but she didn't feel like leading anything until she had warmed up on a few harder pitches.

My own climbing partner, Lana, was crashed out in the back of the van after having eaten an entire box of stale cheerios. She kept moaning something about needing to lose weight in order to "climb the hard stuff;" but we all gathered that her fast was not going well.

"Can this trip be saved?" I muttered to myself, sipping on the penultimate latte of the week.

It was high summer as Jana and I stared up at the too long ridge of Black Peak. My usual sandbag informant had assured me this route was only eight pitches. I hadn't led rock all year, but if we switched off it would only be four leads. No need to get gripped, just yet.

Eight pitches later we weren't even half-way up the ridge and I had a rather sinking feeling about the day. Sinking like the sun actually. I peered over my boots, down the fractured rock, and watched as the party of three guys behind us finished backing off to the glacier below.

Jana glanced up at the rest of the still very long-looking ridge and inquired, "Hey Wendy, would you feel OK if I said I didn't want to do any more leading?"

Hands shaking like aspen leaves in the up-coming autumn, I replied, "Oh, no problem, Jana. I think I can handle it."

Can this trip be saved?

Sure it could be saved; with only eleven more pitches, a midnight black hike out, and a couple of 1 AM phone calls back home. My partner back home had been eating chocolate and having diarrhea while contemplating calling mountain rescue.

Staggering into the 'North Winter' the day after Black Peak, I ran into Sharon, one of my least favorite female climbers. She is well known for telling women who came into the store asking about Women Climber's Northwest, that she didn't know if such a group existed. Sharon had of course been on our mailing list for two years before she scored a boyfriend to lead her up the hard stuff.

Responding to her question of what I'd been up to, I said, "Just got back from Black Peak at three o'clock this morning. Thought it was eight moderate fifth class pitches and ended up doing more than twice that many. But it was a beautiful day to be a slow party in the cascades."

"Yeah. I know, I was out too. We did a second ascent of Balanced Rock. It was about ten pitches. You know 5.9 to 5.11. Beautiful route, not too hard."

Can this climber be saved?! The last I heard she didn't lead rock at all because she "just liked following so much." So much for the concept that all female climbers are also feminists.

Back in the van, Harriet had indelicately pointed out that Alison only led 5.10 when clipping into bolts, and since she didn't know how to place pro, maybe she too could stand to lead a few 5.6's. Alison ignored Harriet's presence and amused us all by reading aloud the newspaper's latest work on the PTL Club scandal. (What does PTL stand for anyway . . . Pay The Lady?)

Speaking of sole saving, I remembered my expletives as I had once again contemplated a Devil's club thicket from the inside out. It all began innocently enough as I staggered off the plane from Japan, having just spent 70 days at sea on a Japanese research vessel. The 14 hour workdays, and all the chundering you could handle in between, had left me pretty trashed. It was Friday night of Labor Day weekend. My climbing partner greeted me at the terminal.

"I knew you'd be too tired for a three-day climbing trip, but don't worry. I've only planned a two-day one", she told me.

Friends were in from Colorado, I really had to go. A mere 1,000 vertical feet later, well into the Devil's Club and slide alder, the Coloradan peered at me through the wall-like vegetation. Though only 10 feet away I could barely make out her silhouette.

"Er, is this the kind of approach 'de rigeur' for the North Cascades?"

In fact we still had 3,000 more feet of the Devil to go, and it wasn't even raining yet. Folks from the lesser ranges sure do wimp out easily, I thought.

Can this trip be saved?

Conversation in the van now turned to food, one of my all-time favorable subjects. I asked the group, "How about an eating contest at the next Women Climber's Northwest climbing meet? You know, like the one's they write about in Climbing magazine."

This suggestion met with scowls of disapproval. Lana revived herself long enough to comment , "That's a terrible idea. You know how many women have problem with eating disorders. You'd just play to the worst side of women's psyches."

Alison seconded this opinion. "Yeah. I think that's a totally unhealthy idea. How about a beer drinking contest instead?"

"Yuck. How politically incorrect can you get?" remarked Jean.

Politically incorrect. Now there was an idea whose time was rampant. For example, politically correct skiing . . . thirteen years of conscientious face planting had not prepared me for the intricacies of this ethical philosophy.

It all began when Jean looked back over her shoulder at Margaret, diligently plodding up the slope behind us, and muttered, "Geez, she's ruining the line."

"Huh?" I inquired.

"Well, check it out girls, she's not following our tracks. She's makin' new ones that come right up the best line. Where's her ethics?"

I guessed Jean had a point, although later that day, and several arguments further along, I realized that we'd only scratched the surface of ski ethics. I stood, poised with fear, on the leading edge of what I believed to be a 5.11 face plastered with snow. I was so busy trying to remember how to calm my breath that I barely heard the directions shouted at me. (Do you count the in breaths or the out breaths?)

"Hey, Goldilocks, be SURE you eight my tracks!"

I ate her tracks? Huh? What had she said? Can I take up parachuting to save my ass on this Suredeathslope?

Full of questions I leapt through the cornice and poured down the slope. The slope ended up looking like a daisy chain with small pox, and I was soundly remonstrated for making far too many divots.

Can this trip be saved?

One thing all my friends agree about is that I am the local guru of bad taste. I swung the van into an IHOP for a caffeine refill and introduced my most promising social event of the week.

"Gang, this is it! A contest to see who can be the most politically incorrect! We'll have it at our April women's climbing meet—absolutely no holds barred."

Everyone had good ideas for entrants in this category. First of all we'd have it at the Peshastin Pinnacles, (now closed). Riding a three-wheeler up the sickly eroded trail to the base of the climbs would start the event off. Climbing in hair curlers, and a ghetto blaster with Barry Manilow at full volume were suggested. Of course an easily offensive entrant would be to bring a guy along, and it was clear that the grosser the guy the more points you'd rack up. I suggested seeing how many bolts we could fit on Porpoise, the classic 5.4 beginner's crack. At that point the girls decided we might have to have some kind of limits.

By now we were rolling up to the Canadian customs window and I thought of my last trip to Canada.

It's not everyone who'd choose to spend their vacation looking like a gortex bag lady. But, lo, I had heard the call of ice climbing. Alison and I had rounded up technical equipment from 17 of our closest climbing buddies, and buzzed up to Banff. Now Alison is the only northwest mountaineer who doesn't like to ski, but I assured myself it would help keep me off the fantastic Rockies powder and into the serious business of ice climbing. Four miles of postholding up a beautiful ski track to a frozen snot-like smear that was "just off the road," and I began to look around for another climbing partner.

Can this trip be saved?

Not to worry, two weeks in the Yosemite of Ice along the Banff-Jasper highway would not reveal a single other female ice maiden. "Sigh." But, learn to ice climb we did. Liz led on up the first day while I read aloud a technical article on how to place ice screws. Two weeks later our ropes looked like somebody had danced the flamenco in crampons on them, but we returned to Seattle victorious and convinced that we had finally achieved the elusive quality of being true Hard Women.

I wheeled the van down the tiny lane and into the parking lot for Little Smoke Bluffs. Now came my least favorite part of any climbing trip. The repartee of the car was over, and the successful glow of having lead my first pitch was still a long way off. In between lay a wasteland of nervous chatter, gear sorting procrastination, and genuine always harder than I remembered it, rock climbing. But I smiled to myself. Unlike most of the others in the van, I possessed the iron clad snobbism of a true northwest alpine climber. Someone who had put in the hard years of apprenticeship that I had learning techniques for brush, ice, snow, crevasses, bears, eight-month long rain would surely be excused a few muttered curses on a low-lying crag, being merely in training for the greater ranges.

Wendy Roberts is a biologist with a degree from Mt. Holyoke College in Massachusetts. She ice climbs throughout the Canadian Rockies and has an ascent of Mount Hunter's west ridge (northern spur) to her credit. Her work as a biologist is far reaching, as her avocations. She has studied alpine meadows in Colorado and the behavior of seals in such locations as the Bering Sea and New Zealand.

No Spare Rib

Rosie Andrews

"I have long believed that physical fitness is the key to woman's emancipation. All over the country women are loosening their girdles, and tightening their abdomens."

Olga Connolly, Olympic Gold—Medallist, Discus, 1956.

The Advent of Hard Women Rock Climbers

While rock climbing has always been male dominated, in the past ten years the involvement of women has increased dramatically. The achievements of the most dedicated and talented women climbers indicate that in rock climbing women have found a sport in which equal status is well within reach. An article published recently in a British climbing magazine stated that women in the U.K. are currently climbing at a standard set by men twenty years ago. Probably this statement is more a reflection of ignorance of women's actual achievements than truth. Generally only those who choose to be vocal about their accomplishments gain recognition for them. Certainly it is far from true in the U.S. While men continue to push the limits of the sport, women are making great strides towards closing the gap.

For men raised in a traditional western culture, learning to lead requires the application of skills closely related to his male heritage. While he may never have seen climbing hardware or have been aware that people climb rock faces, he has generally been encouraged to perform physically, problem-solve, take risks, compete, and learn to rely on himself. These aspects of male socialization provide a foundation that helps instill confidence as he enters into a new, risk-laden sport. Obviously not every western male has had an identical upbringing, but these are traits, which are generally fostered and respected, in the major institutions where socialization takes place.

Women, on the other hand, have been groomed for a very different role. Girls are usually more sheltered and protected, with little emphasis on risk taking. Rather than being prepared for independence, we learn to expect to play a supporting role, which hinges upon reliance on others. Physically active little girls often earn the label "tomboy," and are encouraged to participate in more feminine activities. Thus, for many women, excelling in a sport like rock climbing means going against the grain of social experience, and learning to overcome obstacles created by growing up female.

When I began to climb regularly, in 1978, there were very few other women climbers in the northeastern United States. As a result, I began to develop a reputation as a good "woman" climber, while leading at a standard long since surpassed by men, about 5.8 to 5.9. While the attention was somewhat flattering, there seemed to me to be a flaw inherent in my receiving recognition for something so unremarkable in terms of what was taking place in the sport. The overall impression was that I was doing something remarkable, "for a woman." News traveled of women climbing at a much higher standard in other parts of the country: Coral Bowman was doing difficult 5.11 leads in Colorado and elsewhere. Beverly Johnson soloed El Cap's Dihedral Wall, but they were mythical Western figures, unseen in the more provincial world of eastern climbing. Barbara Devine was perhaps the best known woman who had done hard climbs in the East, but she had relocated in the Midwest.

Six years later, the picture has changed considerably. Female climbing teams are no longer an unusual sight. While women remain well outnumbered by male climbers, those who are good have gained the respect of the climbing community on a more equal basis. At times there have been four or five women climbing at the Shawangunks, all of who lead 5.11 or better. In all major U.S. areas, women have established themselves solidly in the 5.11 grade, and a few outstanding climbers have come far closer to the top of the scale. Visiting Australian climber Louise Shepherd's list of accomplishments included difficult routes in excellent style at many major areas when she toured the Western U.S. in 1982. Among her noteworthy ascents were the Yosemite climbs Tales of Power (5.12b, 1 fall), Separate Reality (5.12b, no falls), and Crimson Cringe (5.12a, 1 fall). Californian Lynn Hill has helped to establish a different perception of women in climbing through her impact on the sport. While attending college in New Paltz, where the

Shawangunks are located, she had done many of the area's hardest climbs, including Supercrack (5.13) and Vandals (5.12). The fact that Lynn has only climbed sporadically over the past two years makes these ascents even more impressive.

The beauty of climbing lies in the variety of skills it requires, and the unique way in which each climb draws upon those skills. The top-level climber exhibits physical and psychological control through movement, problem solving, and maintaining composure under pressure. Because each climb is different, there is no single key to top performance. There is simply a grade, within which many climbs exist, each of which demands varying degrees of strength, technical skill, and commitment. This lack of constants plays a large role in keeping climbing interesting, since failure or success on one climb is no guarantee of similar results on the next. It is also a factor which favors women's participation, since specific features of body type can be as much an advantage as a disadvantage. For example, while women are often hampered by a lack of reach, we also tend to have smaller hands and fingers, a definite aid on thin cracks or small face holds. Thus a natural balancing exists which is lacking in many sports which emphasize traits such as large size, where men have the obvious advantage.

An accurate portrayal of women's participation in rock climbing today is to consider the two major elements of the sport separately. Do women have the potential physical ability to climb the hardest route, and do women have the psychological strength to actualize their physical potential?

The physical portion of this inquiry is more easily addressed. In general, differences in athletic performance between men and women are due to differences in body size and composition. The capacities of the energy systems of the woman are less than those of their male counterpart, and the absolute strength (power) of females is about two–thirds that of males. Physiology has a tremendous impact on women's performance in sports such as running, basketball, football, any arena where size, maximal aerobic power, and absolute strength determine the winner, but in rock climbing, the importance of many of these factors is minimized by the nature of the sport.

While women fall short in absolute strength compared to men, with training they can develop a high strength to weight ratio. The strength needed by the climber is determined largely by physical stature. Lynn Hill, for example, weighs 105 pounds, probably twenty to forty pounds less than even the trimmest of her male counterparts. Women do have a higher proportion of body fat, but this is a characteristic that varies greatly on an individual basis. In a series of experiments conducted in the laboratory, J.

Wilmore, a board member of the American College of Sports Medicine, concluded that for the three major components of athletics, strength, endurance, and body composition (lean/fat ratio), the differences between the best female and male athletes are few. However, because many women do not begin any kind of athletic training program until much later than the average male, relative strength gains are often greater in females than males, following similar weight resistance training programs.

In general, women are considered to have better balance and flexibility than men do when they start climbing. This tendency, coupled with a shortage of strength, often helps women to develop better style and technique in their early climbing experiences. Since use of the feet is critical to compensate for a lack of power, the woman who becomes seriously involved in climbing often has superior technique to complement the strength she gains through climbing and training. Men often face a different task, and must learn how to conserve strength, rather than rely on it.

In reality, the physical limitations on women rock climbers seem to be relatively insignificant. Every handicap seems to have an advantageous counterpart. Given the lack of absolutes in the game, women need only capitalize on their strong points and work on their weak ones to hold their own with the best. Undoubtedly women would be at a disadvantage were climbing ever to become a competitive sport in categories like "World Fist Crack Champion." By the same token, females might well set the standard on slabs and thin cracks. Climbing is climbing, and the major components of the sport remain the same, regardless of the gender of the climber. As we all know, the rock really doesn't care. What matters is that particular blend of qualities the individual brings to the sport. The talents that distinguish the best are both physical and mental. Any seasoned climber recognizes the role positive thinking plays in extending personal limits. For many of us it is the primary source of our addiction. When I am climbing at my best, the only voice getting air time in my internal dialogue is clear and confident. I am convincing myself of my ability to succeed. That other pest, "The Confidence Eroder," scourge of my ambitions, ("It's a long reach, you'll take a forty footer. . .") is held in check, mute. Unfettered by doubt or fear, my body is free to interpret a climb with grace and finesse.

The problem is getting there. Some people no matter how much they climb. never really seem to relax. Others appear blessed with perpetual calm. Women as a rule struggle far more to make the break-through to that state where the inner voice rings with confidence. So while some women are setting a very high standard for their contemporaries. most continue to be hindered from achieving their physical best by an inability to break through the fear barrier. The major reasons for this all find their roots in culture.

An understanding of the traditional female role in western culture helps to shed light on the difficulty women hive taking risks. The roles customarily reserved for women did not require the development of many of the psychological components which earmark the skilled climber. Child rearing anti homemaking are tasks which are rooted in dependence a state which requires far different traits than the more autonomous male roles of provider and protector. Children learn at an early age which behavior patterns are rewarded and receive adult approval and they strive to please.

In a study conducted with schoolchildren in the U.S. (Deck, et al, 1978) the concept of "learned helplessness", the reduction of effort because failure seems certain was examined. Girls were found to avoid academically difficult problems far more often than boys. because they feared failure, and the ensuing loss of teacher approval. In addition following a failure experience girls proved more likely to attribute their lack of success to an innate deficiency while boys explained failure in terms of controllable factors such its lack of effort or a mistake. In fact, academically difficult problems are not the only ones which little girls learn to avoid. In general, girls learn to shy away from situations in which the outcome is uncertain and to stay within the confines of what they can do well. The neatness, docility, and passivity for which girls are rewarded would be considered deviant for a boy, who is encouraged to be more assertive and self-determining.

This contrast between male and female socialization is manifested clearly in the difference between male and female climbing styles. I learned a great deal from an early climbing partner who was a little short on technique but big on bravery. He would throw himself at a problem, pass the point of retreat, and somehow shake and thrash his way upward to the top. Though he often scared me, his drive to succeed seemed somehow to render him oblivious to the danger of the situation (often real). and allow him to jump in and go for broke. I tended toward a more cautious (female) approach smoothly. dancing my way to the point where real commitment seemed inevitable, then beating a hasty retreat. Though I outshone my partner technically. his record of success outweighed my own.

Women climbers are often renowned for their style the grace and finesse with which they execute moves. One friend commented to me that the first time he watched a good woman climber was a real learning experience for him. Her apparent effortlessness alerted him to a side of the sport he'd been missing while relying on his strength to get him up climbs. The problem is that maintaining such tight control makes it difficult to climb near one's physical limit. Many women are held back in their climbing by an inability to push past the point where all is reversible and risk the consequences, even when the actual risk is relatively low. While many men who become involved in climbing seem to thrive on tying in and trying climbs just barely within the realm of their physical ability, their female counterparts shy away from making such commitments, preferring to wait until they feel certain they can do the climb "in good style," i.e., *without falling*.

The willingness to be a bold, aggressive risk-taker is a trait fostered by experience. Freely entering into a new risk-laden situation is a supreme act of confidence in oneself. It is an indication, that the individual believes he has the skills necessary to deal with whatever comes up and to succeed in his pursuit. If more women want to develop sufficient skill to be recognized and respected as "climbers'," rather than "women climbers". confidence is the quality which must be cultivated, for it is the key element underlying any calculated risk-taking. While men are inclined to estimate their capabilities realistically or even a little high, women climbers often doubt their readiness for a given route despite plenty of evidence to the contrary. Many women demonstrate, through a lack of confidence, reserves of energy far beyond what a climb would require by hanging around unable to commit to the difficulties of the route. Unfortunately, failing under such circumstances only serves to undermine belief in one's ability even further.

For many women, a desire to excel in climbing may represent one of the first confrontations with the need to learn to take risks. Though the motivation to do so may be strong, lack of experience can make it far more difficult to assess one's true capabilities. The resultant inner conflict ("I think I can do it/But what if I'm wrong?") can create ambivalence towards one's goal, and prompt an avoidance of risk altogether. While men undoubtedly experience anxiety as well they are subject to more outside pressure to conform to the male norm (take the lead, be aggressive and confident), and compete with their peers. Fitting into the culturally prescribed role becomes a source of motivation which can help offset fear of failure or injury.

Women, on the other hand, have a fairly acceptable escape at this juncture. The supportive role for which women have been groomed is readily available in the position of permanent second. Assuming this function reduces the risk element and the anxiety it generates while allowing involvement in climbing to continue. The fact that many women are introduced to climbing by male friends who are already far more experienced seems to further this trend. While most men eventually experience an urge to get on the sharp end (be autonomous/independent) and get involved with the "real" climbing, many women have the opposite reaction, and decide they would "never want to lead." Women who do take the role of second for an extended period often find the transition to leading very difficult. Despite great technical skill and strength they fall apart leading at two or three grades below what they can follow with ease.

Every individual must determine their own goals and ambitions in climbing, and there is no standard of success which subsumes the personal one. Undoubtedly there are climbers male and female, who derive tremendous satisfaction from following climbs. and there is nothing inherently wrong with this state of affairs. What is most important is that the individual has the opportunity to realize his true. potential. I remember clearly a time in my past when I wanted very much to he a competent climber, but experienced great turmoil 'in trying to realize that goal. I would mentally prime myself to lead a climb only to relinquish my lead, in relief and despair. when fear began to whittle away my resolve. Interestingly, it was often the faith my male friends had in me, and their prodding, that got me over these hurdles insisting that I take my pitch when I would have willingly backed down.

Given the impact of culture. male/female partnerships, particularly those involving couples often make it more difficult for women to develop initially as climbers. This is especially true when there is a big gap in ability and experience. Under such conditions, with the male more experienced it is only natural that he should take more control of the situation, make the decisions,. and deal with the complications that arise. Yet in order to develop the skills necessary to being a confident, competent leader, one needs the experience of getting into and out of real situations, without the sense that there is always someone else to rely on. If the tables were turned, with the female climber far more experienced, there would probably be an initial sense of dependence, but the drive to be in charge of one's own destiny would eventually enable him to function as an equal. By contract, a woman will at times acquiesce and allow the man to make decisions even in situations where she is clearly more knowledgeable.

An additional complication that just as women have difficulty giving up the tendency to rely upon men, men struggle with a feeling: of responsibility for, and tendency to protect their female friends. One friend's boyfriend told her, "I'd never forgive myself if something happened to you." Such reaction is a natural outgrowth of the role for which most men have been trained. In the company of another male friend, responsibility is more easily shared, with each climber looking after himself. But in mixed company, especially when romance is involved, the situation can become far more complex, particularly if the woman is struggling with her own inclination to he dependent.

I once witnessed an incredible example of such role confusion, involving two intelligent friends, a couple, both experienced climbers. When she got to a point of leading her climb where she felt stuck she began to panic and lose faith in her ability to cope with the situation. Rather than tell her to calm down and cope, he attempted to effect a rescue by dangling his leg (!) from his position ten feet above her on a neighboring climb (this despite the fact that he was well above rather shaky protection himself). She chose to go for the leg reached it and fell off anyway adding about fifteen feet to her fall. Although this little drama has been the source of great hilarity among us, it was and remains remarkably telling. What on earth were they thinking? Obviously their responses were far more emotional than cerebral, or the situation would have never taken place. In his desire to protect someone he loved, he lost control of his senses. She chose to let him take charge when things got too committing. In fact, she encouraged him, by appearing to be unable to handle the situation.

Because such dynamics are so deeply ingrained in all of us, many women find that climbing with other women can be an important part of learning to climb well. In 1982, Jill Lawrence, a British climber, and I sent a questionnaire to women climbers in the U.S., asking about their experiences in rock climbing. In response to the question, "Is climbing with other women important to you?", twenty-six of thirty women responded yes. The primary reasons cited were companionship, a greater sense of equality, and a higher degree of self-reliance in the company of other women. Most women felt that more valuable experience was gained in making decisions and taking charge, in situations in which they could not rely on men.

Once sufficient experience is gained most women feel they can return to mixed partnerships on a much more equal footing. Regardless of gender the most successful teams seem to share an even ability and drive. A sizable ability gap between partners seems to hold little value for the less experienced person after a reasonable apprenticeship. It undermines one's sense of accomplishment to do all ant intimidating lead with a belayer who could solo past in sneakers at any time and it only furthers a sense of dependency to stay in a partnership in which the other person s skills are always superior. While the less experienced team is perhaps in a little more danger, it is only through a reasonable acceptance of risk that one can learn what one needs to know.

What does all this mean then, for the woman learning to climb in the next five or ten years? Despite the constraints imposed by culture, there is ample evidence that it is only a question of time before women keep pace with the standards of the day. Men and women are becoming increasingly aware of the benefits of equal status, and awareness is one of the cornerstones of change. Women in the United States today are benefiting to a large extent from the Women's Movement of the 60's and 70's, with far more opportunity to participate as equals in society. Women's Sports are being taken more seriously so that women like Lynn Hill (now 22) can come to climbing at age 16 with a well-developed positive, athletic image, and few mental barriers to achieving her physical best. The words female and athlete no longer seem a contradiction in terms.

Matina Horner, the psychologist, wrote of the development transition in early adulthood marked by change from definition of self by others to becoming self-defining. In males this transition takes place by the time he leaves school (18 years old). In females of our parents' generation, it was postponed until age 50, in the present generation until age 27. As women learn to be more self-defined at an earlier age the demands of climbing will pose less of a threat. Meanwhile, women can learn from men, and recognize the value of the male's ability to take calculated risks and push personal limits. On a very basic level, many women could do more to develop their strength, train harder, sweat more, be more willing to dedicate time to getting into top shape. We can try to recognize more clearly the sources of self-doubt and work to overcome attitudes which are self-defeating by consciously seeking experiences which build confidence and self-reliance. Men can play an important role in encouraging their women friends by not expecting less from them or fostering dependency.

As the best women climbers continue to strive for higher goals, they set standards by which other women can measure their performance, and remove the need for recognition as a good woman climber. In reality, the margin separating the best male and female climbers today is already fairly slim. Setting a separate lower standard only encourages women to expect less of themselves than their abilities allow. Accomplishments should be measured in relation to the sport, not one's gender, and women should not expect public praise for doing routes done by men ten years ago.

In May of 1982, I was with a friend in Yosemite, discussing the role of women in climbing. He stated that although some women might get very good, they would never be as good as men, able to do the *really* hard climbs. Four months ago, the same friend said to me in reference to Lynn Hill, "She's as good as anybody, as good as Moffatt, or.... (he listed several of the best known men). While many undoubtedly would choose to argue this point, it indicated to me a shift in attitude which the impact of women is creating. Once women truly understand their potential in this sport, the only limits to performance will be what is humanly possible.

> Rosie Andrews is one of America's leading women rock climbers, and amongst the first to subscribe to top fitness to all climbers.
> She has worked as an instructor for Outward Bound Leadership School, Outdoor Program specialist at the University of Vermont, and as a manager of *Rock and Snow*, a climbing shop in New Paltz, New York.
> She was one of the owners and a director of Sheer Adventure, a rock climbing guide and lecture service.

Post Cards

Sue Giller

March 24,1982

Dear Molly:

We're seven days into the trek now, and my legs have finally recuperated from all the up and down hiking. Somewhere I read that we gain 40,000 feet and lose 30,000 feet in the 120 miles to Namche Bazaar. If I had known that earlier, I'm not sure I would have come.

So far, all goes so well that it's almost scary. We managed to get all of our equipment through Delhi and the Nepali customs with no hassles and a minimum of expense. Once in Kathmandu, we spent a week buying last-minute food, meeting our Sherpa staff, and packing for the trek. The team has been operating superbly—so far all I've had to do is play bara sahib with a few government officials. Tough life! It's good to be back in Nepal again with such a beautiful mountain as our goal. Wish you were here.

April 15, 1982

Dear Molly:

I'm sitting in Base camp, eating dessert (pop corn) and waiting for the evening radio call, to hear how things have gone today up on the mountain. We arrived here (at 16,100 feet) on April 3rd after fifteen days of trekking. The trail follows the same route that traders have used for centuries in trading with Tibet. Indians and Nepalis would travel up to Namche Bazaar (12,000 feet) with lowland items (rice, sugar, spices, cloth) to trade with the highland Tibetans in Namche.

Our trip has been like a journey into the past, as I doubt the lives of the villagers in this region have changed all that much over the past decades and centuries. It is spring here now, and everyone is out in the fields working on the planting. The lowland terraces are being prepared for the rice planting, which will commence with the onset of the monsoon rains in late May. The men and boys are plowing with their water buffalo, while the women are repairing the terraces and their walls. Although some mustard plants and early vegetables are poking through the soil, the land is generally brown and looks barren. I can remember trekking into climb during the late monsoon several years ago. The fields were lush and green, and I felt as though I were inside a giant greenhouse with water and foliage all around. When we came out in October, the rice and wheat had all ripened and the fields were a golden yellow. Now, in contrast, the land seems so dull.

The trail winds up and down, traversing along the edges of fields and going right through the villages. We got a very good look at the life of the inhabitants, and I now appreciate all the more my home in Boulder, with its running water, electricity, and all those things we tend to take for granted in an industrialized society. These Nepalis lead such a rough, physical life, working from dawn to dusk to support a subsistence-level lifestyle, and prey to all sorts of low-grade diseases. The mortality rate for children up to age nine is apparently 50% in some districts, an awesome percentage. Wood is so scarce now after years of over cutting that it often requires a long day's expedition by the entire family to gather a week's supply of fuel. Many homes are perched on steep hillsides in the middle of the fields, necessitating a one- or two-hour trip for water each day. We saw women grinding wheat by hand. They use large sticks that they bounce up and down in a mortar containing the grain, much like a butter churn with wheat in it. After several hours of this they produce a rough flour used to make chapittis, the flat, unleavened bread tortillas they serve with rice and lentils.

But in spite of this hard life, the people seem to retain a great supply of cheerfulness and friendliness. They sometimes invited us into their homes for tea and potatoes. The porters who carried all of our food and equipment, many of whom are farmers working to pick up a little extra money during slack time in their seasonal work cycle, chattered away with us at the shared rest stops, using limited English and much laughing and gesturing. Even though by their terms we are carrying a fortune in rupees with us, I never feel physically threatened by any of the people I meet here. I think this basic cheerfulness and ease is to a large extent why I've always enjoyed my trips to Nepal so much.

We reached Namche Bazaar, the "chapaty" of the Sherpa people, on March 31. There we traded our lowland porters for hearty, acclimated yaks, and then continued on to base camp. We settled on a sandy beach here, in a small dell formed by several grassy moraines. A small pond provides water and reflects a magnificent view of Ama Dablam and our route. We call the camp Ama Dablam Beach.

We've been working on the mountain for eleven days and seem to be moving along relatively well, although I am getting more and more concerned about the weather. During the first week we had a few showers, but recently we've been getting consistent afternoon snow squalls, and the route has begun accumulating snow. This isn't too bad for the section to Camp I, mostly a long boulder field with little exposure or other hazard beyond a slip with a heavy pack into a hole between two rocks. But the route to Camp II follows a narrow rock ridge and gingerly traverses several steep slabs. They get very slippery, and even with fixed ropes I'm worried about how awkward they might become. A broken leg from a fall on wet rock would necessitate a tricky rescue. Still, I have a great deal of faith in the team members—they were all chosen for their technical capabilities and mountain experience as well as their compatibility.

Another one of my concerns as leader and tactician is the effect the snow is having on the effort to push the route above Camp II. Steep ice slabs predominate there with one rock pitch. I had expected we would take about three days and we still haven't reached the Mushroom Ridge. I originally had Shari, Susan and Stacy fixing lines on this section, but I've asked Lucy and Jini to go up to help with the support, because Shari had said the carries up the rock section were so tiring, and they were all feeling the altitude. Heidi, Anne, and I carried the last load up to Camp II today and came down to base camp to save food higher on the mountain, so laboriously carried up there, and to await word of when Camp III has been established. We will then go back up to Camp II in support of the first summit team.

However, our slowness and these persistent showers potentially create a major problem. We have only so much food for use on the mountain. So if a storm comes in and holds us up for any length of time, or drives us off the mountain for awhile, then I may be forced into a position of having to choose a summit team of only one or two pairs out of the team of eight equal climbers. The rest of us might never get a chance at the summit afterwards. This is a decision I do not want to make. When I accepted Annie's offer to take over the leadership of this trip, I knew I might eventually end up in this position of doling out the prize of the summit to a select few, but I never really understood what such a decision entailed emotionally. How can I make choices among eight healthy, motivated women who have worked for over a year towards one very distinct end? What criteria should I use to pick the lucky two or four who get a chance at the summit?

Indeed, I never really comprehended beforehand how much being the expedition leader would effect my participation in the climb. Certainly on my last two trips to the Himalaya I saw two distinctly different styles of leadership. I was often critical of how certain things were handled, and I thought of how I might handle those situations myself (better, of course). Now that I personally feel the burden of leadership, I begin to see how it changes the perspective of the leader about what is taking place on the trip. I am no longer just "one of the gang" but am an embodiment of some un-named and unearned "authority," both within the group and to the Sherpas and the Nepalese government. I can no longer act only on my own desires. There is something here much bigger than me.

When talking with Annie on the phone and considering her offer to lead the climb, I thought that my job would largely entail logistics—all those de-tailed lists of equipment and food, budget projections, and timetables for the movement of people and material on the mountain. Yet I never predicted how all-consuming this attention to logistics would become. I now feel like a mobile computer whose main function is to see that the correct load is at the correct camp in proper time to be used by camps above—i.e., to have the tents for Camp III taken to Camp II soon enough to be moved on when needed, but not taken up too early, thereby displacing another load that would be needed at that camp sooner. Fortunately we only have three camps, so this organizing is relatively easy compared to the six camps on a bigger mountain. Still, I have already redone my charts three or four times. Due to my own perfectionism, I find the mountain has become a logistics ladder that I am trying to have the expedition ascend in as perfect a manner as possible. In this narrowing of horizons, I now realize, I have lost all per-sonal drive to climb the mountain. I no longer care if I reach the summit at all, and this dismays me.

If I had to answer that silly question, "WHY?," I would say that I climb mainly for three reasons. One is for the enjoyment of using my maximal physical and mental abilities to overcome the physiological and psychologi-cal problems presented by a climb. Another is for the exciting and magical positions I can reach, such as a small ledge 2000 feet up a granite wall or a snowfield 20,000 feet up a large mountain that drops off thousands of feet around me, knowing that I am at a place few people ever reach, enjoying a view shared only with the mountain gods and that special breed of people who are climbers. Lastly I climb for the camaraderie shared by these fellow climbers, fostered by the shared joys and dread encountered in the intense interdependencies of ropemates. On this trip, however, I seem to have lost touch with all of these rewards, and am instead absorbed by logistics. Because of my self-imposed perceptions of "leadership" and "the role of the leader," I find myself experiencing this trip in a totally different way from any of my other big expeditions.

I am extremely concerned with maintaining the elan of the team—its spirit and unity as a force helping us work together for the summit. As one of the climbers on other trips, I also worried about the sense of unity within the team, but I usually felt it was not my "job" to try to maintain this unity, other than during my own one-on-one interactions with the other climbers. If, for example, there were bad feelings between two climbers, I always felt that it was the responsibility of the leader to straighten out the problem. Well, here I am, the leader, and I begin to see this is no small task. As you know, Molly, I am not the world's most communicative person, but I feel that the answer to resolving intergroup problems lies in open communications. It is the role of the leader to expedite discussions and to help relieve tensions by serving as a channel for the exchange of feelings among people.

The other day, Lucy and I were making a carry from I to II and we ended up traveling together. We talked about a lot of things, including the difficulty of the route, the best way to rig the fixed lines, how everyone was feeling about the food and each other, and what Lucy felt about the climb and the others. Normally, as a team member, I would just voice my own opinions, enjoy the time as a good gossip session, and not really think about the comments other than how they applied to me personally. This time, however, I found myself analyzing every comment, searching for insight into how team members were feeling. I kept wondering: how does this effect the group overall? Should I worry about so-and-so not liking someone else? What can I do about it? Are these comments signs of unhappiness and discontent with the operations of the trip or just normal grousing? How will all of this effect the achievement of the summit, our success as an expedition? Will Lucy take what I say as just a comment from a fellow climber, or will it be The Leader speaking? We were no longer just two friends talking.

In order to make decisions that involve the whole team, I find that I want to know what each climber thinks about the progress of the climb, what her desires and ambitions are in regards to leading and climbing, and who wants to climb (or not) with whom. And I feel that I must subordinate all of my own desires to those of the team, to help maintain group unity and not be accused of misusing my authority. The only way that I have been able to successfully perform this role of group moderator has been to withdraw myself to a reserved position some distance from the team and to try and maintain an overall view of the group and events. This has often caused me to feel somewhat isolated from the team—almost a "them and me" polarization. This is not to say that the others treat me so differently, but that I perceive the world differently because of these self-imposed tasks I feel I must assume to be a "good leader."

Well, enough introspection for one night. As you can see, I'm a little down, but I'm sure things will look better when we finally reach Camp III and I can see some chance of success for the team. Overall I am enjoying the trip immensely and am glad to be on this beautiful mountain with such a compatible group of people.

Dear Molly:

Well, we made it! I can't believe it—we actually got everyone to the top. I always thought it was possible to get all of us up, but I didn't dare expect it—someone usually gets sick or loses her drive for the summit. In fact, it was with this loss in mind that I decided on a team of eight instead of six, even though I thought six was a better number for the trip. I figured if one or two dropped out, then four people would be a little too few to assure safety of for the summitting attempt. But this is a great group and it has shown all along. As these trips go, I can't imagine a smoother one.

Ever since we began gathering the equipment and funds, I've felt the unity and drive of the team. We have been able to stay well within our budget, to avoid losing equipment during the long trek, and to remain in good health. The climb itself was nothing short of miraculous. We were only four days off my most optimistic logistics plan; no one was hurt; we had just the right amount of gear and food; and the weather, for all of its threatening at a critical time, held off just long enough for us to climb the mountain.

After my last letter to you, we continued to have those afternoon showers, but the big storm never really materialized. Maybe all my worrying about it did some good. Shari said she never was really concerned about the storms, and didn't see why I kept making a big fuss. But, of course, she is from the Northwest.

Finally, three days past schedule, Shari, Lucy, Susan, and Stacy set up Camp III on the glacier. Once they arrived there, I knew we would get at least two people up and that I no longer needed to worry about the team making the summit. The rest of us moved up to Camp II and we were able to watch the others through binoculars all day as they climbed towards the summit. They seemed to take forever to inch their way up the snowfields, but we finally saw them disappear onto the summit about 3:30 P.M. Then, of course, all we had to worry about was their getting down safely. We had an especially heavy storm that evening, and I finally went to bed at 8:30 with the radio on, anxiously awaiting a call. I could imagine them out in the dark, being coated by the snow, headlamps searching into the void below, slowly and meticulously setting up their rappel anchors and easing themselves down. I hate repelling in the dark, and I didn't envy them the chore even though it was a result of having reached the summit. Finally, at 9:20, Shari came on the radio to announce they were all tired but safe.

Then for the first time on the trip, I felt free to worry only about myself and my ambitions. As an expedition, we were now a success, having placed some climbers on the summit. Therefore any decisions I made in the next few days would no longer affect this success, and would only affect my own personal achievement of reaching the top.

We went up to Camp III the next day, passing the other four on their way down. The day was clear, with no snow, and I took that as a good omen. The first team members looked tired and sunburned, but quietly pleased with themselves. They told us the climbing wasn't difficult, just long, and I mentally girded myself for the physical effort it would entail, trying to regain some personal drive and ambition for the summit. I felt I was just drifting along on the impetus created by the others, aiming for a goal that was a reality for me.

We were up at 3 A.M. the next morning, determined to get going before daybreak. Molly, you've done enough morning starts with me to know what a joy I am before 10 A.M., but I found myself beginning to get excited at last, and I had no trouble rousing myself in time and even eating some awful granola. After the usual wrestling match (four people stuffed into one tent trying to get dressed into the correct clothing without putting an elbow into their neighbor's eye), I stumbled out the door and began buckling on my technical gear. The night sky was dotted with brilliant stars that cast enough starlight to illuminate all the mountains around us and leave the valleys below in shadow. For me, early dawn is such a mystical time to be on a mountain, knowing that the world is asleep at my feet, and knowing that I am about to go where few people ever go. I enjoy that feeling of isolation from the rest of the world, with a single clear goal before me; that paradox of total self-sufficiency yet dependence on my climbing partner.

We finally moved out about 5 A.M., and worked our way up the firm, frozen snow. The climb was basically easy, and we moved along steadily. Unfortunately, clear weather was not our fate. We climbed into thickening fog and snow as we gained altitude, and became totally socked in by 11 A.M. Anne and I reached the summit about 1:15, with Heidi and Jini arriving an hour later. By then it was snowing heavily and we dashed off back down. I was not excited about being on the summit. It looked like any other snowfield in a snow storm. Mostly, I was just glad to be finished moving upward.

We got back to Camp III about 7 P.M. after two rappels in the dark. Thank goodness the first team had marked their rappel anchors—nothing like looking for a little red flag waving in the dark trying to signal you to its haven of security.

The next day we took down the camp and retreated to Camp II and into the worse storm of the climb. My vacation from responsibility was over. As I went down, I could feel myself beginning to reluctantly take on again the cloud of decisions yet to be made to finish the climb: how to safely clear equipment off the mountain, who would be strong enough to help, how to get everything packed up for the return to Kathmandu, what to pay the Sherpas and how much of a bonus to give them, how much cash we would need to clear our debts in Nepal. But, I knew that we had succeeded in my ultimate desire—a Sherpaless ascent of a big, technical mountain with everyone reaching the summit. So worries such as these seemed small.

When we finish all of these details and officially end the expedition, Anne, Shari, Lucy and I are going up to the Everest Basecamp to take a look at the West Ridge. Anne is on an expedition to climb that route in the fall of 1983 and Shari, Lucy and I are considering applying to become team members. It will be fun to travel just as four friends, each of us responsible only for ourselves, and I look forward to the excitement of seeing a part of Nepal new to me.

My perception of events on this climb has been so different from climbs where I was just a team member that I hope I never lead another one. I don't like the feeling of isolation and detachment I have felt on this trip, and I doubt that I could ever change my nagging demand for perfection in details that causes me so much anguish at times. Oh, to be a peon again, to be responsible for only one job, to be answerable for only my own ambitions and desires! I look forward on my next trip to losing myself in the anonymity of being "one of the gang" again.

Aug. 5, 1982

Dear Molly:

Your letter finally caught up with me, the one you sent to Nepal last April that I never received because I had already left the country. It arrived like a ghost from the past, asking all those questions and making all those comments months after our return. But with the perspectives of time, I find I can better answer some of those questions and better understand my feelings about the trip.

As I think I mentioned in some of my letters, I found being the leader a mixed blessing. When I accepted the leadership from Annie, I did so reluctantly, because I felt I didn't have enough experience to lead an expedition to a high mountain. But I wanted to climb Ama Dablam and I wasn't sure I could get on the trip if someone else became the leader. So I accepted figuring I could learn as I went along.

I must admit my ego didn't mind all those times I could say I was The Leader—the title always seems so impressive. In Nepal it definitely carried political and social clout, and I would get to (have to?) stand with the big names at any functions. For example, we had dinner at our sirdar's house in Namche Bazaar, and we were all given katas (white scarves given to guests as a sign of respect). The others all received the standard gauze ones, but I got a big silk one, just because I was the leader. I was even given a fancy teacup, especially for me. But as I discovered during the climb, these perks carry a price. I definitely felt isolated from the rest of the team, and this detachment detracted from my enjoyment of the trip. In fact, even now, months after the trip, I still don't know how the rest of the team feels about the climb. What do they tell their friends about their experience on the mountain? Did they have a good time? Did the trip go as they expected? I can guess what some of them would answer, but I still am not sure.

When people ask me how I feel about the success of the climb, getting everyone to the summit, I say I'm very pleased. But inside, there's a part of me that does not feel that success. Because I did no technical lead climbing, I feel as though I climbed the mountain through the efforts of the others. All I had to do was jumar the lines the others put in; I didn't really earn the summit. I can't even answer the question, "Was it hard?" Jumaring is just physical la-

Sue Giller

bor, and does not reveal if the leading was difficult. I know this is an irrational feeling, but it still detracts from my own personal sense of achievement.

And yet, for all these feelings, I basically had a very good time on the trip. I am still astonished at how smoothly it went, which I attribute in large measure to the experience and competence of the team. We all kept commenting on how little we had to say in our diaries, and that they were boring because of the lack of conflict to write about. Certainly we had some personal confrontations but they were minor compared to what I've seen (and read about) on other trips. In fact, Shari, Lucy and I decided to join Anne on the trip to Everest in 1983. Having tasted the power of being Leader, it may be hard to become just a team member again, but somehow I think I will be quite happy to join the gang and creatively second-guess the leader's decisions without having to pay a penalty for a mistake. Besides, I need all the summit drive I can muster if I hope to climb Everest.

Sue

Sue Giller is one of America's best female mountaineers. She has been part of three Everest expeditions, member of the all woman Dhaulaguri and Ama Dablam expeditions. She is a member of the American Alpine Club, holds a B. A. degree in chemistry from the University of Illinois and has done graduate work in analytic chemistry at M.I.T.

THE OTHER LOVE

LINDA GIVLER

Fifteen years ago I found the man with whom I wanted to share the rest of my life.

He was the most loving, wonderful human being that one could ever hope to meet. I didn't think at the time that perhaps our happiness had to do with two people interacting—I was very young and all I could see was strength and male beauty and kindness and FINALLY someone who really loved me and allowed me to express my feelings and returned my love without any restrictions. I gave myself completely to this person, shared my most intimate thoughts with him, and planned our lives together for ever and always, even taking vows that ended in *"till death do us part."* I shared this wonderful man with only one other woman.

I knew that I was as important to him as he was to me, but always in the background loomed that OTHER WOMAN, always there waiting for her turn to have him. And rather than resenting her, I too loved her. Sometimes we went to her together, and spent lovely days in the *Mountains* where this woman/mountain goddess lives. I felt that it was fair for him to visit her for periods of time, sometimes to teach a class of aspiring mountaineers, and sometimes to stay with her for the duration of an expedition to reach the top of a peak. But it was understood that she would always return him to me. That she would share this man who loved the high places. But, she cheated . . . she became greedy and she had to keep him for herself. Now I am alone, my dreams are dissolving and life has been very bleak indeed.

My husband was killed in a climbing accident ten years ago. It has been a long, difficult struggle to finally accept that he is gone, and that I am still here and that it is OK for me to continue living my life. And more important, that I can be happy again. Women, more than men, have traditionally had to deal with living as survivors. Men go to battle in one form or an-

Linda Givler

other, and often they do not come home. Women in the mountaineering community have recently begun to participate in more difficult and therefore more dangerous activities, but by and large more men than women venture off on trips of extreme difficulty. How does a woman learn to cope with the idea that her loved one may not come home from some trip, and what happens to her if that becomes a reality? I had been very aware of the possibility of Al Givler dying in the mountains, but like most of us, did not imagine for an instant that it would ever come to be. I still remember all too well the words that my dear friend said to me that day in June of 1977, "Linda, Dusan and Al won't be coming home"... so simply put, words that told me nothing yet found their way into my very inner self and triggered something inside of me that I did not know existed. From somewhere deep within me and from some place in the past of women who have experienced this before me came a scream of anguish that symbolized all that I felt then and in the years to come. I found it very comforting to have Louise Sumner there with me at this moment of first impact, but even then, in that indescribable state of mind, I wondered why she came forward from the group to tell me, and why the two men stayed in the background. Louise later told me that she felt she was strong enough to handle this situation; but she, too, has been haunted all of these years by the scream of sorrow and the silent plea that asked that this not be possible.

During the first few months that followed, Diana Jagerska—the wife of the second victim, Dusan Jagersky—and I became inseparable. It was strangely comforting to have another person who was experiencing the same agony with whom to share this sorrow. There was so much to do at first. We flew to Alaska, to Glacier Bay where the accident occurred, and brought with us climbing packs and gear so that we could go up to the mountain and bring these two "bad boys" home because, after all, the others must be wrong and really they were still alive. Flying into Glacier Bay National Monument and seeing the flag at half mast did not deter our thinking in the least little bit. "It's a holiday," I explained to Diana, "they always put the flag at half mast on holidays." Louise and Bill Sumner, who were accompanying us, must have been astounded at our thought process during this trip. Even when we saw Jim Wickwire and Steve Marts, the other two climbers—the survivors—and Jim and Lou Whittaker who had come up on their own to help search for the bodies, still we did not believe. Maybe the sight of the person with the black bag triggered something in me; it was then that I realized that he had in there small pieces of skin and bones and hair that used to be those two wonderful, very alive, human beings who should have been there, too. It seems you have to have such proof to issue a death certificate. We stayed in Glacier Bay for a few days, I think, and we were able to fly around the peak that robbed me of my reason for living. Even now I had to see that this was indeed a beautiful peak, I loved to look at it, I could feel the sense of excitement that they must have had to be the first ones to stand on her summit and feel that incredible sense of accomplishment at having achieved their goal. Then we flew around to the descent and I saw the four thousand foot drop that Al and Dusan went over, and this mountain goddess looked evil and menacing and it made me feel very angry that the place where they ended up was so forlorn looking. How odd a thought, really—does the spirit stay inside the body? I think not.

We returned home to Seattle. The rest of the City went back to living their usual lives, doing everyday things. For me it became an excruciating exercise to force myself out of bed in the morning. What was the point? For a while there were things to be done: arranging this and that, a memorial service which we held at Mt. Rainier National Park, the retrieval of the gear that had been left at base camp, writing to people who sent condolences, and the first viewing of the movie that Steve Marts made of the climb. Then what . . . . I returned to my summer job as a backcountry ranger, thinking that being in the mountains would be soothing and make me feel closer to Al. Fortunately, my friends took it to heart to spend time with me and seemed to have put together some network whereby, as one group hiked out, another group came into my camp and therefore I was not left alone in the woods. At the time it seemed very mysterious, but I later learned to appreciate this wonderful thoughtfulness.

Summer ended and I returned to the University to attempt to finish my studies in Forestry. That, too, had less meaning for me now. Al and I had planned that, during the summers, he would teach and guide while I worked as a backcountry ranger or perhaps helped instruct climbing. Reality began to creep back closer to me and I had to think about how in the world I was going to support myself on three months of work each year. It began to seem like I had to think seriously about planning a new future, even though I had no interest in thinking about such a thing if it meant planning a life alone.

The mountaineering community is a close knit group of people. This had been most comforting to both Diana and myself for about one year after Al and Dusan disappeared. However, we began to feel that perhaps we were being watched all too closely and that it might be time to try to find out what living was like again. In order for each of us to accomplish these goals, we had to get away from Seattle, our families, friends, and the memories that were everywhere we went. She left to be the base camp manager of the 1978 K-2 expedition, and I went to Grand Teton National Park in Wyoming to spend a summer as a ranger.

I felt that I wanted to try to live again, and I knew that I was excruciatingly lonely for my husband. Since it was beginning to seem like he wasn't going to be back for a long, long, time, I decided that I might allow myself to associate with other men. This was a very difficult decision to make. What I really wanted to do was to find someone as much like Al as possible and then mold him into a replica so that my loss would not be so intense. Along with this yet unknown inner desire was the guilt I had for even thinking that I could be interested in another man. All of this made for very interesting encounters. I found that I really had become incapable of entering into another committed relationship and searched out men who were also unable to sustain a long term affair.

What does all of this mean to people who climb? We know that it is a dangerous activity and the chances of an accident occurring are great. Does it make any difference if you are the person going or the person staying home? Will it make any difference when choosing a new partner if you have once experienced this loss to the mountain goddess? I don't think so. What I do see is that this is a subject that appears to be forbidden territory for many climbers. I don't believe that most of us want to admit that death is around us and may creep into our lives against our will. I have never heard of a group of people, other than those who have experienced the death of a family member, talking about the risk that is run each time one or both people venture out to do a climb. It's usually an unspoken arrangement. People marry, have children, and suddenly one or both of them no longer do difficult climbs. Occasionally, my men friends have commented on this subject and admitted that it would be too horrible a thought to imagine leaving behind a wife and children. But they don't say anything more than that. Most of us don't talk about it or admit that the fear is there, because we can't go on climbing if we are afraid. One must always approach the snow or rock with a positive attitude, and know and believe that you will return and once again cheat death. More than talking seriously about the consequences of a bad fall, we tell rotten jokes about how we managed to return home all in one piece. It's hard, if not impossible, to match the thrill that you get from completing a hard climb. And with that physical challenge is the mental one that allows you to fully concentrate on one goal and keep your cool while doing it. Do we ever think about the one who is at home waiting and waiting while someone else is up at 26,000' or maybe only at 1,000' but it's hard climbing and it is dangerous.

Sure, people do think about the ones left behind, but that doesn't stop this burning desire to go out and climb ever more difficult routes or peaks.

I have lived with grief and pain for a long time now, and I have just recently been able to understand and accept what has happened to me. This may seem incredible to most people but it happened and it will continue to happen to others. You can't rush overcoming a loss. I don't feel anger at the mountains, I have no intention to quit climbing; quite obviously if this were the case, it would have occurred a long time ago. I'd just like to be able to explain to others that it does get better. For those who do not climb, who have never felt the wonder and awe when seeing such incredible beauty or the rush of exhilaration when completing a physically difficult portion of a climb it always sounds so stupid to tell them that it was worth it to the one who is gone. To those of us at home—left behind to continue our daily lives—those who died in the mountains have gone to a new territory and we should not be mourning for them. Our grief and sorrow is mostly for our own selves. I know I did not want to live alone. I still do not. But I won't pick a non-climber out of the crowd and I won't give it up myself. It's an addiction. We are far worse off than any drug addict could ever imagine. Our curse takes us to physical and mental highs and satisfies some urge to challenge ourselves. We feel healthy and happy and we don't see that it could ever be wrong to do what we do.

Linda Givler has been involved in all aspects of climbing since the early 1970's. She has climbed extensively in the northwest including some trips to South America and to the Karakorum. Linda attended the school of forestry at the University of Washington and has worked as a back country ranger in both Grand Teton and Mount Rainier National Parks.

In the winter season of 1984 Chris Chandler, M.D. and Cherie Bremer-Kamp made the first winter attempt of Kangcherjunga's North
Face. This was to be Cherie's fourth attempt to climb an 8,000 meter peak, having climbed high on Dhaulagini, K2 and Yalangkong.
All but K2 was 2-person teams without the use of supplemental oxygen Another look at K2 was planned the following summer.

There was every reason to be optimistic for success, perched in a
shallow cave with the summit pyramid towering 2000 feet above.
Yet fate would have it otherwise. Instead, Chris succumbed to a sudden and crippling onset of cerebral edema. Mongol Sigg Tamang,
their Sherpa companion, and Cherie barely managed to get Chris
down 1000 feet, where he died that night.

Frostbitten hypothermic and critically dehydrated, closer to
death than life, Cherie and Mongol took four days to finally reach
Base Camp.

Separated from her soul-mate by death, writing became a tool for
investigating and understanding the pain that followed, using it as
wisely as she dared.

"The Moving Finger writes; and, having writ,

Moves on: nor all your Piety nor Wit

Shall lure it back to cancel half a line, Nor all your

Tears wash out a Word of it."

— *Omar Khayyam*

Horizons

Cherie Bremer Kamp

"And so, Cherie, have you thought about what your horizons are?" The
voice echoed in the overly large room. A feeling grew at the base of my neck,
creeping slowly through the hair follicles to concentrate on the very top of
my head. What's he just done to me? The feeling filtered through my senses
that I had been administered some mind altering drug. Oh God, he'll proba-

bly think I'm stoned. I glanced at the finely built man, dressed in a white polo neck sweater and kind smile, my psychiatrist.

"Horizons, did you say horizons?" He nodded in quiet approval. I laughed nervously at the feeling that enveloped me. I'd be so embarrassed if I lost it here right now. Wanting on one hand the safety of being 'normal' yet lured on to examine just a little longer that curiously raw feeling that lay beneath polite behavior and social graces. Words fell from my lips, obedient to form. I wavered, mid stream. Which shore to swim to? On the other hand, would the current's strength sweep me where it would?

Seconds flew by as I once more experienced the joy of climbing, the thrill and closeness with another human that I shared with Chris-looking out over those distant horizons . . . .

Too soon I realized I was facing a gray wall of granite. I had no need to look down. I knew they were there, those little stubs that remain of my fingers. How could they ever find a purchase on that gray, seemingly impenetrable wall of granite to move nimbly upwards into the clear blue sky?

Where had my friend and lover gone? I stood on the ground in a puddle of impotence; 'I don't see any horizons' I answered lamely.

Struggling in a headlong confrontation with destiny, I tried once more to throw off this feeling of despair that so drained my power and productivity.

It was vital to my survival to preserve the memory of the freedom I found so available in the mountains. To interrupt my everyday existence of running a household and earning a living, exposing myself to cold, fatigue, isolation, and danger interspersed with long periods of confinement in storm-bound tents had a way of stripping away the superficial layers of life. Therefore allowing the freedom to look inward, to examine some of life's great mysteries.

It's observed when log fire and television set are available, most human beings will settle for that life. Only when basic needs are denied, and only then, that people are pushed to their essential depths of experience. Eating and sleeping are some of those most basic needs, and manipulating these needs by stringent rules of fasting and sleep deprivation have been used for centuries to gain insight into Religious truths.

Climbing encompasses that concept of grasping the meaning of life through certain crucial experiences: the death and grief of war, accidents, passionate loves, or great catastrophes of earthquakes and volcanic eruptions. The 'clamity theory' is that people evolve through conflict and struggle. Having led the adventurous life-survived the battleground, debilitating illness or earthquake that wrenched us into awareness-we could be now free to sit back in what may easily become smug complacency, or on the other hand, lured once more to taste the drug of action, as both opiate and stimulant.

Thrill is thought of as a fine tremor; an intense feeling of ecstasy but the word more obliquely can be used as 'to piece, penetrate, or cut through.' Need we ask why climbers climb, and at such great cost?

By studying the concepts of Hindu philosophy as found in the Vedas and Upanishads, we are promised a teaching which cuts through illusion. Perhaps we need not continue in a life of great exploits until death or fear overcomes us, only to be recalled in old age or graveside obituary. Even so, the way of life of a yogi ascetic is not too different from that of a Himalayan alpinist. The simplicity of purpose, paucity of tools, isolation and deprivation blend. Whereas the yogi seeks 'non-action' as a vital meditative tool, the climber has it imposed upon him by the forces of nature pinned down for days or weeks on end by fierce storms, clinging to a small foothold on the edge of existence. In both cases, hardship and deprivation have stripped the ego bare. The mind is now set free to do its necessary work.

Two years ago this winter, Chris and I stood beneath Kanchenjunga's North Face. Today, alone, I face despair. I need to keep in check the impulse to drown out the screaming pain with so many readily available anesthetics. Despair is not necessarily such a bad thing, for when all hope is gone, there is no fear. From that deep despair, a beauty is born and new possibilities can arise.

The idea of freedom that is born from despair is that one may not be able to do anything to alter the situation or set of circumstances that makes one a powerless victim of destiny. The release of power and freedom comes by developing the ability to change the context in how we view a particular situation. This is a continually difficult idea that I struggle with. Several months before the expedition was to leave San Francisco for our second alpine style attempt in Kanchenjunga's North Face in far eastern Nepal, our base camp manager Lori came to me with an urgent request. She needed to tell me about a dream she'd had. We both had just completed a hectic night shift in an intensive care unit and my emotional energy was drained. More from politeness than interest, I gave in to her request. With her eyes focused on some place far from where she stood, she began to describe a scene of three people on a mountainside. It wasn't clear if they had reached the summit or not. One person sat alone close to some rocks looking on, almost as though he was guiding the efforts of the other two who were climbing down very slowly. She broke the narrative, twisting her facial muscles up in intense concentration. One person was yelling at the other who seemed hesitant and unsure. There was a problem communicating, almost like a language barrier, and something was terribly wrong.

To this point, I had shown patience, but now I broke free of her grasp on my arm. I'd heard enough. Why implant subconscious messages on my brain—that Chris and I would be out of harmony on the mountain? I was acutely sensitive to the 'problems' in our relationship that usually arose from frustrated effort, yet these problems had a way of dissipating in our shared passion of climbing.

I dismissed the incongruity of three people instead of two on the mountain to some Freudian symbolism of an 'alter ego.' From the moment of conception, the climb had always been a two-person attempt. She had caught my initial interest and attention, now it had gone too far. As I walked away, her voice trailed after me "there will be much falling."

"So, do we live or do we die?" I responded sardonically.

"That won't be known until the very last moment." I had pressed the button to the elevator and waited impatiently, but she insisted on continuing. "Cherie, you've got to do something about your hands, promise me. Your gloves . . . you lose one or drop one." I assured her that we always took an entire wardrobe of extra gloves along and that if anything froze, it would most likely be my feet. Finally, the elevator door opened, I stepped in, the door closed. I had escaped . . . or so I had thought. I never mentioned the incident to Chris.

It was hard enough wading through the mire of anxiety that our friends and loved ones often unwittingly projected at the beginning of a big trip, and I couldn't spend time on what I considered simply environmental noise. I had difficulty enough sorting through my own mental static and I did not want to add to Chris'. Usually it would take until we reached the flanks of a mountain, perhaps in the chill of an early morning sunrise to make that important connection with those inner feelings. I could be patient.

Hectic preparations for the trip soon overwhelmed us and the dream faded, until the night of January 5, 1985. I lay on a small platform that had been hacked out of hard winter snow. Mongol, our Sherpa companion, lay on a similar one, a few feet to the left, and the body of Chris several feet below. My hands, although frozen into rigid claws, remained precious. I cradled them against my cheeks. My wooden legs lay in urine soaked down. I had little expectation of surviving the bitter cold of night. Overcome with

Cherie Bremer Kamp

grief and despair, I stared up into the abysmal blackness of the night sky. Only then did I remember the dream and its significance in our present situation. Calm and peace replaced crippling fear and cold. Although it was still 'unknown' if Mongol and I were to survive the descent or not, I was no longer afraid and faced what lay ahead with calm acceptance.

Today I ponder that pivotal question. What was the purpose of Lori's dream? Given foreknowledge, how much could I have altered the course of events, if at all?

It is the exceptional person who does not retract from the possibility that our futures are fixed in cement, yet that night high on the side of Kanchenjunga, I marveled at the unfolding events. The multiplicity of choices we discussed, each leading to an alternate future that could have replaced the one I was now experiencing.

No one can say that any event has 100% probability of occurring until all the conditions for its occurrence have been satisfied. Finally, that night, it had all fallen into place. Rather than reacting with horror at this realization, I was filled with perfect stillness, suspended by wonder of the universe.

It seemed important at the time that we take active part in vital decisions, to exercise our free will that unwittingly led us on in what became a seemingly inescapable part of a greater cosmic design. Rollo May explains it that: "It is a paradox that destiny is significant only because a freedom of choice exists, that freedom being born from how we relate to our destiny."

Skeptics representing the ultra-materialists could well argue my subconscious mind, open to suggestion, was "programmed" to run the course of events just as it was related in the dream. I doubt my cleverness at such self deceit and manipulation of events, and besides, what was my motive? Yet this remains an often-quoted argument against fulfillment of prophecy. Unfortunately, the whole subject of precognition and distant viewing suffers credibility as much from "true believers" as it has from critics who have difficulty in accepting any scientific data on the subject.

The governments of Russia and the United States of America are regarding the phenomenon seriously enough, for them to budget large amounts of money for these carefully controlled experiments. The results of were published in a congressional report in June 1981. It suggested an interconnectedness of the human mind with other minds and matter, and implies the human mind is able to obtain information independent of geography and time.

So, if our lives are laid out before us in one Grand Design and our puerile calculations and awkward efforts do give into a higher plan, why should we not as Omar Khayyam suggest in the Rubaiyat-take the cup, drink the wine, and while away our time in licentious pleasures. Eastern philosophy's answer to how we should respond to this question is embraced by the concept of Karma.

Suppose there is an infinite variety of responses to one's Karma. It would depend on the quality of our thoughts as well as our actions with the consequence of either further enslavement in the wheel of suffering or release to final enlightenment. With Eastern philosophy blending with Rollo May's idea that our freedom is born from how we choose to relate to those events that make up our destiny, it seems the temptation to focus on manipulating the external events by peering into crystal balls, consulting oracles, or other methods could be better directed to the internal process of developing understanding and meaning from it. Nonetheless, it would be foolish to suggest crossing an avalanche prone slope when instincts and gut reactions cry out not to; or not to try to develop the ability to distinguish between mental clutter and valid intuitive, possibly life saving, information.

In situations such as skiing avalanche country or climbing big mountains where all the facts cannot be known, this sensitivity would seem a most valuable tool and something, which Chris and I were at pains to develop. How then, could I have allowed such a powerful message as Lori's dream to slip by unrecognized, as well as all the other clear signs and messages and feelings pass unacknowledged? Or were they? Looking back, it seems as though there was a gigantic blockage between information given and information acted upon. What created that information block? A ready answer would be Blind Ambition and Prestige Seeking, but was that really it? If that was the prime motivating force, however much we denied it, surely we could have chosen a larger team with logistics that would ensure success.

We knew how small the odds were of our reaching the summit and it was a bit of a game to test them, always trusting that little voice inside to speak up when it was time to turn back. The summit was a goal and worth maybe the tip of a toe or two but not our lives. We often laughed about adding to our list of unsuccessful attempts. Mental stress was more likely responsible for interfering with our being in tune with our inner feelings. However, to dissuade someone from going into the mountains because inherent stress might block hearing that voice within would be like recommending a diabetic not to take his insulin. The mountains were a place where stress was ameliorated rather than accumulated. Sometimes now, perhaps when com-

Cherie Bremer Kamp

ing across a forgotten photo of the climb, I recall unexplained feelings of sadness that at the time I chose to ignore with resignation that the future was out of my hands anyway. So I go on, in a tangle of intuition, imagination, intellectualization, and emotion.

I sit here staring at a Christmas card my sister sent me and think about Kant's idea that the state of mind of the beholder influences what he perceives in life, and our minds not only conform to reality, but reality conforms to our minds. The card is a small black and white drawing by the Australian cartoonist, Luenig. A man is pulling a rickety homemade cart across a vast expanse of land that reminds me a lot of the Outback. In the cart are three small creatures. The sky is black except for a circle of light that surrounds the little travelers. As they move toward an endless horizon, their gaze is fixed upon a star that is hanging from a pole that has been rigged to the cart. They have smiles on their faces, which are radiant with hope and a sense of purpose.

Cherie Bremer-Kamp, a native of Queensland, Australia, is trained and educated as a nurse and midwife. She has lived and worked in Nepal, Holland, New Zealand and the United States. In 1978 she was a member of the American K2 expedition. In 1985 she and her husband, Chris Chandler attempted the north face of Kanchenjunga on which Dr. Chandler died and Cherie suffered severe frostbite resulting in the loss of her fingers and toes. She is the author LIVING ON THE EDGE an account of her attempt of the world's third highest mountain the 28,168 foot Kanchenjunga.

Cho Oyu–The Turquoise Goddess

Magda Nos King

My parents, who were avid hikers and campers long before equipment was sold in stores, introduced me to the outdoors at a very early age. I have very fond memories of our summer vacations in the Pyrenees, near our hometown of Barcelona, Spain. Every year, we would put up camp near a river—never further than a day's walk from a small village—where my father would go once a week to buy food and supplies.

We had an A frame canvas tent that my grandmother had made for us, and we would lay our wool blankets on top of a soft bed of pine tree branches that my father would replace every few days. We would normally spend the entire month of July or August exploring new territory on day hikes near our camp, and seldom would we encounter any other hikers.

My first experience with ropes was while spelunking with the group of scouts I had joined, but about a year going down into my first cave, a friend invited me to try to up a rock climb. I was instantly hooked on rock climbing and I never went back to spelunking.

Through rock climbing I made many friends and as time passed, some of those friends introduced me to their friends, who told about their experiences in remote peaks in South America and Asia. I looked up to those heroes returning from the Andes and the Himalayas with tremendous respect and admiration, often asking myself if I would ever have the opportunity of going to one of those Himalayan giants.

But, of course, I knew that I could never share such thoughts with any of my climbing partners. They would have thought that I was crazy, or even worst yet, they may not have allowed me to continue climbing with them! My attempts to find female climbers only turned up an occasional climbing partner, and always under the condition that we would only attempt an easy climb ant that I would do all the leading. In the late sixties, women climbers in Spain were very rare, and the ones I knew, at maximum dreamed of climbing in the Alps with their boy friends.

However, I kept to my dream, and over the years I found myself attempting harder and higher mountains all over the world. Having married and moved to Colorado with my American husband, I had climbed many 4,000-meter peaks and in 1978 I felt ready to attempt a 5,000-meter peak. I decoded to go to Mexico. I organized a small group consisting of a couple from Barcelona, my husband and myself, and we all reached the summit of Popocatepetl without difficulty.

Being able to climb to 5,000 meters gave me tremendous hope that I might also be able to reach the top of a 6,000-meter peak and for the next few years I kept on organizing climbs to Kenya, Tanzania, Peru, Bolivia, and other South American countries.

By 1984 I had climbed enough 6,000-meter peaks to feel confident about attempting my first 7,000 meter-peak and I went to India. The South East Ridge of Nun, only climbed once before, that appeared to me even more appealing than anything I had ever attempted before. But this was quite a big mountain, requiring more time necessary. I returned home very disappointed and for the next two years I went back to the more dependable mountains of South America.

Finally, in 1987 I found myself with what I considered to be most valuable piece of mail I had ever had in my hands. I had written to the Ministry of Nepal asking for a permit to climb Yalung Kang, 8,505 m (27,905 ft). Also known as the West summit of Kangchenjunga, it is the 6th highest summit in the World and lies in remote eastern Nepal, bordering Sikkim.

Now I had a very official looking registered letter from Nepal, surely their answer to my request, but what would it say inside? Would they grant me such a privilege? . . . In spite of the extreme excitement, I managed to control myself enough to carefully open the large oatmeal colored envelope and, as I read its contents, I suddenly felt a burst of happiness like I had never experienced before. Over 20 years had passed since I had first heard the fascinating stories of my friend's friends climbing in the Himalaya and now . . . I had in my hands my very own permit to attempt one of those Himalayan giants.

I came out of the Post Office as if, instead of having a letter in my hands, I was holding on to a huge helium balloon that was lifting me from the ground. I would not have traded that climbing permit for all the money in the world.

Yalung Kang turned out to be a very intense introduction to 8,000-meter peak climbing. The expedition lasted three and a half months and during that time I had plenty of opportunities to test everything that I had ever learned—not only about climbing, but also about survival.

As I was reaching last camp at 7,700 meter, a gusty wind ripped away from my hands my down parka, and with it went all my chances of continuing up the mountain. On the way down, a huge snowstorm caught me. Trapped for 5 days at Camp 1, with hardly any food or fuel, I fought for survival with all my will and whatever strength I had left in me by that time, until finally on the 6th day I was able to reach Base Camp.

There, looking at me as if he was seeing a ghost was Narayan, our Sirdar. Standing in the kitchen, next to the cook, they were the only two people remaining at Base Camp. Everybody else had left, thinking that on one could have ever survived such a storm.

It had been an expedition of superlatives and extremes. Like any important first event in one's life, my first time on an 8,000-meter peak was forever engraved deep into myself, along with the hard lessons I had learned in the process of going there, and even more important of coming back.

As hard as this expedition had been, back in Denver, I kept on remembering how disappointed I had felt at last camp. Not able to continue myself, I had wished I had a female climbing companion with me—someone who could have finished the climb and changed the female climbing records of my home country, Spain.

Living in the United States, I'd followed with great interest the success of the first American all female expedition to an 8,000-meter peak, Annapurna, lead by Arlene Blum. I hoped that some day women from my country could stand up to such honor.

Later, with the announcement of Barcelona hosting the 1992 summer Olympics I also wish: to have the first women from Spain to climb an 8,000-meter peak carry the Olympic flag to the summit.

I decided on Cho Oyu—8,201 meter (26,907 ft) as our climbing objective. Then, armed with all my enthusiasm, and hoping to find an all female team from Spain, I traveled throughout Spain looking for the right people, but this proved to be difficult since up to then, there had been no female expeditions from Spain to any 8,000-meter peak.

When I finally found three other women willing, able, and capable of making a good team, the access to Cho Oyu, the mountain I had chosen, was closed. Due to the pro-democracy clashes in Tiananmen Square, all spring expeditions to Tibet were canceled.

Since our expedition was to depart in August, there was still hope that the situation would improve and we would be allowed to enter Tibet.

In the meantime, there was plenty to do organizing all the logistics of the expedition, and trying to find a sponsor who would believe in our project. This was a monumental task, and the lack of a track record did not help. Potential sponsors would not believe that four women, alone, were capable of climbing an 8,000-meter peak, and were not willing to finance the project.

With insufficient funds to cover the total budget, came the withdrawal of two of the women who could not obtain personal loans to finance the remaining deficit, and automatically total disbelief fell onto my only remaining climbing partner, Monica Verge, and me. Jokes were started about us not even been able to find Base Camp, but we were determined to go no matter what, and totally committed to give Cho Oyu our best try.

However, with the new changes in our team, I felt that our safety had been jeopardized. If one of us was to fall into a crevasse, it could be very difficult, if not impossible, for the other to do a rescue all alone. I discussed my concerns with Monica and we decided to hire a climbing sherpa to accompany us on the climb. Finally, everything was ready, and in early August of 1989, the news of our departure was spread by the media in the midst of curiosity and amazement that we had gotten as far as we had.

Unable to afford a direct flight from Barcelona, we happily accepted the kind offer of some of friends to drive us to Paris for our flight to Kathmandu. Caught in the euphoria of having actually left for Cho Oyu, or small expedition early came to and end as the Pan Am ticket agent at Orly's airport bluntly asked me how many people were in my group! We had felt quite accomplished at having been able to compress the nearly 300 kilos of food, gear and supplies into only 12 duffles, but international flights in Europe allow only 20 kilos per passenger, and we had no money to pay for the excess weight.

I could not allow for my expedition to end right there, when we had already overcome so many difficulties and, somehow, I managed to convince the agent to let us go for free!

In Kathmandu we met our Sherpa, Ang Furi. We purchased our last food and supplies and quickly left for Cho Oyu via Kodari at the border between Nepal and Tibet.

Since our approach march was through Tibet, we used yaks to carry our loads to Base Camp and it is thanks to the stubbornness of the yak herders that Monica and I got some extra acclimatization. Unable to convince them to carry our loads to our choice location for a permanent Base Camp, they dumped all gear at "their" choice location and it took us an extra week of ferrying loads to what we then called Advanced Base Camp.

This incident proved to be very valuable to us allowing for a perfect acclimatization and rapid progress in establishing the higher camps. My plans was to climb Cho Oyu as a lightweight expedition, stocking Camp 1 at 6,600 meter, placing a tent and some supplies at 7,200 meter (Camp 2) and from there, continuing in alpine style to the summit.

However, when we reached the site of our Camp 2, a lot of snow had accumulated from recent snow storms and avalanche danger was too high to make a summit attempt, so, we decided to return to Camp 1 and wait for the snow to settle.

Around 3:00 p.m. we opened our radio to notify our cook at Base Camp that we had returned to Camp 1 to wait for an extra day, and just as our cook signed off and closed his radio, a new voice appeared. It was the anguished voice of Thirta, the Nepali high altitude porter contracted by an Italian expedition also attempting to climb Cho Oyu. He and an Italian woman had been caught in an avalanche at around 8,000 meter while trying to reach the summit. He could not tell his own location due to the heavy fog, and he had no idea of what my have happened to the woman. His voice was coarse from the snow that he had inhaled, and the batteries of his radio were nearly finished.

Our attempts to contact the rest of his team, at their Camp 3 to organize a rescue party were useless since they either did not have a radio, or did not have it on. It was a desperate situation. Heavy fog prevented all visibility. Thirta could not even tell his own location and nightfall was not far away. I knew that his hope for survival depended on our ability to keep him awake, but how long would his radio batteries last.

Finally, around 5:00 p.m. a miracle happened. As the day was ending, the fog lifted for Thirta to see the tent that we had placed at 7,200 meters, and it was well within his reach. We felt a mixture of relief and sadness for the life that had just been spared, and for the woman, woman's bad luck. Our next communication was to be once Thirta had reached the tent, but we were totally amazed at the news that he gave us when he went inside. Valentina, the Italian woman climber, had been taken down the mountain for nearly 800 meters and miraculously, the avalanche had deposited here only a few feet away from our tent. Badly bruised, but still conscious, she had been able to crawl inside, where Thirta had just found here, still alive.

The following day, we went back up to help the Italians improvise a rescue system to take Valentina down. Our North Face tent had survived the avalanche with minimal damage. The Italians started down and we decided to spend an extra night there to insure better snow stability for our summit attempt.

The next day, we packed the necessary food and supplies, as well as two lightweight Gore-Tex tents to be used on our final summit bid, and we climbed to the rock band following compacted snow of the avalanche. At 7,700 meter we found a large overhanging rock under which we built a small platform to spend the night. At 2:00 a.m. a heavy fog was rising toward us from the valley and by 3:00 a.m. the weather had not improved enough for us to leave our tents. As time passed, I grew worried with concern that it may be getting too late. We had wanted to leave at 2:00 a.m. to have enough hours of daylight to reach the summit and safely return to our tents before dark.

Finally, at 5:00 a.m. the fog lifted and Cho Oyu—"The Turquoise Goddess" gave us a chance. As the first rays of sun lit other Himalayan summits, we left our tents. We walked in silence, submerged in our thoughts, with each step forward our hope for success growing yet stronger. Around 8:00 a.m. I stopped for a drink and looked at my altimeter and on its face was the magical 8000m

My heart took a leap, and for just one second, I allowed myself to belief, that this was the day, we would stand on the summit.

Success was not ours yet, and I needed to direct all my energy towards that final step that would allow us to savor the moment of reaching the summit. Now the snow was soft and knee deep. We took turns in opening track into what seemed an endless horizon, slowly placing each foot in front of the other, totally determined to keep going until we could not climb any higher. At last, at 10:45 a.m. we stood on the summit, and on the precious day of September 19th, 1989 as the Barcelona Olympic Flag waved into the air, a new chapter was written into the history of women climbers in Spain.

In 1989 Magda Nos King changed the history of women climbers in Spain as she led the first all-woman expedition from Spain to an 8,000 metre peak.

Her successful ascent of Cho-Oyu (8,201metres) played a major role in encouraging other women from Spain to attempt

8,000 meter peaks. She has also reached the summit of Shisha Pangma (8,008m) and made high camps on five other 8,000m peaks: Yalung Kang, Gasherbrum II, Broad Peak, Everest and Kangchenjunga.

She has organized cleaning efforts that removed over one ton of garbage from Broad Peak BC and 1,140 lbs from Kangchenjuga B.C.

When Women Were Women in the NE

Laura Waterman

Not long ago I went back to the Shawangunks. I walked the short path from the highway to the carriage road, as I had for the last 25 years. There was the usual throng of climbers bouldering, top-roping, and telling stories around the ranger's truck. I saw two women climbing "Apoplexy." Nearby, another woman was leading a man up "Retribution." These climbs are rated 5.9 and 5.10. Fifteen years ago people would have stopped to watch a man lead either climb. By the mid-1980s, no one particularly noticed. Women were regularly leading hard climbs at the Gunks.

Yes, we've come a long way.

But these and other talented women climbers are simply re-establishing a tradition of women climbers that has a glorious past in northeastern rock climbing circles of more than 70 years ago.

Judged by the standard of their times—the only fair way to judge any climber—the women who climbed when climbing was first establishing itself in the Northeast were remarkable.

In the beginning was Miriam O'Brien Underhill. She has been called America's greatest woman climber.

"She was a beautiful climber, like an example from a climbing text," wrote New Englander Elizabeth Knowlton, a Himalayan veteran, and a contemporary who knew Miriam from her earliest climbing days. "Naturally graceful, she moved steadily and easily in rhythm, sort of flowing up the rocks. It was a pleasure to watch her."

Kenneth Henderson, an American alpinist of distinction, and good friend of Miriam's, unhesitatingly called her, "technically your top climber." He also pronounced her the only woman leader of her time.

Miriam climbed in New England, but she made her name in the Alps.

By the late 1920s and early 1930s, she had not only climbed many of the Alps' classic routes, but had begun to lead confidently herself on major routes without the services of a guide. In those days guideless climbing by women was frowned on.

In 1929 Miriam took a further step: she began a period of "manless" climbing, as an all-women's rope team was then called. For years she remained in the vanguard of a very small group of women who were doing manless ascents of difficult alpine peaks. Among her most notable climbs, major routes all of which were first ascents by a woman's rope, were the many-spired Grepon in 1929, the snow-and-ice covered Monch and Jungfrau in 1931, and the great massive pyramid of the irresistible Matterhorn, a real plum, a year later.

One might say that climbing without men (either guides or amateurs) in those days was just not done. In fact it was officially disapproved by the Ladies Alpine Club of London. Miriam wrote about this very controversial subject: "I have grown to recognize the fact that when a man lets a woman 'lead' it is, for him, just a pleasant little fiction . . . . A woman cannot really lead if there is a man at all in the party . . . . And so if she wants to lead she must climb with other women." She went on to say that if a man is in the party he will just naturally take over if an emergency arises; after all, what man, she wrote, "wouldn't feel a certain final responsibility when doing a climb with a woman? Call it illogical if you like, or perfectly natural, but I have tried out quite a lot of them, and they are all made that way." Miriam pointed out that during those years when she and a handful of other women pioneered on routes without men there never was an accident to a "manless caravan," of even a forced bivouac. But she was also aware that certain mothers who packed their daughters off for the Alps on a climbing holiday made them promise they "wouldn't climb with Miriam!"

Although Miriam did not happen to make her mark in the Northeast, several of her feminine contemporaries did—and did so just as the sport of rock climbing was beginning.

In 1928 four of the five big cliffs of the White Mountains in New Hampshire were climbed for the first time. It was a year, as historian Barbara Tuchman says of another era, "of vigor, confidence, and forces converging to quicken the blood." It proved but prologue: the following year saw even more spectacular advances, and major new climbs were racked up throughout the early 1930s from New Hampshire's vertical playgrounds to the cliff-bound mountains in Maine, back over to the comparatively isolated Adirondacks and down to the populated Hudson Highlands of New York. Women were along on many of these pioneering ascents.

Climbers from Boston opened up the White Mountain cliffs. Some of the women who were along on the earliest ascents included:

- Marjorie Hurd, Boston lawyer, who said she climbed because she liked people and added, "The more strenuous the trip, the more interesting the people," was on the first attempt of the Pinnacle (direct) in Mt. Washington's Huntington Ravine in 1927.

- Jessie Whitehead, daughter of the famous philosopher Alfred North Whitehead, and noted for her ability, as Ken Henderson put it, to "push the leader up the rock with a good string of profanity," was on the team who finally climbed the Pinnacle (direct) in the Fall of 1928.

- Margaret Helburn, A Bostonian, who had an abiding love of mountains all her life, was with a party who explored far-off Katahdin's rock in 1928, led by Robert Underhill (Miriam's husband).

By the early 1930s women were climbing every route which had been worked out by the pioneering Boston climbers on New England's cliffs:

- Old Cannon on Cannon Cliff;
- Whitney-Gilman on Cannon;
- The south face of Willard in Crawford Notch;
- Huntington Ravine's *Pinnacle;*
- The Standard route on Whitehorse Ledge;
- The Standard route on Cathedral Ledge;
- Katahdin in Maine (many routes);
- Mount Desert in Maine (many routes).

In the Adirondacks Betty Woolsey joined John Case to put up the first route on Wallface in 1933. A brilliant athlete, Betty successfully fused a life as a climber with that of a champion skier. She was on the US. Olympic women's ski team in the mid 1930s.

In 1935 fifteen Boston climbers went to Katahdin, under the able leadership of "Hec" Towle. In a week of climbing they put up eight new routes and the Armadillo was the prize, a long, complex route in the middle of the cirque called the South Basin. Not technically hard—Towle's route was about 5.5—the exposure and overall length as well as the remoteness of the cliff put it right up with the explorations done on New Hampshire rock of a few years earlier. On one day five of the men explored it and completed the route. Two days later, after waiting out a rain, 12 climbers did the route! Four of them were women, including Thelma Bonney, (later

Towle when she married "Hec"), Marjorie Hurd, Helen Chase, and Gretchen Cleaves, all well-known in the Boston and Appalachian Mountain Club climbing circle.

In this age when we all pay meticulous attention to the ratings of climbs, and even 5.13 is subdivided (5.13a, 5.13b, 5.13c, 5.13d), it is difficult to place ourselves back in the context of the 1930s. Then there were no ratings. If you were a rock climber, you climbed all the routes. So any really active woman climbed just about everything the men climbed. In those days of hemp rope and genuine commitment in leading, few climbers led. That's where a sex gap developed: few women led. But in climbing per se, there was not the large gap between men and women which developed during the 1950s and 1960s. Thus, Marjorie Hurd, and Jessie Whitehead on pioneering New Hampshire climbs, Betty Woolsey on the first ascent of Wallface, Thelma Bonney on the second ascent of the Armadillo.

This historical fact is little realized today. We all tend to think that the achievements of Lynn Hill and other women who climb as well as men today are unprecedented. These achievements are indeed impressive, because of the mental roadblocks and prejudices of the last generation which had to be cleared away. But in the early days a greater degree of parity had existed. A look at the historical development of one eastern area, the Shawangunks, is revealing.

As every climber knows, the Gunks were discovered in 1935, sighted in the clear air that follows a thundershower by Fritz Wiessner from the top of Breakneck Ridge. And so began the era of modern rock climbing.

A close look at the climbing history of the Shawangunks, the East's most prominent rock climbing center, reveals a startling fact: for that area at least, more women were climbing at the top of the prevailing standard in the 1940s and 1950s than at any time since then.

A careful perusal of three guidebooks (Art Gran's was published in 1964 and Dick Williams' in 1972 and Todd Swain's in 1986) reveals that women were particularly active in first ascents during the 1940s. In the 1950s the number of routes put up nearly doubled, and the number of women involved in them stayed the same. During the 1960s the number of new routes again doubled, whereas the number of women climbers on first ascents dwindled markedly.

There have, of course, always been women climbers at the Gunks, some of whom led at the top of *their* standard. But the following breakdown is in terms of men and women who have been involved in first ascents only, as this information can be documented by the guidebooks.

Laura Waterman

1940-1950: The total number of documented climbs put in was 63. A total of 32 of these had women in the party—or 51 percent.

1951-1959: In these years the total number of documented new climbs nearly doubled to 109. The number of climbs with women in the party stayed the same at 32, so the percentage of total number of climbs which included women was nearly cut in half—29 percent.

1960-1970: The total number of reported new routes more than doubled—221. The number of climbs with women in the party decreased to just 11 climbs, reducing the percent to a low of 5 percent.

1971-1979: In the explosion of climbing's popularity, 561 new routes were recorded. Though the number involving women doubled, to 21, their percentage remained low: 4 percent.

1980-1985: With 683 new routes entered in the guidebook, and 63 involving women, the proportion began its slow return toward earlier levels: 9 percent for the first half of this decade.

Who were these women participating in just about half the new routes climbed during the 1940s and early 1950s?

To begin at the beginning, in 1935 the very first route put up at the Gunks was Old Route at Milbrook, and a female, Peggy Navas was in the party led by Fritz Wiessner.

Among the top climbers of the early days at the Shawangunks—men or women—a name that stands out right after Hans Kraus and Fritz Wiessner, who really opened up the area, is Bonnie Prudden.

Physical fitness crusader and sometime television star, Bonnie Prudden was from the late Thirties to the mid Fifties a rock climber extraordinaire. She climbed all over the Northeast, in the West (the Tetons and Estes Park), and in Europe, especially the Dolomites.

Hans Kraus, a dominant early figure at the Shawangunks, recalls her as "the best woman climber in the area." If you look through the list of climbs in Williams' 1972 guidebook, Kraus' verdict gains support. The star-studded names of Jim McCarthy, Williams, Kraus, Gran, and Wiessner are the men who put in the most numbers of new routes at the Gunks. Then comes Bonnie Prudden.

Bonnie has a documented thirty first ascents taking place in the years 1946 to 1955. Among these is the famed Bonnie's Roof, rated 5.8. (Gran's guide and many a dangling leader rate it a 5.9). Bonnie put in the route with Kraus and she led the roof, using a sling for aid. This was in 1952. The aid was not eliminated until 1961, when McCarthy and Williams managed to climb the big ceiling free. The route remains a testpiece for climbers breaking into a higher standard. Gran writes in his guidebook, "It's a great route to bear one's name."

Among Bonnie's other notable climbs are Something Interesting, a tough 5.7 put in at the early date of 1946. Grand Central came the following year. In 1951 she climbed with Hans Kraus Never Again, rated 5.6a$_1$, at the time, and today goes free at solid 5.10. That year she and Hans climbed Hans' Puss, a truly fine route and one of the longest at the Gunks. Triangle followed in 1954 and Dry Martini a year later. Aside from documented climbs, Bonnie recalls many nameless routes at Lost City (which she remembers being called "Secret City") and other outlying crags. The hardest free moves on these climbs were respectful 5.7, done at a time no one was climbing 5.8.

Bonnie holds a place in the climbing history of the Shawangunks that has yet to be superceded by any other woman climber, especially in terms of her first ascents, in leading climbs at the top of her standard—in fact at the top of the standard of the area—she was unique among women climbers of her day. Only with the advent of the remarkable Lynn Hill in the early 1980s has any woman approached Bonnie's challenge. The climbers of Bonnie's time remember her vividly, describing her as "tops" or "the best," among all women climbers. Bonnie was a luminary in the climbing scene for more than a decade.

Krist Raubenheimer was a potent force at the Shawangunks in the mid Fifties. An aggressive leader on many of the area's then-harder routes, Krist also put in several first ascents of her own, which ranks her right behind Bonnie among women pioneers, though a long way down the list among the men.

Krist put up some very fine climbs. Among them, The Raubenheimers Special was rated 5.5 in Williams' guide, but it's a rating many climbers felt hardly did the climb justice when they were clinging desperately to that utterly blank crux. At least 5.6! Swain's guide moved it up to that rating. Krist is also responsible for the very popular Bunny (5.4) which she climbed with Ann Church—an all female climb, one of the very few at the Shawangunks.

Although Krist does not really come close to Bonnie Prudden in her number of first ascents, she was as good as there was and Hans Kraus recalls her as next best among the women climbers. She, like Bonnie, led climbs at the top of her standard.

Back in the Forties, another woman climber whose reputation stands high in the memory of old timers in the area, is Maria Millar. Although the marvelous route that bears her name is one of just two first ascents of hers in the guidebook, she is recalled as a capable leader on the harder established routes of the day. The intensely competitive Bonnie Prudden once said, "I never met another woman other than Maria Millar who could really climb."

Maria was a born climber. Before she discovered rocks she climbed water towers, traversed churches, chimneyed doorways, climbed balconies on hotels, climbed over slowly moving freight trains, and of course, climbed houses and trees. At the Gunks she is remembered—now only by the oldest of old timers—as a brilliant natural climber, sparked by tremendous enthusiasm and spirit.

The climbers of the Shawangunks owe a lot to Maria, as it was she, and her husband David, who took Hans Kraus to the Gunks for the first time.

Mary Perry and Del Wolcott each have five first ascents to their credit, though neither are remembered as leading at the level of Bonnie or Maria.

Betty Woolsey, who was with Fritz Wiessner and Bill House on Mount Waddington, also put in four new routes at the Gunks in the early Forties. Among them the classic jam crack "The Baby" is rated 5.6 and was put up in 1941 by Fritz Wiessner, Betty Woolsey, and Mary Cecil. The popular beginner's route, The Betty, memorializes Ms. Woolsey, who put it in also in the same year. She is remembered as being a very competent climber.

Ann Church was on three first ascents, two of which were put up with Krist Raubenheimer in 1955, making them the first all-female rope doing first ascents at the Shawangunks.

Ruth Tallan is one whom Maria Millar remembers as a climber of natural grace and skill who developed into one of the area's better climbers, and eventually chairman (this was before the years of "consciousness raising" terminology like "chairperson") of the dominant club climbing at the Gunks, the Appalachian Mountain Club.

Dorothy Hirschland was another who did outstanding climbs and also led at a respectable standard for the times.

These were the outstanding female leaders of the Forties and Fifties, although many other women were active in the then-smaller climbing circle at the Shawangunks. By the end of the Fifties and the early Sixties, women were far less prominent either in making first ascents or leading at the demanding new standards then being pushed by McCarthy, Gran, Williams and others.

Why the change? Why were women so much more active at the forefront of Gunks' climbing in the early days? Here are a few conjectures.

1. The climbing population was small, not more than 10 to 25 climbers on a weekend, and more like 8 to 10 climbers in the early days of the Forties. A reasonably high proportion of these climbers were women; certainly a

much higher proportion than are found at the cliffs today when a pleasant, sunny weekend will bring out hundreds of climbers at the height of the season.

2. Somehow the social scene in those days was conducive to women leading and following climbs near the top of the standard for the area. The small number of climbers at the Gunks might have contributed. Also, everyone knew each other. This, as well as the fact that climbing then was not unduly competitive seems to have produced a context in which women could advance.

3. The Appalachian Mountain Club, the dominant group at the Shawangunks during the Forties and Fifties employed a system of advancing leaders that was rather formal and restrictive, but at least had the merit that it did not discriminate between male or female. In fact, as mentioned, Ruth Tallan served as chairman of this group for a time.

4. Hans Kraus and Fritz Wiessner, who put up many, many first ascents liked to climb with women. Hans was happy to have women lead. Fritz liked to have women along in his party, so often one or two women's names accompany his in his roster of first ascents.

Reasons unique to the Shawangunks, however, are probably not a sufficient explanation of the prominence of women climbers in the early days, because other Northeastern climbing areas, as we have seen, show a similar leading role by women during the Twenties and Thirties. In fact by the Forties, Jan Conn was putting in routes like the very serious Conn Course on Cannon Cliff, in which she alternated leads with her partner Herb Conn. The first Adirondacks' rock climbing guidebook was written by a woman, Trudy Healy, who knew as well as anyone cliffs large and small of that region.

Yet some time in the Fifties there was a definite diminuendo in the role of women climbers in the Northeast. The statistics on first ascents at the Shawangunks, cited earlier, gave dramatic evidence of this change. What might be some of the reasons?

1. After 1960 the average difficulty of first ascents increased to 5.8/5.9, and in the 1970s many of the old aid routes were freed, most going at 5.10 and harder. Generally, women just hadn't convinced themselves, at this point, that they could climb at that level. Very likely the strenuous nature of the climbs put them off.

2. After 1960 and particularly in the Seventies, climbing became more competitive than it was in the more relaxed early years. Possibly, this predominantly male competition that goes on at the upper end of the standard

drives out the women climbers. Vera Watson, a former Gunks climber who was a team member of the all-women expedition to Annapurna in 1978, commented that she had done much of her climbing with women and found "more of a feeling of camaraderie, less competitiveness."

3. The climbing population has increased markedly since the 1940s and 1950s. The increase had brought many more male climbers than female to the cliffs, thus reducing the chances that women climbers would be on first ascents.

4. One old Vulgarian (these were the climbers who were setting standards during the early Sixties) maintained that Vulgarians liked to have women around for other purposes than strictly climbing . . . (Several of the women who were climbing during this period don't support this point, however, as they claim that these men encouraged them in their climbing).

In the Sixties and early Seventies there were certainly good women climbers at the Gunks. Several of these women were doing harder climbs than Bonnie Prudden and Krist Raubenheimer, but the standard of climbing had increased so fast during the Sixties that in retrospect their climbing seems not as impressive as that of their predecessors. So that although these climbers were doing free moves that Bonnie or Krist never attempted, they were climbing at a level far behind the standard set by the men.

Gerd Thuestad, who climbed at the Shawangunks from 1950 to 1969, led all of Vulga-tits (5.6), put in by an all-female party. Gerd also did a lot of leading and at the top of her standard. She climbed a lot with women, and remembers getting into very funny situations on her all-female climbs. Muriel Mayo did some very capable leading, including a first ascent of After You (rated 5.7).

Patty Crowther and Cherry Merritt were two women who were leading hard climbs. Cherry led Art Gran's classic thin-face climb Never Never Land rated 5.10 by Gran and 5.9 by Williams and Swain.

But these women were exceptions to the trend. Despite the impetus of the "Women's Movement" emerging in the 1960s, most women climbers were leading far below their standard. None was following at the highest standard of the men.

The 1970s, though backward in many ways, saw the first signs of change. Women were climbing more with other women—and not just on the easy grades, but at a moderately hard level. In 1977 Mountain reported, "Another development [at the Shawangunks] has been the appearance of increasing numbers of competent women climbers, operating at the top grades." This well-known British climbing magazine went on to name

Barbara Devine as "the most successful of the female climbers."
Climber-historian Al Rubin commented that by the mid-Seventies he noticed a definite increase in good women climbers, and that women were
climbing together more.

The *wunderkind* of the Seventies was without doubt Barbara Devine.
She stepped into the vacuum left by the Sixties, and, with no female role
models for inspiration, worked her way up to the stratosphere of the highest
grades, becoming herself a model for her followers.

Barbara began climbing in 1970. She was taken to the Gunks by her boyfriend Kevin Bein—a Gunks habituee—who proceeded to drag her up
Northern Pillar (5.2). Terrified, Barbara resolved never to climb again. But
the idea of overcoming her fear took hold, and she returned to the cliffs for
another try. Barbara Devine came to stay. Two years later she accompanied
Kevin to Yosemite and did her first 5.9s. In 1973 (now married) the couple
moved to New Paltz and became probably the most constant presence at the
cliffs; climbing "literally every day," training intensively, bouldering hard,
and striving constantly to improve their standards. Tall and thin, Barbara
developed a phenomenal strength-to-weight ratio (she has especially strong
fingers) when she took up serious training. By 1974 she led Retribution,
possibly the first female lead of solid 5.10 in Northeastern climbing. That
was just the beginning. By 1976, she had done Foops and Persistent, both
5.11. In 1977 she did Kansas City (5.12) and such desperate 5.11s as Open
Cockpit, To Have Or Have Not, and Wasp Stop. Barbara was moving fast.
In July 1983 she did the first female ascent of Supercrack, plus other 5.12s
of that day. Like her husband, Barbara was always subjected to an un-
der-current of whispers about poor style—willingness to accept a top-rope,
lengthy sieging, and a preference for nearby protection on leads. For sheer
technical virtuosity, however, there was no denying that she was far and
away the outstanding woman climber in the Northeast during the 1970's.

A top climber of the Eighties, Rosie Andrews, said of Barbara that in the
late Seventies "Barbara Devine was perhaps the best-known woman who
had done hard climbs in the East." Rosie pointed out that Barbara is an example of what women can do—and yet still be limited. Technically she was
impeccable, but she was possibly not willing enough to step out on her own,
since she rarely climbed outside of her husband Kevin's circle—all brilliant
climbers, but predominantly men.

By the Eighties, women were willing to step out on their own.

By about 1980 Iza Koponicka, a graceful climber with superb technique
was leading 5.9s and occasionally 5.10s. Annie O'Neill and Laura Chaiten

were right up there too. These women, though, were not leading (or even following) at the top of the area's standard as was Bonnie Prudden.

But perhaps the next woman after Barbara with a substantial independent impact on female climbing was Rosie Andrews. Rosie took striking out on one's own seriously. By 1980 she was leading consistently in the 5.10 range and had moved up to the thinner air of 5.11 by 1981. Unlike many other strong women climbers at that time, Rosie never really had her name linked with that of a strong male climber. Once she got good, she seemed to maintain a kind of independence that was possibly unique among Eastern women climbers. By doing this, she became an extremely effective role model.

Rosie comes close to being the first woman since Bonnie Prudden to put in the climbs at the area's standard. In 1981 she stunned the Gunks community by leading a crux 5.12 move on a first ascent of Point Blank with Russ Raffa. Though Russ ultimately first led the entire climb, word got around about Rosie leading that one desperate move.

Rosie led a growing movement toward more independent self-contained women climbers in the early 1980s. She was the first woman to guide professionally in the East, working for International Mountain Equipment in North Conway, N.H. in 1982. In the mid 1980s she guided at the Gunks, influencing many women to "strike out on their own." Her landmark article on women climbers published in *Mountain* in 1984 was avidly devoured.

Another climber of independent mind was Alison Osius. A journalist whose sage and amusing articles appear often in the climbing press, she is at home leading 5.12.

In 1983 a 21-year-old slight, slender, attractive California woman came East. Lynn Hill had been a gymnast, swimmer, and hiker from childhood. Gifted with uncommon strength, but even more flexibility and grace, she took to rock climbing with ease. Before she left California, she had climbed 5.12. But when she arrived in the Northeast, her climbing activity level, physical fitness, competitive instincts, and mental attitude came together to make her a top-flight climber. Not a top-flight woman climber; simply a top-flight climber. In 1983 she was one of four Gunks climbers to master the region's first 5.13, Vandals. In 1984, making one of her few trips to North Conway to sample local test-pieces, she took on Tourist Treat, a problem which had been stumping local climbers for years; she led it on sight, with but one fall, perhaps the most difficult first ascent in the north country at the time. In the same year, back at the Gunks, she led the first ascents of Organic Iron (5.12 plus) and the original aid line on Yellow Crack

(5.12 plus with scant protection), the latter called by Russ Raffa, himself a 5.12 leader with a reputation for boldness: "the best lead I've ever seen in my life." When the 1986 guidebook was published, the cover photo unselfconsciously showed Lynn Hill leading Open Cockpit. That long-time observer of the Gunks scene, Kevin Bein, pronounced her, in 1986: "the best climber in the Gunks now." Most observers declined to set any one of the seven or eight top 1980s climbers ahead of the rest, but the point was clear that no man was climbing significantly better than Lynn Hill. Bonnie Prudden's long-awaited heiress had arrived at last.

Though cited here as exceptional "women climbers," these women of the 1980s were beginning to think of themselves simply as "climbers." The distinction was significant. Rosie Andrews, Alison Osius, Lynn Hill and others vehemently disclaimed special recognition as women and sought to be accepted as climbers. Their example spread. Alison insisted, after a first free ascent of the Labyrinth Wall on Cannon Cliff, with three pitches at 5.11 and six at 5.10, wherein she shared the lead with Neil Cannon: "There's no intrinsic reason why women can't climb as well as men. So we shouldn't get congratulated for lesser accomplishments."

Women had caught up. Actually, only Lynn Hill. The general level of female climbing was still well below males'. But clearly barriers had been removed, and it appeared unlikely that another "dark ages" could return. The new outlook owed much to the path-breaking by Barbara Devine, Rosie Andrews, Alison Osius and Lynn Hill, but the real story written in the 1980s was by the anonymous multitude of women who climbed well and independently, perceiving themselves once again in the mainstream of northeastern climbing.

Laura Waterman is a pioneer of women rock and ice climbing. She was the first woman the Black Dike ice route on the beautiful Cannon Mountains. The author of the 1979 book, "Backwood Ethics: Environment Concerns for Hikers and Campers," and the co-author, with her husband Guy, of "Forest and Crags: A History of Hiking, Trail Blazing, and Adventures in the Northeastern Mountain"(1989), a contributor to the *Backpacker* and *New England Outdoors* magazines.

Early Climbs

Elizabeth D. Woolsey

My first climbing adventure came close to ending in tragedy. I was thirteen when I wandered off from a school picnic in Mt. Carmel near New Haven, and followed a path that skirted the base of a cliff. Impulsively, I decided to climb it.

The climb went easily the first few feet, gradually grew more difficult until I was stopped by a holdless section some thirty feet off the ground. I then discovered that it's easier to climb up than down. I was spread-eagled there for what seemed like hours; my muscles began to cramp, my legs to shake; my heart pounded and although it was a cool, fall day, I was drenched in sweat.

I held on for agonizing minutes and then fell off backwards. I remember nothing of the fall itself and landed in a bushy evergreen tree, the only one growing from the rocks of the talus slope. I crashed on down to the ground, landing on a bed of broken branches, twigs and needles. I had cuts and bruises, but no broken bones and my faith in my guardian angel was unshaken.

This accident in no way dampened my interest in climbing, though being stiff and sore I temporarily became an armchair mountaineer. I read Frederic Burlingham's How to Become An Alpinist in which it became apparent that he greatly admired the women climbers of his day. Of Mrs. Bullock Workman he writes, "The American, not long ago ascended to the tremendous height of 23,300 feet in the Nun Kun Range in Kashmir as she has been eight times in the Himalayas it would not surprise her friends to read, almost any morning that she is at it again."

From an account of the second ascent of Mont Blanc by a woman, Mlle. d'Angeville, he has this to say, "Owing to the rarefied air she sank down exhausted . . . by pure will power she ordered the caravan to proceed, and exclaimed, 'Promise me that if I die on the way you will carry me to the top.'"

Burlingham reassures his readers that the lady did, in fact, reach the top alive and "after dancing a quadrille in the snow at 15,781 feet she said she wanted to go higher than Mont Blanc, and climbed on the shoulders of the guides. Enthusiasm such as this will lead one almost anywhere."

We have little clue as to what Miss Annie Peck, the conqueror of Mt. Huascaran, in Peru, really looked like as there is not an inch of skin exposed in her studio portrait. A floppy hat is pulled down over her forehead and she is wearing a face mask over goggles. Her laced boots reach the knee and bloomer-like knickers end above them. The space between is covered by what appears to be long, white underwear.

Although I had lived in the shadow of the mountains for many years it wasn't until I was 15 that I got above tree line on a trip to Europe with the Winslows, the parents of a classmate, Nancy. I was promised that after a certain amount of educational sightseeing we would go to the Pyrenees and then on the Geneva, where Dr. Winslow was due to present a paper before the League of Nations.

I kept a diary with fairly equal space devoted to food (generally not to my liking), to museums, castles and other historic sites. In Les Baux, for example, which I admired for its fortifications, perched on a limestone crag high above the valley, I comment, "Had the worst dinner of my life, with dishwater soup, then omelet saturated in kerosene. The climax was a stringy chicken, with head attached."

Dr. Winslow remembered his promise about climbing and sent Mrs. Winslow ahead to Gavarni with the luggage when we left Biarritz. He, Nancy and I hiked to the Lac Du Gaube where we would spend the night before traversing the Vignemale, some 3,298 meters, coming into Gavarni on the far side of the mountain. Our guide woke us before sunrise and the route started with easy mountain walking. Then, "We had some exciting times crossing deep snow on the almost perpendicular side of the mountain . . ." I was exaggerating, but this was my first mountain and I was only fifteen.

Shortly after our arrival in Geneva we motored to Chamonix where I was impressed by the great peaks and aiguilles—or sheer rocky spires—of the French Alps rising just outside town. The streets were full of mountaineering types and, through a telescope set up in the town square, I watched a group struggling through deep snow on their descent of Mont Blanc. Lunching on the terrace at Montenvers, overlooking the Mer du Glace, I saw a threesome that was to have a profound influence on my life, a slender, sunburned woman, quite old I decided (probably around thirty), with two

Elizabeth D. Woolsey

men all in nail boots and carrying rucksacks, ropes and ice axes. They were handsome, vital and about to head for unknown adventures in the mountains. I was suddenly overcome by a desperate longing to become a member, some day, of such a party. This, I now realize, was a turning point in my life.

Back in New Haven I found my first climbing companions, the Whitney brothers, both undergraduates at Yale. Roger, the older brother was tall and blond, Hassler equally tall and red-headed. Both were good climbers and excellent teachers. From them I learned how to handle the rope; methods of belaying, and how to pendulum. We practiced long, free rappels from the "Nose" of the Sleeping Giant, which involved placing a doubled climbing rope around a solid object such as a tree or a rocky knob and sliding down it. The rope could then be retrieved at the foot of the cliff by pulling down one end. The Mt. Carmel cliffs were of no great extent, but had enough variety for practice in chimney and crack climbing as well as friction climbing on smooth slabs. My next sister, Anne, about my size, joined us on many of the climbs and did very well.

My father gave me a climbing rope for Christmas and I took it along to New Mexico in 1927 where Anne and I met Ashley Pond and George Massey, also friends from Yale. Our first climb was to the top of the Enchanted Mesa, a steep-sided, flat-topped butte west of Albuquerque in the Acoma Indian Reservation. We followed a relatively easy route via a series of chimneys, finding solid wooden pegs pounded into the rock cracks that could be used as hand holds. On top we admired the view of the ancient village of Acoma, perched on its own high mesa and still inhabited, and decided to take another way down.

As we had my 120 foot climbing rope, we decided to descend a sheer side in a series of rappels. The top section went well as we found a ledge every 40 feet or so with a convenient knob to anchor the rope and repeat the procedure. But the last pitch above the valley floor was much further than my rope would reach. We couldn't climb up as we'd come down over a series of overhangs and were in a jackpot.

It was blistering hot on our unsheltered ledge; we had no water and were in a remote area (in those days) of the Acoma Indian Reservation. The ledge we were trapped on continued around the face of the mesa ending in a sheer cliff.

Without much hope—but it was better than just sitting and waiting for complete dehydration—I followed the ledge and found that there was a chimney between the cliff and our shelf which had been hidden from sight until I was directly above it. There, hanging down and reaching all the way to the ground, was a rope, possibly left by climbers who had found themselves in the same predicament that we were in. A shout brought my companions to my side. We tested the rope; it was solid and we were soon all down on the valley floor. I have always been grateful to our unknown saviors—and to my guardian angel.

Although Mesa Verde had been made a National Park in 1906, it was still largely undeveloped and unexplored in 1927. The four of us borrowed camping equipment from the Ponds who lived in Santa Fe, stocked the car with food and headed north to Colorado, following the New Mexican-Colorado border until just before the Four Corners, where Arizona, Utah, Colorado and New Mexico touch. There we turned south on the road leading to the top of the plateau where park headquarters were located.

Anne and I pitched our tent near the rim of the mesa with a wonderful view over the deep canyons that lead from the plateau. We found several eccentric characters camped there who had preceded us. There was a lady dressed in Chinese clothes who spent most of her time sitting on a log playing a flute. Another had her sleeping bag laid out on a narrow ledge, protected by an overhang of rock. Rumor had it that a magnificent mountain lion came to curl up beside her every night, taking off at dawn. Anne and I inspected the eyrie while the lady was away, and were delighted to find the pad marks of a big cat in the dirt under some nearby cedar trees.

We were given permission to explore the park as long as we left all undisturbed in the cliff dwellings that it contained. We would pack a lunch, fill our canteens with water, and spend the days hiking and climbing. We found many cliff dwellings, most of them perched high above the floor of the canyons. These we would climb up to from below when possible, or rappel down into them from above, using trees to anchor our ropes. We spent a tense hour under a great vaulted niche, full of broken pottery and bones, during a violent cloudburst while the lightning flickered around us and the thunder reverberated from the canyon walls.

My first chance at real mountaineering came the summer of 1928 when Anne and I were sent to Europe with Alice Lowell, of Boston, as chaperone. It was not an ideal arrangement as Anne and I (or was it chiefly I?) wanted to be in the mountains and Alice preferred the Salzburg Festival where she had a chance to sing in the chorus.

After a walking trip in the Black Forest we arrived in Salzburg where I found a letter from the Whitney boys waiting for me. They suggested that Anne and I meet them in Switzerland for some climbing. I immediately cabled my father for permission and the answer was "Certainly." This reply was no surprise as father had always been supportive of my climbing, indeed had given me my first rope. I suspect that he found life as a consulting forester a bit quiet in contrast to the challenges of his early years as a ranger in New Mexico and the service overseas with the American Expeditionary Forces in World War I. I am sure that he took pleasure in listening to my own tales which evidently evoked memories of his own active years.

The Whitneys and their cousin Bradley Gilman (who became the president of the American Alpine Club in 1953) met us in Montreux and we immediately headed up into the Alps Vaudoises for training climbs, sleeping in various alpine huts. After a few days Anne and I had learned how to move along without getting tangled in the rope, leaving too much slack or jerking the climber ahead, things many pure rock climbers never learn as they are apt to move one at a time.

It was a wind-still day on top of Les Diablerets and we ate our bread and cheese with a semicircular view of the alpine giants: Mont Blanc just over the French border and the great peaks of the Oberland and the Valais whose snowfields and glaciers were all glistening white. To me it was a vision of the Promised Land.

Then what intense pleasure it was to come down off the sunbaked cliffs to the first alp, or mountain pasture, and drink great gulps of ice cold water from streams flowing through meadows of green grass and flowers. There were dark blue gentians, anemones, white and pink saxifrage with small yellow centers, and most beautiful of all, the alpenroses.

There would be cows and goats grazing, many wearing bells of different tones that made lovely music as they moved along. I envied the cheese makers who summered with their flocks, rarely leaving their picturesque, weatherbeaten huts in the high, cool uplands to go down to the hot valleys.

We spent our last night in a mountain inn, a bit more than a hut but less than a hotel, where we ate six-egg omelets and drank quarts of warm milk, fresh from a herd of Brown Swiss cows. There was a piano and we stretched out on the floor after dinner while Hassler Whitney, who is a talented musician as well as mathematician and mountain climber, played many of the Bach fugues from memory with hardly a false note, a performance all the more remarkable as his fingers had been handling a climbing rope, or been curled around an ice axe, all that day.

The innkeeper brought out bottles of wine and by midnight we had formulated plans for the next few weeks. My sister Anne decided to join a school friend in Paris; I, with the memory of that threesome setting forth for unbeknown adventures from Montenvers still clear in my mind, chose to stay in the mountains especially as our destination was to be Chamonix.

We traveled directly to Montenvers: the two Whitney boys, Bradley Gilman and myself. I came this time, not as a tourist, but as a mountaineer proudly equipped with a rucksack, ice axe and crampons. I looked with scorn at the "trippers" on the terrace who were following Mark Twain's recipe for climbing: "Hotel veranda! Bottle of whiskey! Telescope!"

The solid Chamonix granite that we found on l'Aiguille de l'M delighted us and we resolved that the Grepon would be next. I reread Mummery's light-hearted account of his first ascent with the guides Burgener and Venez and amused myself by trying to estimate the number of alcoholic drinks they consumed during the climb. The text was full of references such as "libations should be duly poured; . . . having restored our spirits by a quiet consideration of a certain flask" and, on the summit, they opened a bottle of champagne. Mummery comments, "it has been frequently noted that all mountains appear to be doomed to pass through three stages: an inaccessible peak—The most difficult ascent in the Alps—An easy day for a lady."

The Grepon was not really I thought, "an easy day for a lady." I had climbed harder pitches on Ragged Mt. and other cliffs in Connecticut, but the exposure was awesome on most of the traverse of the narrow, crenelated ridge and this made all the difference. The route is largely hidden from below and the climber has a series of delightful surprises as he discovers the flaws in the mountain's defenses.

Two days later we headed for the Grand Charmoz and had the misfortune of following an Englishman, sandwiched between two guides whose idea was to reach the top as soon as possible.

The unfortunate client was poked with an ice axe from below and hauled from above like a piece of baggage until he was reduced to exhaustion and tears. No sooner on top, the two guides (who looked very much like gangsters) prepared a rappel for the descent. To my suggestion that they give their client a rest one replied "Foutez moi la paix" (roughly translated, "Mind your own business") and lowered their unhappy Englishman off the summit tower.

It was early in the day, a fine one, and we lazed on the summit rocks, ate bread, cheese and chocolate and admired the view of the great Chamonix aiguilles. Hassler had his head buried in the "Guide Vallot," which gave detailed descriptions of the various routes. He suggested that rather than returning the way we had come, we do the traverse, a much more demanding climb. I seconded the motion but Roger and Brad were meeting friends in Chamonix and had to hurry down. So we parted company, each party taking one rope.

"Hass" and I had a delightful climb on the slabs that formed the broken arete of the Charmoz, stopping often to consult the guide book. We then, as directed, headed down the steep face which involved several long rappels. Our single rope was barely long enough and I was soon in trouble; first to go down, I found myself at the end of the rope, hanging against a sheer rock wall. There was no way I could climb back up the rope so, remembering our maneuvers on the Mt. Carmel cliffs, I started swinging back and forth in ever widening arcs until I was directly above a ledge a few feet below me. I took a chance—I had to—and jumped, landing on the ledge and keeping my balance.

As soon as I stopped shaking (the tension and effort had been great) I called up to Hass, who was out of sight but could hear me, to move the rappel point till it was directly above me. He did so and joined me with no difficulty on the correct route that had been hidden from above and now seemed obvious when seen from below. We hurried on down to the glacier and rested, eating our one can of sardines washed down with sips of melting snow water. This was our last climb as a storm boiled up from the south, coating the mountains with a layer of snow and ice.

The next two summers my only climbs were on eastern cliffs, ranging as far north as the White Mountains, as far south as West Virginia. New friends included Tom Rawles, an instructor at Yale, Bill Willcox, a Yale graduate student (presently editing the Franklin Papers) and his brother Alan, a New York lawyer.

They proposed a climbing holiday in Zermatt and I jumped at the chance. I should mention that these weekend trips and this trip to Europe were possible as I had a small, independent income that permitted me to travel as I pleased, within reason.

We met in Zermatt in July, 1931. Although I had seen many photographs and paintings of the Matterhorn, they hadn't prepared me for the reality: "a pointed mountain, pointing at the stars, looming up above its white encircling glaciers, dark and beautiful."

We dined formally our first evening at the Monte Rosa, our hotel, the men in dinner jackets, I in a dinner dress, as such was the custom set by the chiefly British climbers who headquartered there. Dinner over, we adjoined to a large living room for coffee and were joined by Bernhardt Biner who was to be our guide.

Bernhardt was blue eyed and blond, tall, and well built, who spoke with an English accent, because, as he told us, he had spent a year in England. He was the "chef des Guides" in Zermatt and our visit was interrupted when another guide hurried in and asked what to do about two guideless Germans stuck high up on the Matterhorn. Bernhardt gave the guide instructions in German and then turned his attention back to us, confiding to me that "he was not the best guide in Zermatt, but was the best lady's guide," an opinion I was never to dispute.

For training we started on the Untergabelhorn, an easy climb but involving a lot of height difference. Part way up we found an Australian lying on the turf and groaning. He explained that he climbed as fast as he could, "till I become bloody sick," and "No, I don't want any help." So we left him on his green sick bed, reached the top and descended in a downpour that lasted a week, piling up new snow on the peaks.

It cleared one day, as it does, and after several days climbing on the Riffelhorn and on boulders north of town we walked up to the Trift Hotel to sleep before climbing the Obergabelhorn. On the descent from this peak I had my first experience with an avalanche. It was a hot afternoon as we worked our way, rather tediously, down unstable scree slopes.

Bernhardt spotted a long steep snow gully that he thought might afford a quick route to the valley below. He anchored himself on the edge of the couloir and payed out rope as I climbed down into it. The snow was wet and I sank in to my waist.

"I don't like this" I called out to Bernhardt who was now out of sight. "Keep going till you reach the middle and then head straight down," he answered. I struggled on till suddenly, without a sound, the top layer of snow avalanched, taking me with it. A few seconds later there was a tremendous jerk, and I hung onto the rope, fighting for breath through the snow that was still pouring down from above. The avalanche ran its course and I was safe but angry. Bernhardt called down "Too dangerous," an opinion that I fervently agreed with as I climbed back up and out of the gully. This incident left me with a lasting respect for steep, wet, snow slopes.

That night, over coffee, we held a council of war. Bernhardt proposed a snow climb and suggested Monte Rosa from the Italian side, a steep 8,000-foot crescent-shaped face comparable to the Brenva face of Mont Blanc.

This face is bisected by the Marinelli Couloir, into which most of the falling rock and ice from the upper section of the mountain finds its way. The first man to climb this face, a guide, was killed repeating his route as he was

Elizabeth D. Woolsey

bivouacking near the edge of the Marinelli. The Italian Alpine Club now has a hut at an elevation of approximately 10,000 feet and we would sleep there the night before our climb.

We took on another guide, Hugo Lehner, and left by train for Domodossala, then transferring to an ancient Fiat for the drive to Macugnaga, the village nearest the base of our peak. There we left the car and hiked up the dusty trail in the broiling Italian sun to the Belvedere Hut, or Inn where we arrived perspiring freely. The grass was soon littered with damp socks, shirts and alpinists. A rustic meal followed, with fowls wading in the soup, roosters pecking at our bare toes and a large and unusually hairless pink sow watching us with her one baleful eye.

We continued after lunch and in the course of the next four hours discovered one of the most tedious and hot hut trails in the Alps. I was puzzled to see on the slopes above me what appeared to be clouds of smoke coming right up out of the rocks. As we drew near the Marinelli I saw that the source was the hut itself where we found three French boys and their guides trying to cook supper over a smoky fire in a battered iron stove. We added a pot of soup, with bits of sausage to thicken it and, with bread and cheese, this was our dinner.

Evening in the hut was not exactly cozy. When we stepped outside for a breath of fresh air the intense cold drove us back inside and we resigned ourselves to sleeping in the interior. We divided the four mattresses among the ten of us and I, at least, was tired enough to sleep soundly.

We crossed the quiet Marinelli Couloir at 3:30 the following morning, and then had two hours of easy climbing on rock. We pushed on, now over snow, and our second breakfast was on a small rock island below a steep snow slope. Almost directly above us we could see the rocks of the summit ridge that looked about three hours away. They looked closer here than they did for the next six.

Just below us we could see the other party bound for the Nordend. Beyond the sea of cloud that covered the Italian plain, were the Ortler, Cresta Agutza and other distant peaks silhouetted against the sun and glowing with marvelous colors. In the foreground the tops of the peaks loomed up through the clouds like black islands floating in a misty Aegean sea.

We strapped on our crampons and climbed steep snow slopes between the Marinelli that we wanted to avoid, and the ice fall on our left. This slope finally merged into the couloir and forced us to find our way up through the seracs that finally barred our way effectively. The tension increased almost unbearably, for me at least, as we hurried across the Marinelli to reach the base of a rudimentary rock ridge. At the top of the rib we had another rest and watched avalanches of flour-like snow pour off the terraced cliffs of the Nordend.

The sun was now hot and the first rocks were beginning to shoot down the couloir, about a hundred yards wide here, with a horrid, whining sound. We crossed it for the last time, slowly because of the steep angle of the slope and the wet snow sticking to our crampons, trying to ignore the stones that were now coming down almost continuously. Safe on the far side, I watched Bill and Alan, on the second rope, dive for the shelter of a small crevasse just off the couloir to escape a shower of large rocks that just missed them. Although the main stone fall was down the Marinelli chute, we were exposed to some stones from above for the next three hours with only one protected spot, behind a big serac where we took another rest.

The fresh snow on the route was wet and formed great balls on the bottom of each crampon and climbing was exhausting work. I would drive my ice axe in as far as I could reach and pull myself up with my arms. The bergschrund, where the snow and ice breaks away from the underlying rock leaving a crevasse-like chasm, was in this case a hundred meters or so below the rocks of the summit ridge and filled with snow. We crossed it easily and above was the only ice slope we found on the whole face.

We climbed to some small rocks projecting through the snow, anchored ourselves and tried to ignore the rocks that were whizzing down for the half hour it took Bernhardt to cut steps up to the cliffs of the summit ridge. We had joined both ropes together and with this protection were able to hurry up the steps to Bernhardt who was belaying us from his rocky perch.

It was a tremendous relief to finally be out of the line of fire. Without helmets, or protection of any kind, it was a helpless feeling and the danger had lasted for many hours. I am sure that this climb should be done earlier in the day, before the sun has had a chance to melt the snow and ice that cement the rocks in place, and turn the Marinelli into "the greatest avalanche through in Europe."

We had our third meal of the day on a rocky perch with a spectacular view down the east face, and beyond, the green valleys of Italy. In perfect safety we watched several avalanches, some of rock, others of snow and ice, roar down the Marinelli. The larger boulders gouged great trenches in the snow leaving ugly, black streaks where they uncovered the ice beneath.

The route then led over snow and ice-covered rocks to the summit ridge and on to the Dufour Spitze, at 15,203 feet, the highest point on Monte Rosa, which we reached at 2:30, just eleven hours after crossing the

Elizabeth D. Woolsey

Marinelli for the first time. I found slabs on the summit that were not only level, but also dry, and I stretched out in the sun, suddenly very tired and not a bit hungry.

I lay on my stomach with my chin resting on my crossed hands and looked down on the Matterhorn and the other great peaks of the Valais surrounded by their world of ice and snow. Dozing, I thought of the many who had climbed Monte Rosa since its first ascent in 1854. I had a series of dream-like images: of Winthrop Young, slowly and perhaps painfully, making his way up on the one leg left him after World War I; of Queen Margherita of Italy, with her big entourage and her two little dogs romping through the snow; of Vittorio Sella, the great Italian mountain photographer, muffled against the cold during the first winter ascent.

Bernhardt persuaded me to drink some sweet lemon-flavored tea. I was soon completely restored and we raced down to the Betemps Hut in an hour and fifteen minutes. We walked up to the Riffelberg, and caught the train down the Zermatt, all delighted we had climbed the East face and I, for one, resolved never to repeat it.

Alan and Bill Willcox, Tom Rawles and Bernhardt all came to the station to see me off as I was leaving before the rest of the group. I was relectant to leave my friends and the mountains and spent the trip down to Visp leaning out of the train window for last glimpses of the Matterhorn.

I had just settled myself in my compartment in the train for Geneva when Bernhardt came bounding in and sat down beside me. He explained that he had "business down the valley," so had hopped on his motor bike and roared down to Visp. We talked of the climbs we had done, planned future expeditions and I promised that I would return as soon as possible, preferably in winter or spring with a pair of skis.

I realize that I was very fortunate to have climbed in the days when it was possible to explore and make first ascents in reasonably accessible ranges rather than to have to travel to the "ends of the earth."

In retrospect I realize that I enjoyed the challenge of exploring unknown ranges, the route finding on unclimbed mountains and the unique sensation one has when setting foot on a virgin summit, more than pure rock climbing which is deliberate and slow. The latter takes a great deal of patience, a quality I am somewhat lacking in.

Elizabeth D. (Betty) Woolsey was born in Albuquerque, New Mexico and started her climbing career in the Sandia Mountains of New Mexico. Vassar educated, Betty spent a great deal of time climbing with the likes of Fritz Wiessner and Hans Kraus in many of the great mountain ranges of the world, doing first ascents in the Alps, the Tetons and the Canadian Rockies. Betty was also responsible, or at least partly so, for the refinement of ski mountaineering in the Alps. She was a member and captain of the American Women's ski team from 1937 to 1940.

Recollections of Margaret

Annie Whitehouse

I miss Margaret in her baggy pants and loose cotton shirt, pockets heavy with her altimeter, note cards and pencil. For those who knew Margaret Young, that image alone will bring a smile and stir memories of shared adventures and climbs. For those who didn't, I hope to recall the curious and pioneering nature of a very special woman! My desire for 5.12 and high mountain ascents began with my association with Margaret. Picture a sixteen year old girl, sturdy and able, offered the opportunity to fly over the Sierra Nevada in a Cessna 180 piloted by this enigmatic woman and then to climb the steep couloir of the North Palisade in January. I had been climbing some at that time. I was both excited and intimidated, for until that time I had the vague notion that climbing was a group undertaking.

Under the insightful and keen tutelage of Phil Arnot and David Lunn I was taught basics of climbing through a high school class. Instead of studying the 3-R's we were often out climbing, en masse, in various locations throughout the Western states. We were to meet at her house for an early morning start. Grey metal shelves lined the entrance, on which were stacked pitons, ice screws, fossils, airplane parts, a dog food dish, dusty pieces of wood, books and various manuals. Advancing further I noticed an automatic chart of the elements taped to one of the kitchen walls, under which she sat. She was on the telephone getting a pilot briefing for our flight. She scribbled the flight information directly onto her kitchen table in what seemed to me to be a confusing mess of abbreviations, elevations and arrows.

I stood and watched, thinking that her kitchen looked more like a laboratory; nesting sets of measuring cups, metal bowls and labeled plastic containers on metal shelves. The sun had not yet risen, but if it had, little light would have come in. Black spray-painted 10 gallon plastic water containers sat on even more metal shelves in front on the south facing windows. These, she later told me, were an experiment in solar heating.

As I think back, I realize Margaret's house was not the chaotic array of things it might have seemed, but an efficient work space. The out of doors; clean, pure and ordered by nature was where she felt at home.

As a novice climber I was only too eager to charge up a mountain, oblivious to the world around me. This was not Margaret's approach. Margaret liked to dream up the most improbable, outrageous schemes and then carry them out with meticulous attention to detail. The continuity of her approach became more tangible as we drove to the airport. The high cirrus clouds above us in Palo Alto were an integral part of the weather projection, she repeated to me. Not only did they mean high winds aloft for our flight, but also high pressure and possible windy conditions for our climb.

The entire plane shook and shuddered as she 'reved' the engine during the pre-flight inspection. I sat, buckled in; looking out the window at our small red and white airplane's little tires. They belonged on a toy car rather than a plane. Blind faith and naively abound in youth!

Once up she asked me if I wanted to fly for awhile. Over the roar of the engine I learned how the rudders, yoke and ailerons worked. She shouted, "If you want to go left, push in on the left rudder and turn the yoke to the left at the same time. To go up pull the yoke towards you, and to go down, push it in. O.K., now fly at this elevation and keep the heading indicator at 170°." I was sure we were going to get hit by a Greyhound bus. She gazed out the window, jotting down numbers on the acre chart held in her lap. My neck and shoulders felt as though they would turn to stone. I knew that the Greyhound bus was out there somewhere. She took the controls back over Fresno. By then I was kind of having fun.

We landed, tied down quickly and called a friend to give us a ride to the road's end. As we approached the North Palisade, Margaret's slow; steady pace was occasionally interrupted to photograph snow, delicately balanced on a branch or to ponder the geologic events leading to the rock formations we passed. Last fall while climbing in the Schwangunks I felt something remiss. Many times had we parked our car alongside the road, walked along the carriage road to the base of the climb and then climbed. Many climbers, including myself, seemed oblivious to their environment. Only the powerful pull of the cliffs held our attention. In Margaret's world both the climbing and the surroundings would have intrigued her. I can picture her questioning the rangers ranger at the Uberfalls about where one can legally camp, what kind of trees were those and how many climbers paid fees today? Margaret was introduced to climbing in the Schwangunks. During the early 1950's she studied physics and chemistry at the Massachusetts Institute of Technology (MIT) On weekends and school breaks she joined the MIT outing club's sojourns to the "Gunk's" wild overhangs, finding a pleasure and niche in climbing. Later she moved to Palo Alto, California for both its proximity to the mountains and its growing scientific community.

The industrious climbing section of the Sierra Club offered Margaret climbing partners and opportunities for challenging climbs. When I joined Margaret on a Sierra Club climb I sensed her fellow climbers were both amused and respectful of her indomitable nature. The more complicated the approach and the less straightforward the climb, the more Margaret seemed to enjoy herself. Being the impetuous, on trips ranging from the first winter ascent of 14,000' Mount Tyndall to a more imaginative Trans- Sierra winter crossing on snowshoes, her reputation as a strong-willed, determined climber was firmly established.

A July 27, 1968 Palo Alto Times article reads, "A doctor, a student, two scientists and a homemakers. Put them together and what do you get? A mountain climbing team. . . *en route* right now where they will climb Chimborazo and Cotopaxi. Being the only woman in the party does not faze Mrs. Young. "I have been on quite a few climbs as the only woman. Besides, you can never tell who you will meet on the mountain."

Margaret found being a woman and a climber easily congruent. I adopted that attitude without question, besides you can never tell who you will meet on the mountain. I recall meeting skiers swooshing through the powder snow of the Bugaboos while Vera Watson, Margaret and I plodded across the cirque on snowshoes after climbing S. Hauser Tower in sub-zero temperatures. They seemed surprised to see three women with heavy, packs walking through the knee deep powder. They refused my offer of trading their skis for some used climbing equipment and a frustrating pair of snowshoes. Having accomplishments under or overrated because I am female seems odd and unnecessary. Certainly there are differences between men and women. To objectively recognize those differences and to climb using individual talents only makes sense.

Though there has always been rivalries and rule setting in climbing, Margaret has unfortunately missed the controversies present today. To Margaret climbing was not in need of a definition. A climb was defined by the skill and objectives of the person climbing. You usually started from the bottom and did what you wanted to do to reach the top. Or started from the top, as she did when making her "Glen Canyon first and last ascents". In this case they started from the rim of the canyon, repelled down and rafted along the base of the cliffs as the waters in Glen Canyon rose. Several "first and last ascents" were made and captured on film as the climbers ascended the now underwater sandstone walls in the bluff.

I am certain that Margaret would find some of the controversies interesting and worthy of thought, but not to be solved in concrete terms. She valued the individualistic nature of climbing far too much to be obliged to follow other's rules and opinions. A progressive thinker, Margaret would have been delighted to trade her black polyester climbing pants in for a pair of green and pink lycra and give hangdogging a shot.

In 1963 Margaret flew her Cessna to Alaska. The unclimbed South East ridge of Foraker and Moose's Tooth were her objectives. Unsuccessful in reaching the summit of both, she returned the next year to the virtually unexplored area of 'Little Switzerland' southwest of McKinley to make several first ascents. Later she returned to climb the S. Moose's Tooth, this also being a first ascent. Climbs in Bolivia, Nepal, Afghanistan, Russia and Africa were interspersed with her frequent trips to the Sierras.

Determination was one of Margaret's strong points. Something I learned early climbing with her was that given halfway decent conditions you can usually get to the top by just keeping going. On Noshaq in 1972 she set the altitude record for American women by climbing it in her "own alpine style." She and Bill Griffin set out to climb the west ridge one day after she arrived at base camp. Seven days later she arrived at the summit solo. Her climbing partner turned back because of cold feet. Arlene Blum, the leader of this expedition, described Margaret as careful, but unconventional. She refused to abide by Arlene's plan of climbing in expedition style, preferring to slowly acclimatize by ascending in a slow, focused manner.

Margaret was dead by the time I joined the 1983 American expedition to climb Everest's west ridge. She died of cancer after a horseback accident left her partially paralyzed. The day Renny Jackson, Eric Reynolds and I ascended the Hornbein Couloir in hope of attaining Everest's summit was cold and clear. The hills and valleys of Tibet, muted shades of brown and pink, were far below. We were above even the surrounding icy white Himalayan peaks. Each laborious step drew me upward, wanting to take another. Sometimes vivid recollections of Margaret, her solid determination and spirit, spurred me on. The two cold oxygen less nights we spent at 27,000' were uncomfortable and at times scary. Again, thoughts of Margaret among other fleeting recollections of life and loved ones kept me going. She probably would have enjoyed it up there.

I appreciate the introduction Margaret gave me to climbing. Sometimes I wonder, what is this thing called "climbing", a quest or an obsession? What is this thing that takes my body and mind, shapes and molds it, giving and taking strength? My answer will change, but the mountains, rocks and plants I pass along the way will not.

Annie Whitehouse is recognized as one of America's foremost female expedition climbers. In 1983 she set the American women's altitude record by reaching 28,000 feet On Everest's west ridge. She has been a member of an expedition to the north face of Mount Everest and was on the 1978 all women expedition to Annapurna. She has contributed articles to National Geographic and Outside Magazines.

Women On the Rocks: Way Back Then

Ruth Dyar Mendenhall

Because of the passage of time, I have advanced from climber to pioneer woman climber.

I started climbing rocks in Southern California in 1938. Alpine techniques had been introduced to both the Los Angeles and San Francisco areas in 1931 during Robert L. M. Underhill's visit from New England. A Rock Climbing Section (usually referred to as the RCS) was established in the mid-thirties in the Southern California (now Angeles) Chapter of the Sierra Club. At the time I took up the sport, the popularity of climbing was rapidly rising. Most of the pioneer rock climbers were men, but several outstanding women climbers had already retired from climbing or overlapped with me. Now that I am considered a Pioneer nearly fifty years later, modern women climbers have expressed an interest in the status of women climbers of that day. A question occasionally asked is whether we climbed with men or mostly with each other. The short simple answer to that is that we did not have enough climbers to sort them out by gender.

There were seldom more than three or four serious women climbers in Southern California at any one time, often only one or two compared to, perhaps, six to a couple of dozen men. Besides that, the boys and girls enjoyed climbing together. Most respected their own and each other's abilities and limitations. A few fellows, usually young gymnasts, seemed to feel diminished if a girl made a pitch they couldn't. But I remember very little machismo, or for that matter machisma, among us. Of course, a mixture of these attitudes did surface occasionally. For example, at a Tahquitz Rock climb, the man who was trip leader was arranging the ropes for the day's climbs. He asked me to lead a visitor from Switzerland up the Fingertip Traverse. Although I had made the climb, I was in my first season and somewhat lacking in confidence. I was on the verge of declining when another man nearby, who really had nothing to do with the matter, spoke to me:

"Ruth! You shouldn't! You had only three or four hours of sleep last night." That decided me. I agreed to lead the rope, off-handedly collected my equipment and my second, and went. Years later I discovered by chance that I had acquired a modest fame in Europe as a rock climber.

Other women in our club had been making their mark in the climbing world: Mary Jane Edwards, Adrienne Applewhite (Jones), the first woman to climb the East Face of Mt. Whitney, LaVere Daniels (Aulie), who appeared in a professional movie short, "Three on a Rope," and was the first woman to climb Temple Crag, 12,999 feet. May Pridham, who had made assorted climbs with her sister and other girls before she ever heard of rope techniques, and who provided our newssheet with skiing and climbing cartoons so pertinent that they are famous in Sierra Club publications to this day. Elsie Strand and Agnes Fair. We didn't think of ourselves as women climbers, but as women who liked to climb. The field of mountaineering and rock climbing was wide open to all comers.

I had grown up having outdoor adventures with various of my three sisters and occasional cousins (our brother was too conservative). We had hiked, backpacked, camped, and gone on wilderness fishing trips. Though we had never heard of rock climbing, we had indulged in ascents of some of the basalt formations in Spokane, Washington. I later classified some of these climbs as fourth class; we should have been roped. Though all my sisters climbed to some extent in later years, I was the only one to develop such a passion for climbing that I pursued it for thirty-five seasons.

From Spokane, I had come to Southern California as a college graduate in need of a job, my school having assigned all its scarce job openings that year to men. A relative offered me secretarial work with one of the State Relief Organizations of the time. I was lonely, homesick, and displaced in both occupation and geography. When I discovered the Ski Mountaineers Section of the Sierra Club, my life improved immeasurably. When I found out that many of the skiers became rock climbers when the snow melted, I thought I had been catapulted into Eden. Don't laugh! After all, there allegedly was an apple tree in eden. And due to a childhood of tree climbing, I soon realized that apple trees are the horticultural equivalent of sound granite.

My situation was not unlike that of many young people of that time, the latter years of the Great Depression. Some were unemployed; many held poorly paying jobs and worked hard not to lose them. We hungered for fun, adventure, and companionship. These were available in the skiing and climbing set—and at that time had the added advantage of not costing much.

In the late 1930's there were no ski lifts except for a few short rope tows. The Ski Mountaineers gave instruction. They also raised money and provided the manpower to build and maintain ski huts in nearby mountains. Hut fees were twenty-five cents a night. Entertainment, often complete with a member's accordion at the end of a steep trail, was free.

Rock climbing was even cheaper. Our club furnished most of the equipment. Ropes were 90-foot and 130-foot seven-sixteenth inch manila, the best yachting line available. We compensated for its lack of stretch by dynamic belays. Steel carabiners were imported from Germany. The same was true of soft iron pitons until the duty became so high that local manufacture was arranged. Quarter-inch manila was used for slings and prusiks. We sewed leather patches onto pants and shirts to protect us from the friction of body rappels. We wore old jeans and very jaunty, individual felt hats. Ice axes and piton hammers were personal equipment, and we often had only one to a rope. For footgear in the high mountains, we had men's work shoes or old leather ski boots nailed with tricounis. For rock climbing we wore tennis shoes or crepe-soled basketball shoes. With this gear, the better climbers of the time put up routes judged very difficult to this day, and others followed them. In recent years a male climber remarked in my hearing, "Imagine climbing the Mechanic's Route (at Tahquitz) in tennis shoes!" I said, "I don't have to imagine it. I did it."

In my first season, I attended RCS climbs almost every weekend. There were one-day or half-day instructional climbs locally, at Stony Point, Eagle Rock, and Devil's Gate Dam (until the authorities plastered it with concrete). Here anyone could learn elementary rope handling, belaying, and safety. Weekend climbs were held at Tahquitz Rock. This thousand-foot wedge of glorious granite rock, on the south side of Mt. San Jacinto above Idyiwild, seemed to offer endless possibilities for new routes. Only ten had been established by early 1938. And for three-day weekends, we went to the High Sierra, its stupendous East Face readily accessible from the south. Climber's vacations were usually spent in the Sierra. Foreign climbing, except for a rare venture to Canada, was at that time beyond the scope of our group.

Over the weekend of July 4, 1938, I had my first taste of scaling one of the fourteen-thousand-foot peaks in the Palisades, west of Big Pine in Owens Valley. The backpack was three or four miles of easy trail to Third Lake at about 10,000 feet. Parties attacked North Palisade (14,242 feet) and Mt. Sill (14,162 feet) by assorted routes. I was one of two ropes that made a new route up the North Buttress (now called the Swiss Arete in climbers' guides). We had two experienced rope leaders. The rest of us were all in our first season of climbing. The two men, whose bent was really not rock climbing, didn't seem to appreciate the exposure. I was so exhilarated by my first ascent of a real mountain, by the elevation and difficult moves, and by the lovely surroundings that, though I kept my cool, I was running over with sheer joy. We made the summit and descended by an easier way. For years afterwards, my rope leader twitted me about our return to camp. He claimed that, when our friends came into view beside their little campfires, I exclaimed, "Let's run, so they don't think we're tired."

Over Labor Day that year, eleven RCS members, nine men and two women, made the strenuous backpack, largely cross-country, over Pinnacle Pass to camp at East Face Lake at over 13,000 feet. Next day we all climbed 14,495-foot Mt. Whitney's East Face by the Sunshine-Peewee Route (now more decorously referred to as the East Buttress). The difficulty of the pack-in made a much more lasting impression on my mind than the climb itself.

Backpacking equipment of the day included Trapper Nelson packboards of wood and canvas, tortuous for neck and shoulders. Many of us had made our own sleeping bags. A pillow factory blew goose down into the tubes. Down cost $3 a pound, but as we often remarked, down was going up. A shelter was rarely needed, since it "never" rained in the Sierra until after nylon and plastic were invented. Our foods came from the grocery store in the form of cheese, sausage, spaghetti, cereals, dried fruits, crackers and candy. We didn't miss freeze-dried or "instant" foods since there weren't any. But we did have Primus stoves from Sweden.

On our trips the mountains rang all day, and sometimes far into the night, with puns, jokes, yodels, shouts, and laughter, and with the singing and pinging of pitons going deeper into the cracks with each whack of the hammer. It was a gay and happy period in our lives, certainly not carefree, but light-hearted and filled with good comradeship. Both men and women became close friends through their mountain activities and related pursuits.

We were often together evenings as well as weekends. We held meetings, gave parties, promoted "ski rallies" to raise funds for the ski huts, and published our Ski Mountaineers and Rock Climbing Sections' newssheet, The Mugelnoos. For many a year I was chief honcho for The Mugelnoos, named after what is now called a mogul and our Ski Mountaineers chairman George Bauwen's Austrian accent. I kept the newssheet crammed with puns (one issue claimed forty-nine puns), cartoons, and facts that made climbing history. The first ascent of the Eigerwand was noted in August , 1938. We also had a correspondent from Byrd's third Antarctic Expedition of 1939-40. The Expedition's official artist, Leland Curtis, was a member of the Ski Mountaineers Section.

Transportation to Section affairs posed the usual problems. Most of the men and a few women drove old cars, and the rest of us were courtesy or paying passengers. Some of the crowd still lived at home, a very few were married, others occupied rooms or apartments, alone or with friends. Gradually a few of us, whose situations and yearnings were similar, conceived the idea of starting a cooperative coeducational boarding house for climbers and skiers. We weren't quite ready for a serious romance, though that came along soon. We weren't into what are now called relationships. Our mutual and overwhelming desire was a place to live that would be spacious, enjoyable, and of necessity economical—A HOME. The concept was rather far-out for the times. That it actually became a reality—and a success—seems a little surprising even now.

Ideas had been exchanged, and the prospective personnel reduced to six for a start: three men (Howard Koster, Glen Warner, and John Mendenhall) and three women (Olga Schomberg, my sister Joan Dyar (Clark), who had recently joined me in California, and I). We were between the ages of twenty-one and thirty. The men and I were dedicated climbers and also skied. Olga and Joan climbed a little and skied a lot. Our first practical need was to find the right house.

All the rental houses we had looked at up to late April 1939 were unsuitable—inconveniently located, too costly, too stark, too small. Then came an incredible stroke of luck. En route to a ski mountaineering venture on Mt. San Gorgonio, John and I took a look at a house for rent in northeastern Los Angeles. There it was! Big enough; on a streetcar line; cheap enough ($60 a month); and fully and nicely furnished, right down to table linens, a radio-phonograph, an encyclopedia, a piano, a fireplace and a mantel clock. On top of all that, the landlady, Grace Schults, had been a Sierra Club member. She seemed to have neither questions nor qualms about our unconventional plans. We telephoned our prospective housemates to inspect the place and went off skiing. Early the next week, the chosen six assembled to look together at this gem of a house. The decision seemed so momentous that for a short time we even ran out of wisecracks. We voted *"yes."*

The rooms were apportioned among us without problems. Joan and I had the big upstairs bedroom and Olga the small one. John, who needed a little peace and quiet for his engineering studies, had the third. Howard and Glen took the big downstairs bedroom. Mr. and Mrs. Schults retained a small corner apartment. Their son occupied a little knotty-pine building at the back of the lot. That was Monday. The next Saturday, May 5, 1939, we moved in.

Six people arrived with their accumulated belongings. These turned the ample front porch into a sort of junkyard of hickory skis, bamboo ski poles, desks, boots, carpets, a drafting board, lamps, ropes, a typing chair, canned milk, and my typewriter. Before getting organized, we looked again at our brown stucco palace. Enthusiasm mounted. Glen and I were so pleased at the back lawn that we turned somersaults all over it. Roses, syringa, and apple blossoms were in bloom. Mrs. Schults, with what turned out to be typical kindness and thoughtfulness, had cooked us a big pot of split pea soup and disappeared into her own rooms. Pea soup became a symbolic delicacy that for many years was ceremoniously served at Base Camp anniversaries and reunions.

A few days later, as all gathered at our new home for dinner, we held a house meeting. Our residence had to have a name, of course. After contemplating the fact that we had all heard of Green Gables and Seven Gables, Howard suggested Composition Roof, and Joan came up with Clark Gables. Eventually we chose Base Camp. We decided to try out this system of housework: a girl and a fellow would buy food and cook dinner together for one week (breakfasts were individually prepared, and we were seldom home for lunches); a girl and a fellow would wash dinner dishes; and a girl and a fellow would do the cleaning, yard work, household laundry, and everything else. We would have the same partner for three weeks, then switch partners and start all over. This plan worked so well that we stuck to it with trade-offs and variations, for the duration.

None of us had ever been in charge of running a household, and we found the job novel and even hilarious. Before we moved in, our contemporaries told us it "wouldn't work." It did, and so did we. Of course we didn't have the same tastes and talents. Some were better cooks than others, Howard the best of us all. One of our male visitors did remark that he "just couldn't see why the men should be compelled to cook." It really took two to run the 1915 washing machine in our small back cellar. It had two large copper tubs, leaky hoses, an electric wringer, and frightening gears. We kept each other up to a high standard of living. I once overheard Olga reprimanding Glen for getting out a clean tablecloth. Glen replied firmly that he would rather eat off newspapers than use the dirty one.

Dinners were nutritious and tasty, though sometimes we were up till midnight the preceding evening preparing jello, shelling peas, and other tasks. Mother's Day came around soon after we were settled, so we planned a special dinner for the five available parents and grandmothers. Olga and I planned the menu: roast beef, gravy, new potatoes, asparagus, aspic salad, rolls, coffee, and strawberry pie. Much preparation had to be done the preceding afternoon, since most of us planned to attend a practice climb Sunday morning. It had been my custom to rush off to climbs at the earliest possible moment, and return as late as feasible, and the fellows were even more addicted to this procedure. That Sunday Glen left early to take the ropes, which were stored in our living room window seat, to Eagle Rock. But the rest of us were putting the finishing touches on the dinner preparations. I was baking pies and dusting, Joan fixing bouquets, Howard doing the wash, and John cleaning house and preening the parking strip. I put the roast in the oven and set the timer to turn it on at noon; those who stayed home watched breathlessly to be sure it did. Eventually John, Olga and I were off to the climb, where we were greeted by remarks about our lateness. I explained that we were too busy keeping house to climb, a shock to those who knew us.

When we returned to Base Camp, the roast was snapping away in the oven. John had set the table for eleven. Chairs, plates, and silverware were carefully arranged so the guests would have the best. Our invited guests duly arrived, and the affair went off smoothly. The older ladies seemed properly impressed. After their departure, we spent the rest of the evening praising ourselves, cleaning up, and hurling insults at each other.

During that summer, we entertained countless guests, sometimes too many. We gave special dinners for aunts, cousins, old friends, and mostly our climbing and skiing friends. Drop-in guests sometimes seemed a bit startled by in-house arguments about who would stake them to the meal (twenty cents a head). Later we decided we should argue it out in private.

Since early 1938, I had been editing our newssheet and putting it out at my apartment, with a few assistants both regular and ad hoc. The first time The Mugelnoos was mimeographed and mailed at Base Camp, a gang of thirty friends turned up for the occasion, probably more from curiosity than volunteerism. During the week, I had collected and rewritten the news and cut the stencils, with John and Glen helping me. The mimeographing, an inky procedure, fitted ideally into the back porch. Our friends were perfect guests. They invited themselves, did most of the work, entertained themselves and their hosts, cleaned up the place, and went home.

Ruth Dyar Mendenhall

Mugelnoos-night parties became traditional, and Base Camp was turned into a social center as well as a source of information about almost anything. There was a lot of togetherness, but our rooms were strictly private territory.

Guests or not, there was always something going on at Base Camp. Joan on the piano and Howard on his tuba played duets. Some of us were always poring over mountaineering books such as Climbing Days by Dorothy Pilley and The Romance of Mountaineering by R. L. G. Irving. Four who were taking a first aid course had hysterics over prone-pressure artificial respiration. At dinners, the male cook was to sit in the armchair, which we called the Papa Chair; but if the male cook was absent, the female cook did the honors. There was a decided advantage to having two cooks—no matter what was fixed, there was always one other person to praise it.

We were heavy on economy, especially Howard, who occasionally overdid it. On one occasion he spied an uneaten cob of corn among the garbage, and indignantly bore it into the kitchen to add to the lima beans he was preparing. I intervened in sanitary horror. Howard was adamant. A wrestling match ensued, during which I succeeded in messing up the corn so even Howard admitted it was unfit to eat. Then we settled down to a laughing spree, and for several days our jokes seemed to center around garbage.

At dinner, humor seemed to be at its height. We often had jello for dessert, because it was cheap and easy to prepare. Its basic ingredients became a matter of speculation. Howard advanced a theory that it was made from horses' hooves. The encyclopedia revealed that gelatin was indeed extracted from animal tissues. Horses were not specifically mentioned, but it was not uplifting to read of hides, glue, coated pills, and isinglass. When the first course was over, Glen leaned back in his purple shirt and said, "Well, bring on the isinglass." I glanced at the color of the dessert being served, and inquired if it was "strawberry roan." On another evening Joan had received a message to telephone a climber who was an intern. As she rose from the table, she remarked, "I have to call General Hospital." John inquired sternly, "Has your meal taken effect already?"

Sometimes we laughed so loudly that we would glance up and notice the next-door neighbor peering at us from her kitchen window and laughing right along with us. This neighbor was such an avid church-goer that we referred to her as the Christian Lady. We were somewhat surprised one day when she told Joan that we were "finer young people than some of the Christians she knew." Our landlady, Mrs. Schults, told us from time to time that we took better care of her property, and kept our house neater, than any tenant she ever had. Along with all this virtuosity, domesticity, and high jinx, we were living more economically than had seemed possible. About twenty dollars from each of us monthly covered all expenses, rent, food, telephone, newspaper and utilities.

We were usually gone weekends, climbing with each other and non-Base Camp friends. John D. Mendenhall had been attracted to the climbing scene since he was a child in Missouri. He is credited by Chris Jones in Climbing in North America with being the first known person "to consciously belay in the Sierra Nevada." He had figured it out from library books and practiced with like-minded friends. That summer John and I went on many private climbs together. Our main goal was to make pioneer ascents of the north side of Strawberry Peak in the local mountains. The cliff could be seen from the Angeles Crest Highway and was approached by a long hot trail and by way of a firebreak amid Southern California's chaparral. Our first route occupied us for several Sundays, and was so devious that we named it the Strawberry Roam.

Over the weekend of July 4, 1939, John and I planned to join the Rock Climbing Section's trip to the Minarets in the Sierra. We had spent our evenings the week before poring over maps and guidebooks. Our entire household was preparing for other trips. Ropes were inspected for flaws, crampons were tried on, boots waxed, pants patched. And our household duties were always with us.

John and I both had to work Saturday morning. After that nothing went quite right. Our transportation didn't leave till mid-afternoon. We reached the end of the road at midnight. John and I staggered out of our bags at 5 a.m. and backpacked seven miles to the RCS camp, easily identifiable because in those days our climbers rarely saw anyone else in the mountains. Due to inexperience and over-optimism, we thought we could make an afternoon climb of the Underhill-Eichorn Route on Banner Peak (12,957 feet). The approach seemed long, but we moved fast when we got on the rock. The difficulty increased as we climbed, and by 6 p.m. the summit was still far above us. We bivouacked. We always had extra food in the rucksack, but it was a cold cramped night on our ledge. We slept, we shivered, we nibbled on our Famine Ration of horrid drugstore bargain chocolate. We laughed: climbers always seemed to think the worse the conditions, the funnier. It was a new experience for me, and I thought that since I was there I should make the best of it. The cliffs dropped precipitously below, a star fell, the Banner Glacier gleamed in the moonlight. A red star rose over

White Mountain Peak across Owens Valley. At around 4 a.m. the eastern sky was filling with an orange light. Before 5, pale sunlight lay across our ledge. We ate snow and our last lemon drops for breakfast and descended to camp. We were teased for years about this bivouac, as a couple of weeks later we announced our engagement.

When we told Howard about our plans, he exclaimed, "But you can't get married and move out of Base Camp." It turned out that we could and did. But Howard, true to his philosophy, in early 1941 brought his own bride to live at Base Camp for a few months, presumably under housekeeping tutelage of the residents.

By mid-August of 1939, the Romance in Mountaineering had struck again. Dick Jones and Adrienne Applewhite announced their engagement. Our household and its circle of friends rose to the occasion. On my birthday, August 16, a surprise party was arranged at Base Camp for the two recently engaged couples. My gift from John was an ice axe, the peak of my desires. He had die-stamped in the steel head the words *"Happy Birthday 1939"* on one side, and *"Ruth From John"* on the other. After that presentation, Cupid came, in the flesh of a brawny mountain climber dressed in pink tights, a grass skirt, and wings, carrying a small bow and arrow. Gifts proliferated. The party ended with a turmoil of tissue paper, paper dishes, and cake crumbs in the living room. Glen said in his sage way, "Let's put the cake where the mice won't get it, and go to bed."

Despite mountain peaks and diamond rings, housework went on. Howard edged the front lawn, John mowed the back lawn, and I followed up with the sprinkler. I cooked a huge pot of stew that, with side dishes, kept dinners going for nearly a week. Green apples were falling from the tree that had been in bloom when we moved in. We picked them up for sauce and pies. Times were changing. Dick and Adrienne went on a Mass Honeymoon with a group of friends. Over Labor Day they bivouacked while down-climbing the East Face of Mount Whitney. On the same weekend, John and I put up a new route on the East Buttress of Third Needle south of Whitney. The next Mugelnoos commented that our two-man rope was soon to be spliced. I quit my job: hereafter we would divide work differently. In the midst of a terrible 109 degree hot spell, we were married at the home of John's parents in the San Fernando Valley and left Base Camp for our own home. Two girls and a man replaced us. The Schults family moved out to make room for more new residents.

The institution of Base Camp as a residence and social headquarters for skiers and climbers continued for over two more years. Sixteen different young people lived there, the maximum at any one time being ten, and the minimum six. This number included nine women and seven men. Base Camp was reluctantly disbanded in October 1941 because of the difficulties of keeping up the number of residents; defense work and the draft, higher education and romance were taking their toll. John and I, on the brink of leaving the Los Angeles area for war work on the East Coast and elsewhere, put up a new route on Mount Whitney, the Southeast Face. World War II scattered our crowd all over the world and changed our lives. But when we returned four years later, the mountains were waiting.

Wartime research had made great changes in mountaineering equipment and techniques, as well as in other things. Both men and women found changes in many aspects of life. And in another fifty years, women climbers of 1988, now Pioneer Women Climbers themselves, will find out how they fit into the climbing world of 2038.

Ruth Dyar Mendenhall began climbing in 1938 and continued for thirty-five seasons. In those thirty-five years she was responsible for routes all over the world.

Ruth was a member of the American Alpine Club and served on its board of directors and, for years, edited American Alpine News. Ruth wrote books and articles on climbing for beginners, about backpacking and outdoor cookery.

Ruth died in Seattle, Washington, in the Spring of 1989.

ABOUT THE AUTHOR

Dr. Mikel Vause is the author of the collection of essays "On Mountains and Mountaineers" and the editor of the original "Rock and Roses" (Mountain N' Air Books), "Wilderness Tapestry" (University Of Nevada Press, Reno, NV 1992) and "The Peregrine Reader" (Gibbs M. Smith, Layton, UT 1997).

Dr. Vause numerous articles, poems and short stories have appeared in magazines and journals such as *Climbing, The Climbing Art, The Journal of Evolutionary Psychology, Weber Studies, Popular Culture Review, The Trumpeter, Utah Foreign Language Review, Wasatch Review International, The Junction, Word Works, Rough Draft,* and *The Himalayan Journal #53.* He has recently completed a collection of poems under the title, "I Knew It Would Come to This" and is working on a archival study of the British mountaineer, Sir Christian Bonington and on a philosophical study entitled "Doug Scott: Pragmatic Mystic" with Doug Scott, C.B.E. also a British mountaineer.

Dr. Vause holds a Ph.D. from Bowling Green University and is a Full Professor at Weber State University and is currently the Director of the Honors Program.

Beverly Johnson
April 4, 1947—April 3, 1994

She touched stone, and enriched all our lives.

The Beverly Johnson
Memorial Scholarship Endowment Fund
for the Teton Science School

This fund was established in 1994 by Mike Hoover, Doreen and Ed Johnson, and members of their families, and it includes contributions donated in honor of Beverly's memory by friends and business associates.

The income from the fund is now used to provide scholarship for economically disadvantaged Junior High School students, most specifically but not limited to children from the South Central Los Angeles area. The scholarship is intended to cover the full costs for the child (or children when enough funds exist) to attend a two-weeks session of Teton Science School summer program.

If you wish to make a donation, please contact:
Teton Science School
Beverly Johnson Memorial Scholarship Endowment Fund
Jack Shea, Teton Science School executive director
P.O. Box 68
Kelly, WY 83011

Call: (307) 733-4765
Fax: (307) 739-9338
On line information: **www.tetonscience.org**